NO MATTER WHAT YOU SAY, FURI-SAN IS SCARY!

vol. 4

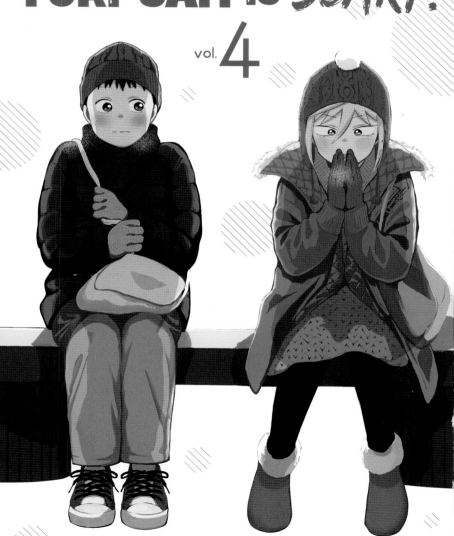

Contents

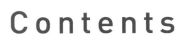

Chapter 27 ——— 003

Chapter 28 ——— 017

Chapter 29 ——— 033

Chapter 30 ——— 049

Chapter 31 ——— 065

Chapter 32 ——— 081

Chapter 33 ——— 097

Chapter 34 ——— 113

Bonus Chapter ——— 129

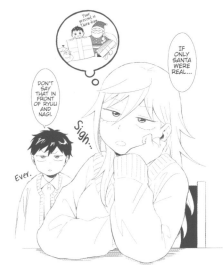

Your present is Taira-kun.

IF ONLY SANTA WERE REAL...

DON'T SAY THAT IN FRONT OF RYUU AND NAGI.

Sigh...

Ever.

Chapter 27

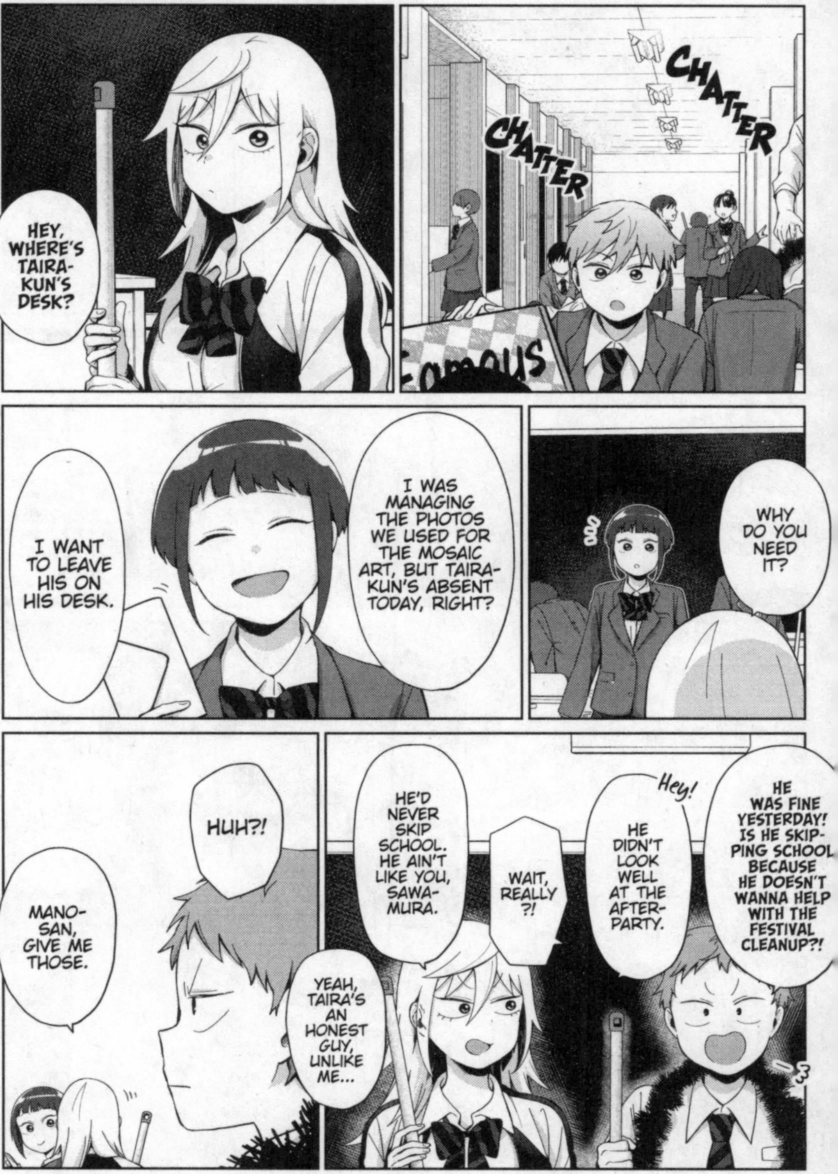

CHATTER
CHATTER
Famous
HEY, WHERE'S TAIRA-KUN'S DESK?
WHY DO YOU NEED IT?
I WAS MANAGING THE PHOTOS WE USED FOR THE MOSAIC ART, BUT TAIRA-KUN'S ABSENT TODAY, RIGHT?
I WANT TO LEAVE HIS ON HIS DESK.
HE WAS FINE YESTERDAY! IS HE SKIPPING SCHOOL BECAUSE HE DOESN'T WANNA HELP WITH THE FESTIVAL CLEANUP?!
Hey!
HE DIDN'T LOOK WELL AT THE AFTER-PARTY.
WAIT, REALLY?!
HE'D NEVER SKIP SCHOOL. HE AIN'T LIKE YOU, SAWAMURA.
YEAH, TAIRA'S AN HONEST GUY, UNLIKE ME...
HUH?!
MANO-SAN, GIVE ME THOSE.

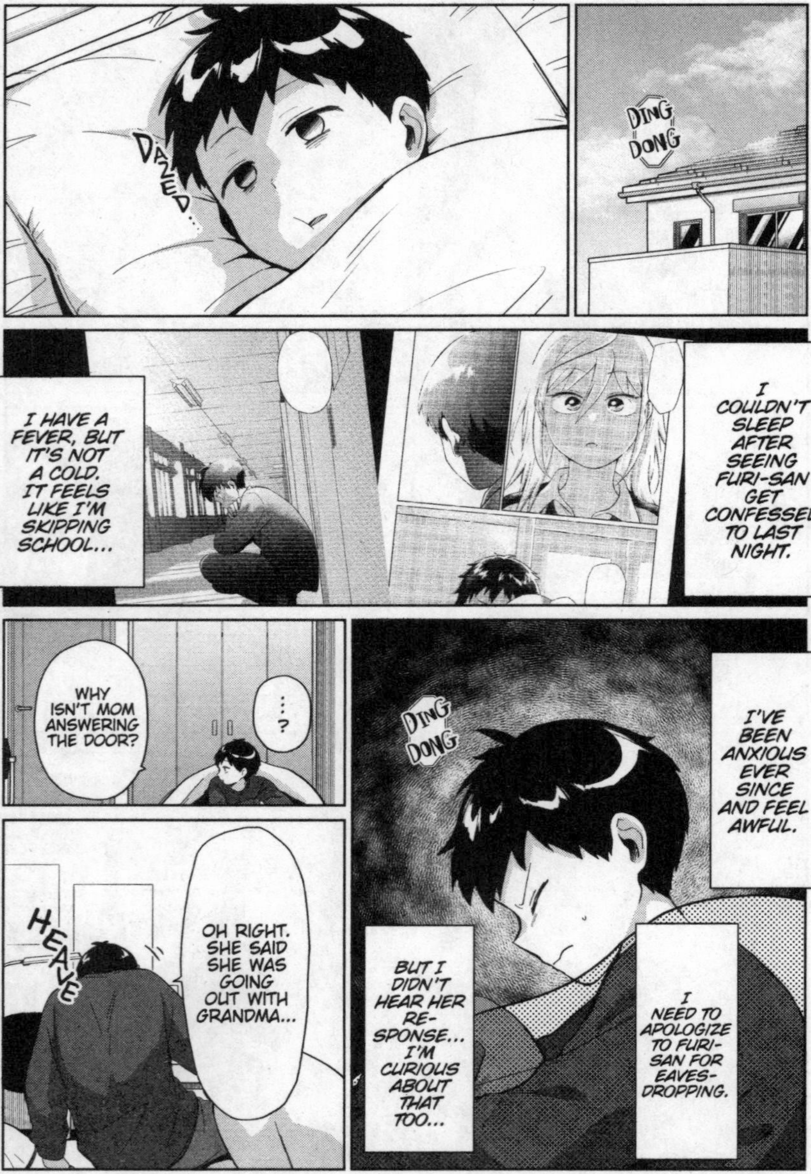
DING DONG
DAZED...
I COULDN'T SLEEP AFTER SEEING FURI-SAN GET CONFESSED TO LAST NIGHT.
I HAVE A FEVER, BUT IT'S NOT A COLD. IT FEELS LIKE I'M SKIPPING SCHOOL...
I'VE BEEN ANXIOUS EVER SINCE AND FEEL AWFUL.
DING DONG
I NEED TO APOLOGIZE TO FURI-SAN FOR EAVES-DROPPING.
BUT I DIDN'T HEAR HER RE-SPONSE... I'M CURIOUS ABOUT THAT TOO...
...?
WHY ISN'T MOM ANSWERING THE DOOR?
OH RIGHT. SHE SAID SHE WAS GOING OUT WITH GRANDMA...
HEAVE

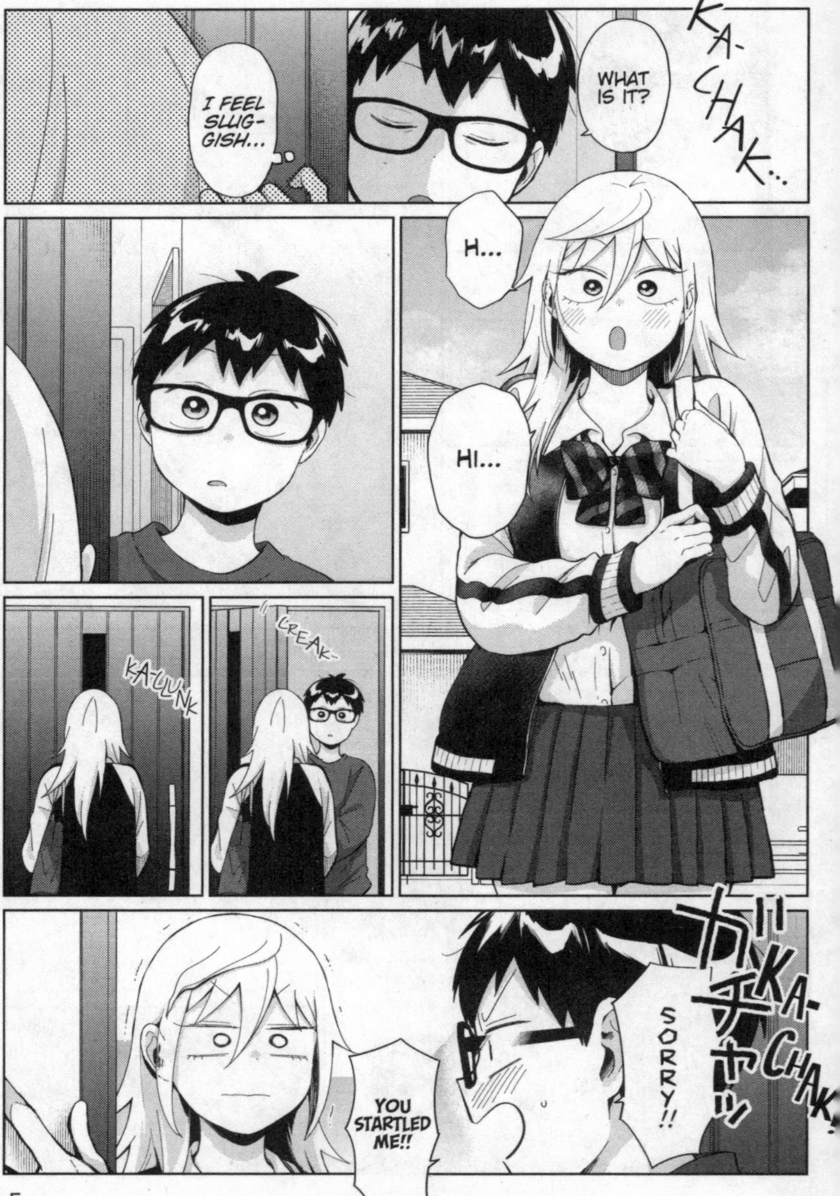
KA-CHAK...
WHAT IS IT?
I FEEL SLUGGISH...
H...
HI...
CREAK...
KA-CLUNK
ガチャッ
KA-CHAK!
SORRY!!
YOU STARTLED ME!!

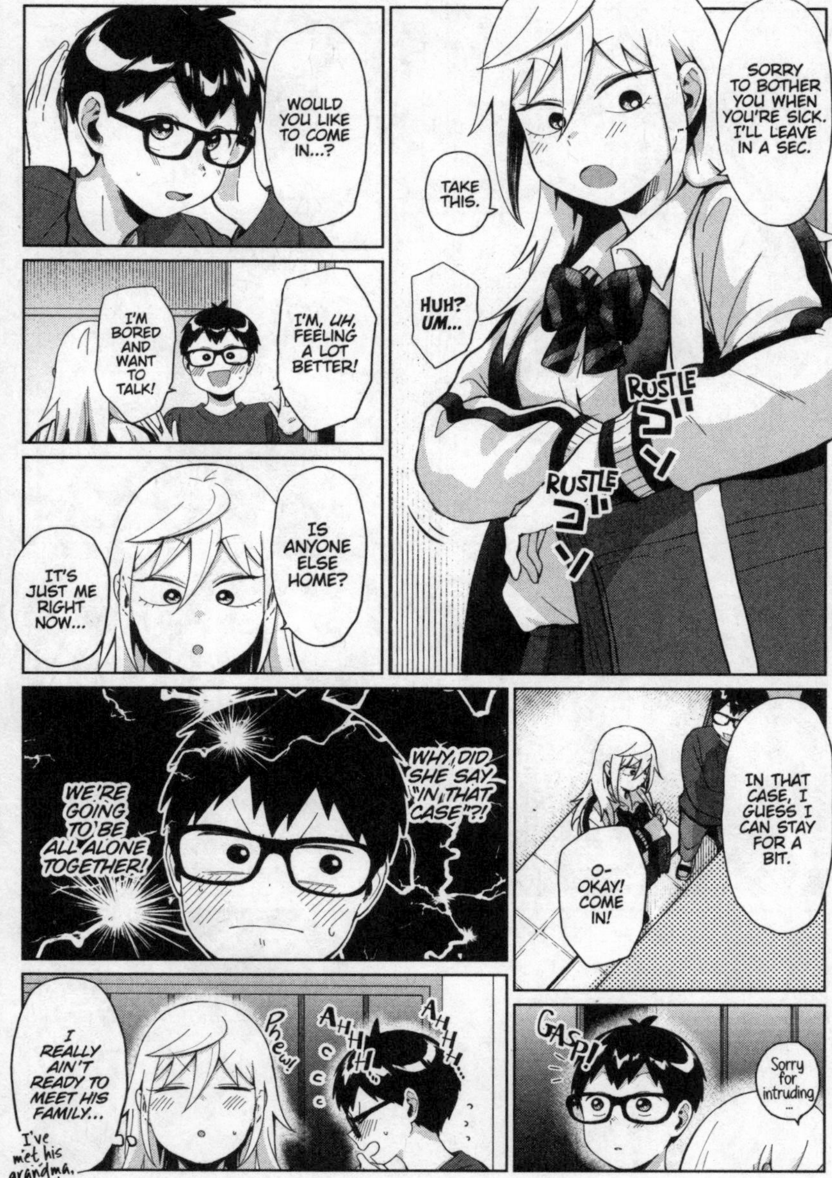
SORRY TO BOTHER YOU WHEN YOU'RE SICK. I'LL LEAVE IN A SEC.
TAKE THIS.
HUH? UM...
RUSTLE
RUSTLE
WOULD YOU LIKE TO COME IN...?
I'M, UH, FEELING A LOT BETTER!
I'M BORED AND WANT TO TALK!
IS ANYONE ELSE HOME?
IT'S JUST ME RIGHT NOW...
IN THAT CASE, I GUESS I CAN STAY FOR A BIT.
O-OKAY! COME IN!
WHY DID SHE SAY "IN THAT CASE"?!
WE'RE GOING TO BE ALL ALONE TOGETHER!
GASP!
Sorry for intruding...
AHHHH...
AHHHH...
Phew!
I REALLY AIN'T READY TO MEET HIS FAMILY...
I've met his grandma, though.

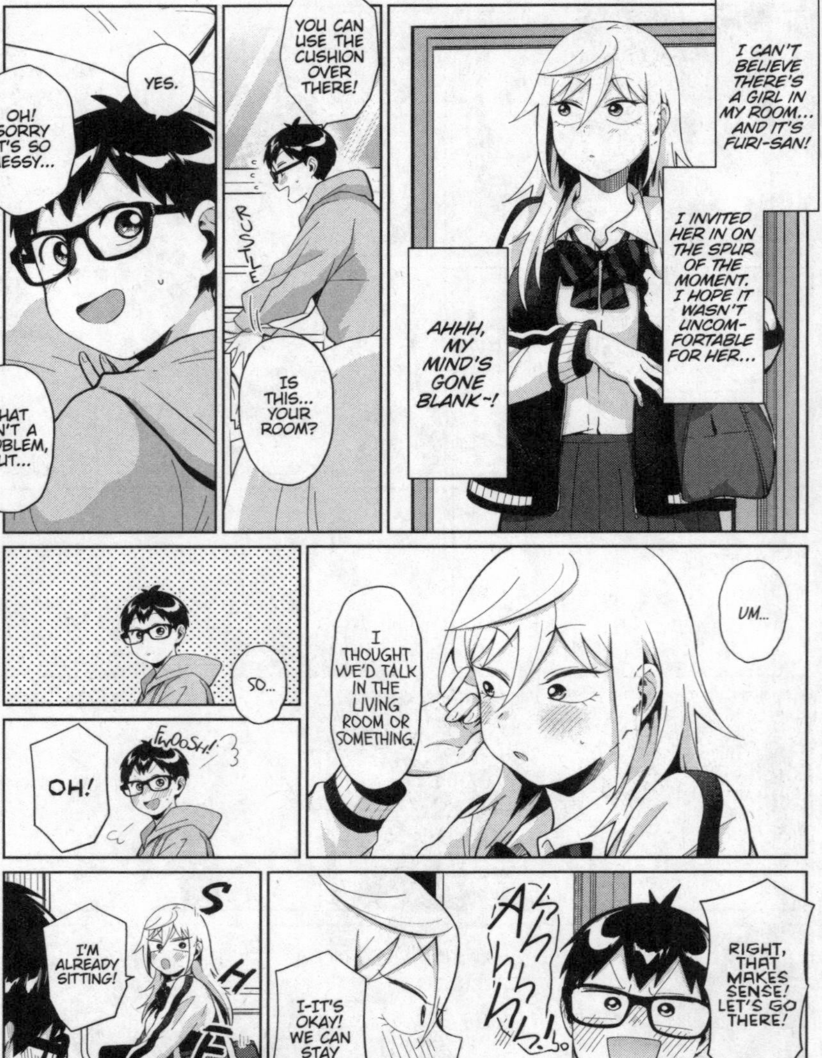
I CAN'T BELIEVE THERE'S A GIRL IN MY ROOM... AND IT'S FURI-SAN!
I INVITED HER IN ON THE SPUR OF THE MOMENT. I HOPE IT WASN'T UNCOM-FORTABLE FOR HER...
AHHH, MY MIND'S GONE BLANK~!
YOU CAN USE THE CUSHION OVER THERE!
RUSTLE
IS THIS... YOUR ROOM?
YES.
OH! SORRY IT'S SO MESSY...
THAT AIN'T A PROBLEM, BUT...
UM...
I THOUGHT WE'D TALK IN THE LIVING ROOM OR SOMETHING.
SO...
FWOOSH!
OH!
RIGHT, THAT MAKES SENSE! LET'S GO THERE!
I-IT'S OKAY! WE CAN STAY HERE! DON'T WORRY!
SHF
I'M ALREADY SITTING!

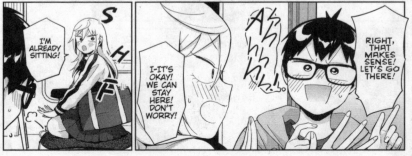

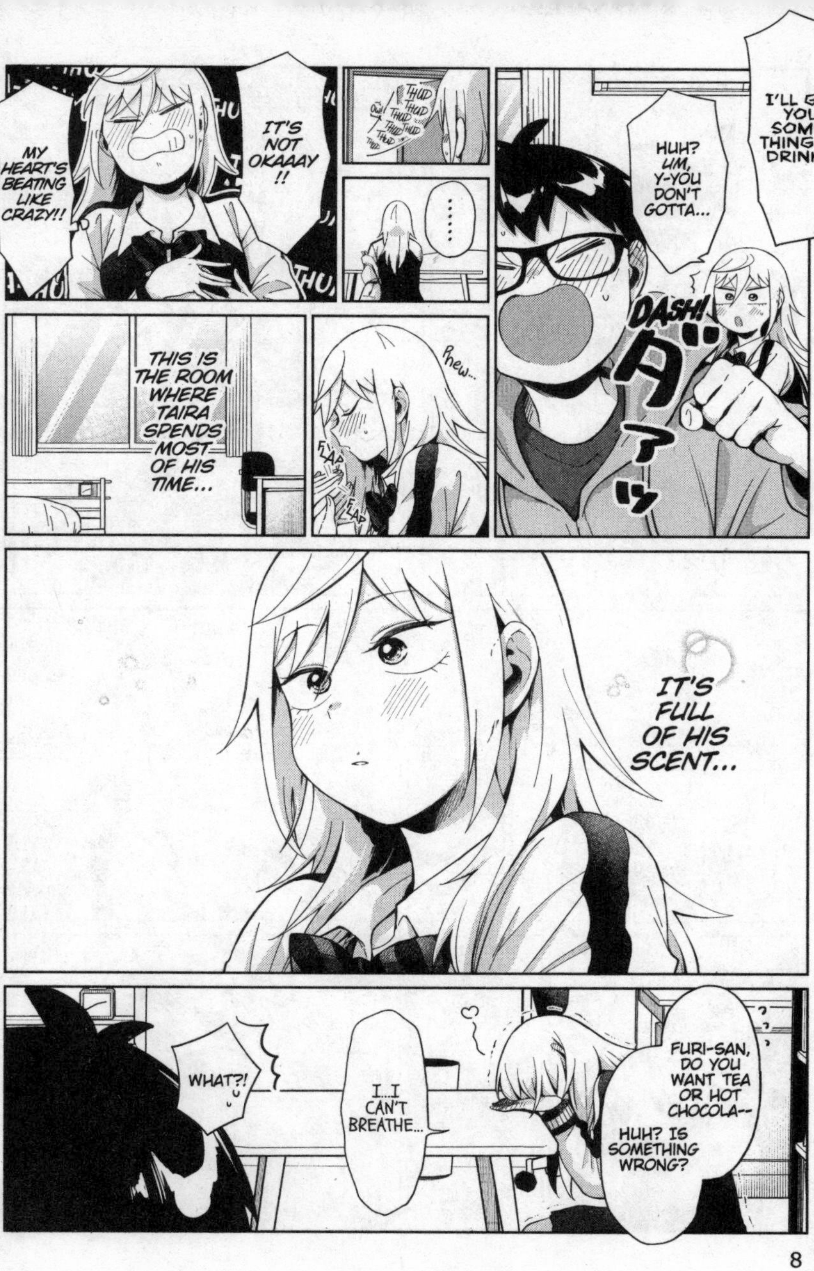
I'LL GET YOU SOME-THING TO DRINK!!
HUH? UM, Y-YOU DON'T GOTTA...
DASH!
ダァッ
THUD THUD
OW!
......
IT'S NOT OKAAAY!!
MY HEART'S BEATING LIKE CRAZY!!
Phew...
FLAP FLAP
THIS IS THE ROOM WHERE TAIRA SPENDS MOST OF HIS TIME...
IT'S FULL OF HIS SCENT...
FURI-SAN, DO YOU WANT TEA OR HOT CHOCOLA--
HUH? IS SOMETHING WRONG?
I...I CAN'T BREATHE...
WHAT?!

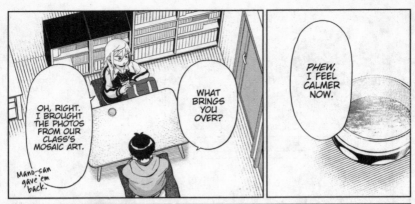

PHEW, I FEEL CALMER NOW.
WHAT BRINGS YOU OVER?
OH, RIGHT. I BROUGHT THE PHOTOS FROM OUR CLASS'S MOSAIC ART.
Mano-san gave 'em back.
THANK YOU FOR GOING OUT OF YOUR WAY TO DELIVER THEM TO MY HOUSE.
WHEN I WAS SICK, YOU BROUGHT ME OUR CLASSWORK, DIDN'T YOU?
OH, I DID DO THAT.
BACK THEN, I THOUGHT FURI-SAN WAS SCARY.
IT'S HARD TO IMAGINE THAT NOW.
I'M GLAD YOU'RE OKAY.
YOU DIDN'T LOOK TOO GOOD AT THE AFTER-PARTY LAST NIGHT. YOU SEEMED KINDA... GLOOMY?

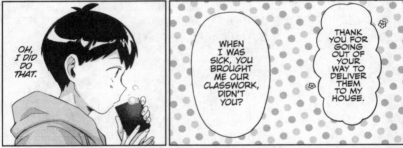

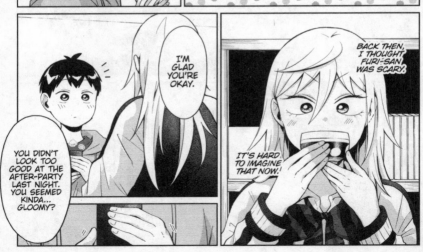

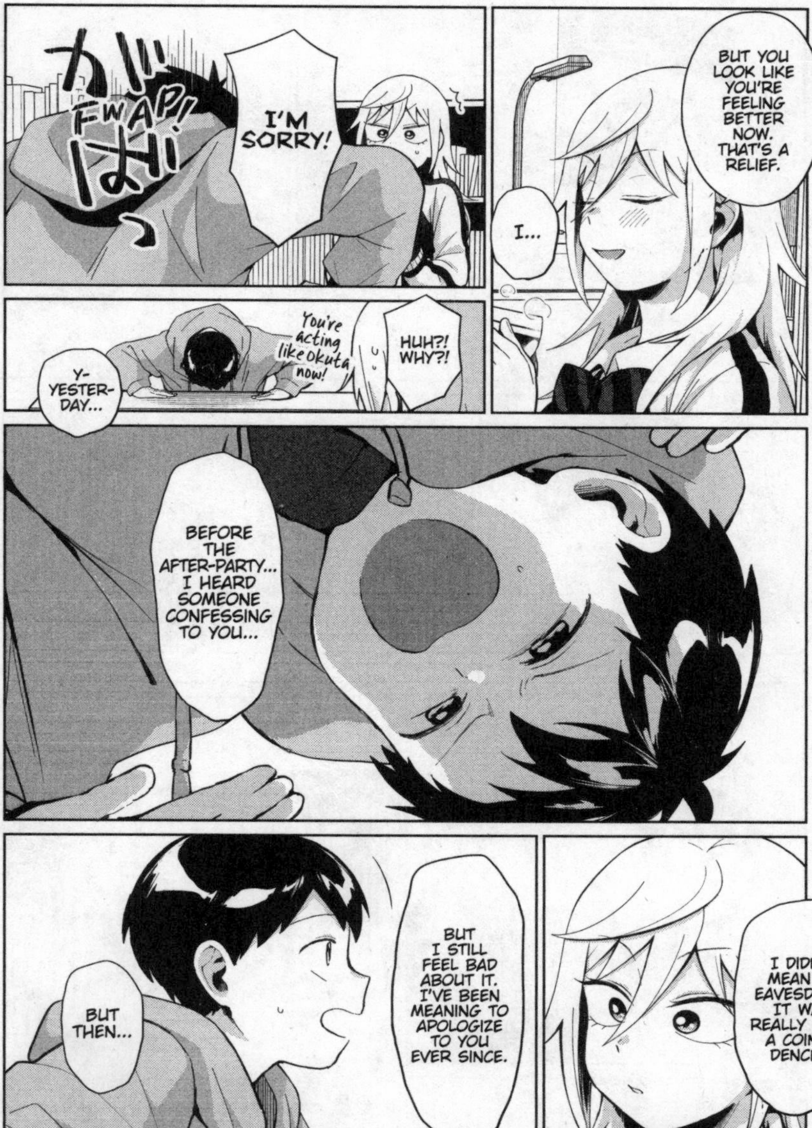
BUT YOU LOOK LIKE YOU'RE FEELING BETTER NOW. THAT'S A RELIEF.
I...
I'M SORRY!
FWAP!
HUH?! WHY?!
You're acting like Okuta now!
Y-YESTER-DAY...
BEFORE THE AFTER-PARTY... I HEARD SOMEONE CONFESSING TO YOU...
I DIDN'T MEAN TO EAVESDROP. IT WAS REALLY JUST A COINCI-DENCE...
BUT I STILL FEEL BAD ABOUT IT. I'VE BEEN MEANING TO APOLOGIZE TO YOU EVER SINCE.
BUT THEN...

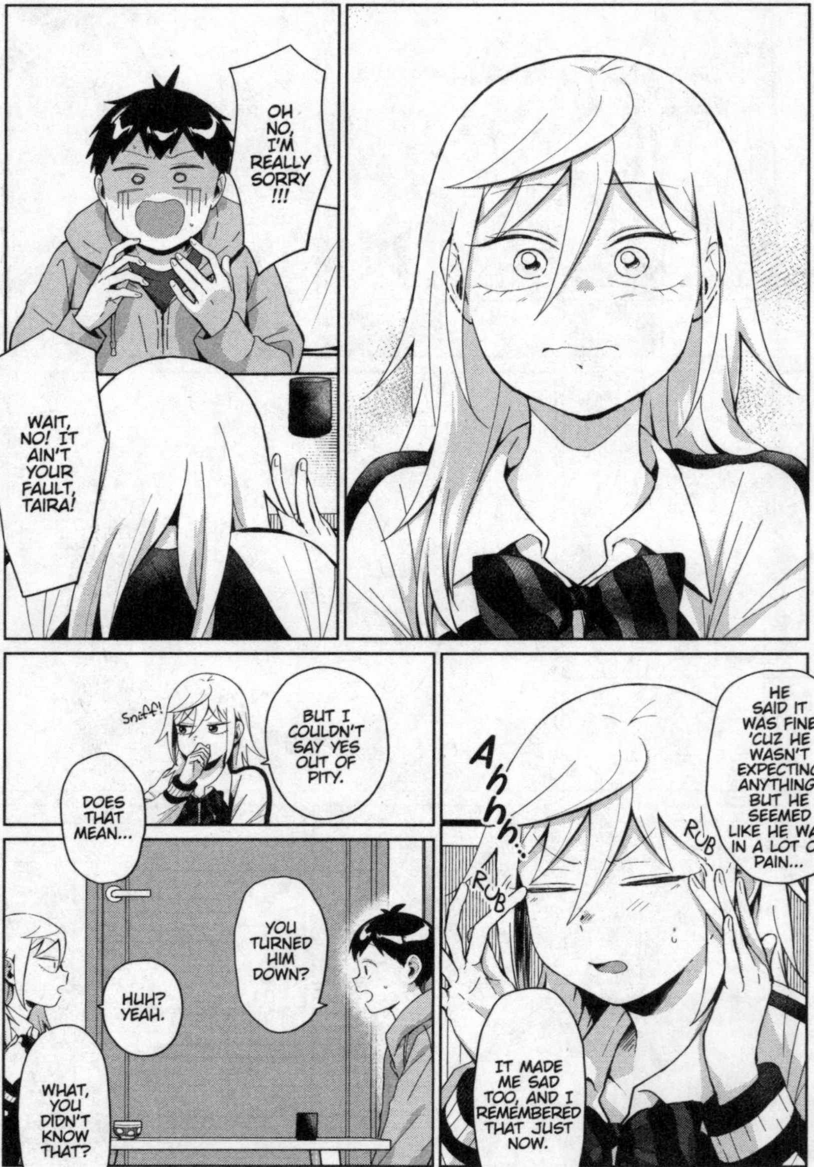
OH NO, I'M REALLY SORRY!!!
WAIT, NO! IT AIN'T YOUR FAULT, TAIRA!
HE SAID IT WAS FINE 'CUZ HE WASN'T EXPECTING ANYTHING, BUT HE SEEMED LIKE HE WAS IN A LOT OF PAIN...
Ahhh...
RUB
RUB
IT MADE ME SAD TOO, AND I REMEMBERED THAT JUST NOW.
BUT I COULDN'T SAY YES OUT OF PITY.
Sniff!
DOES THAT MEAN...
YOU TURNED HIM DOWN?
HUH? YEAH.
WHAT, YOU DIDN'T KNOW THAT?

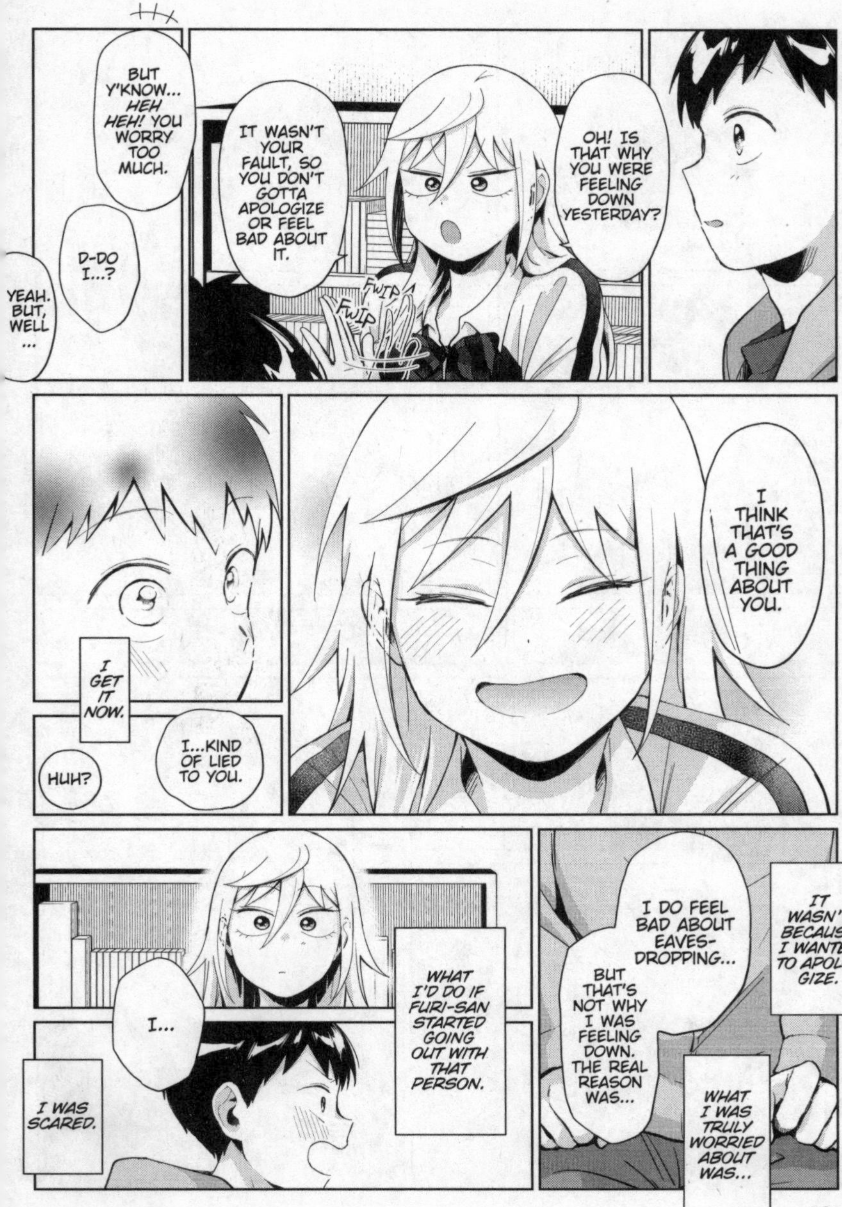
OH! IS THAT WHY YOU WERE FEELING DOWN YESTERDAY?
IT WASN'T YOUR FAULT, SO YOU DON'T GOTTA APOLOGIZE OR FEEL BAD ABOUT IT.
FWIP FWIP
BUT Y'KNOW... HEH HEH! YOU WORRY TOO MUCH.
D-DO I...?
YEAH. BUT, WELL ...
I THINK THAT'S A GOOD THING ABOUT YOU.
I GET IT NOW.
I...KIND OF LIED TO YOU.
HUH?
IT WASN'T BECAUSE I WANTED TO APOLO-GIZE.
I DO FEEL BAD ABOUT EAVES-DROPPING...
BUT THAT'S NOT WHY I WAS FEELING DOWN. THE REAL REASON WAS...
WHAT I WAS TRULY WORRIED ABOUT WAS...
WHAT I'D DO IF FURI-SAN STARTED GOING OUT WITH THAT PERSON.
I...
I WAS SCARED.

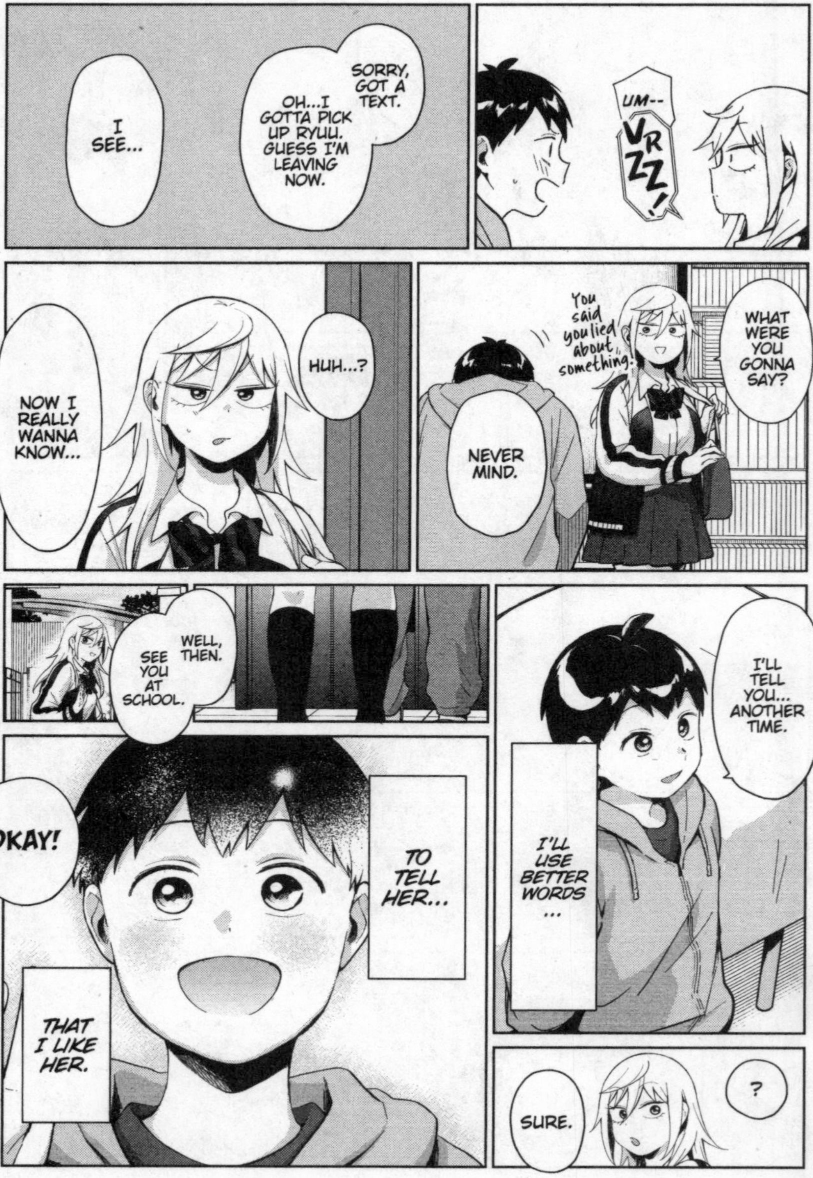
UM--
VRZZ!
SORRY, GOT A TEXT.
OH...I GOTTA PICK UP RYUU. GUESS I'M LEAVING NOW.
I SEE...
WHAT WERE YOU GONNA SAY?
You said you lied about something!
NEVER MIND.
HUH...?
NOW I REALLY WANNA KNOW...
I'LL TELL YOU... ANOTHER TIME.
I'LL USE BETTER WORDS ...
?
SURE.
WELL, THEN.
SEE YOU AT SCHOOL.
TO TELL HER...
OKAY!
THAT I LIKE HER.

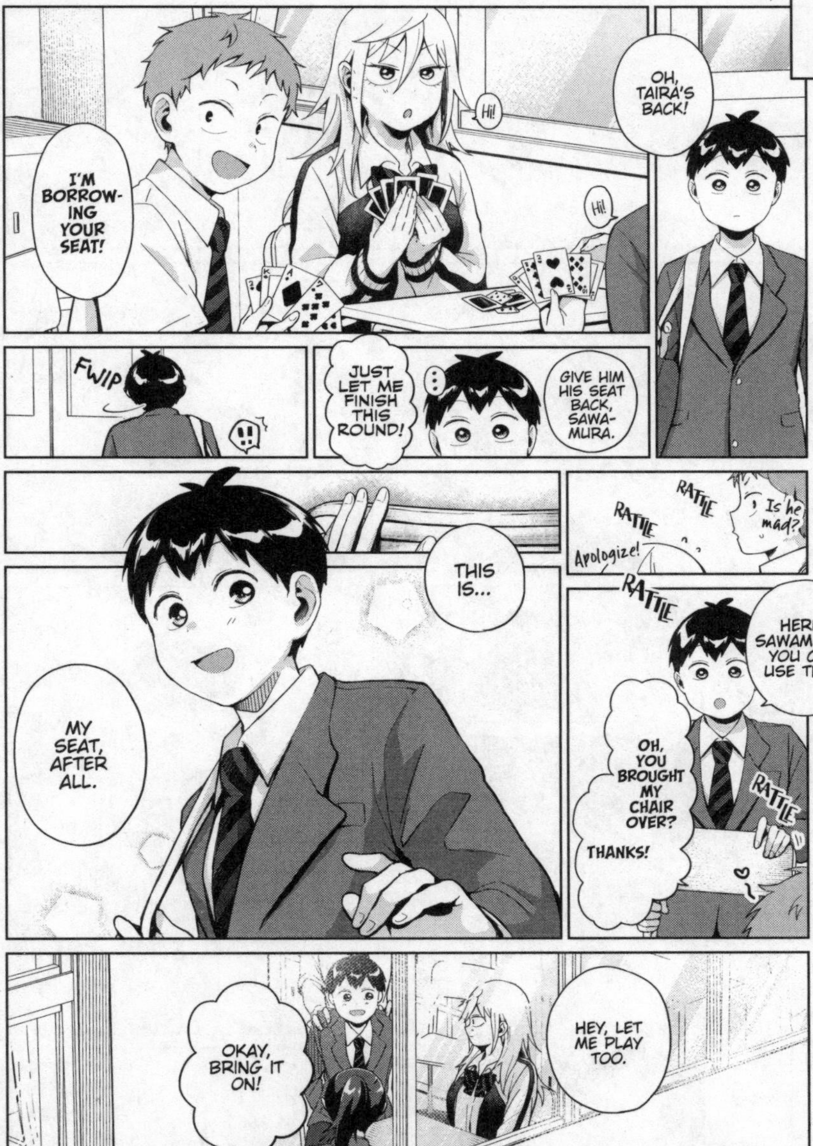
OH, TAIRA'S BACK!
Hi!
Hi!
I'M BORROWING YOUR SEAT!
GIVE HIM HIS SEAT BACK, SAWAMURA.
JUST LET ME FINISH THIS ROUND!
...
FWIP
!!
RATTLE
RATTLE
Is he mad?
Apologize!
RATTLE
HERE, SAWAMURA. YOU CAN USE THIS.
RATTLE
OH, YOU BROUGHT MY CHAIR OVER?
THANKS!
THIS IS...
MY SEAT, AFTER ALL.
HEY, LET ME PLAY TOO.
OKAY, BRING IT ON!

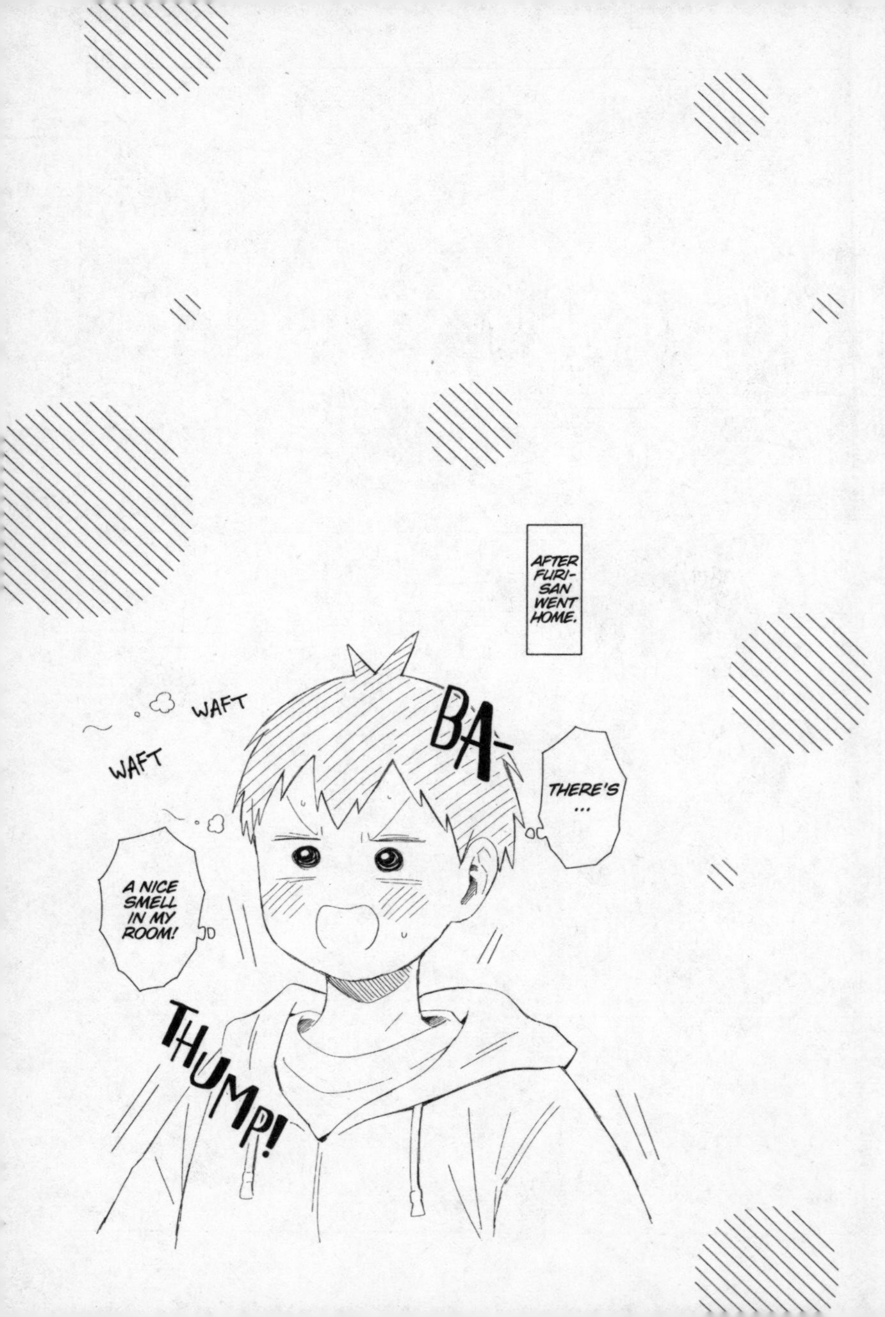
AFTER FURI-SAN WENT HOME.
BA-
THERE'S ...
THUMP!
WAFT
WAFT
A NICE SMELL IN MY ROOM!

Chapter 28

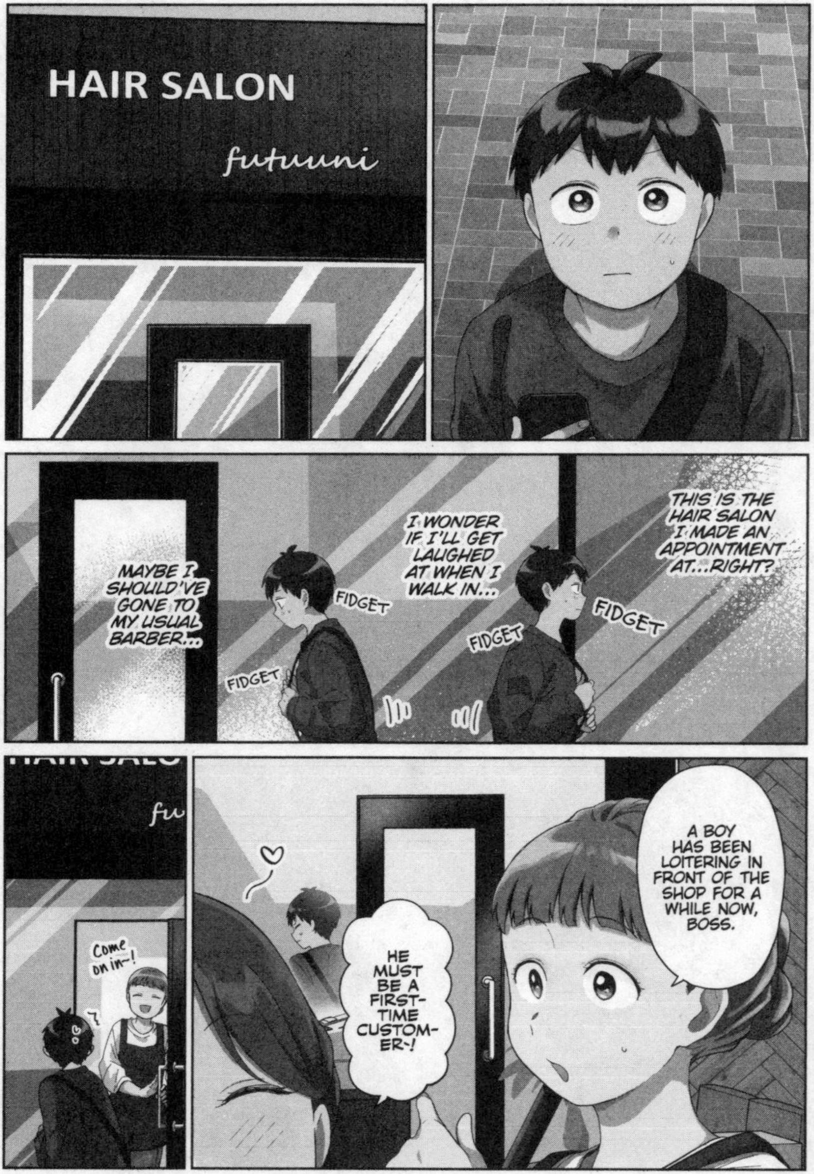
HAIR SALON
futuuni
THIS IS THE HAIR SALON I MADE AN APPOINTMENT AT...RIGHT?
FIDGET
I WONDER IF I'LL GET LAUGHED AT WHEN I WALK IN...
FIDGET
FIDGET
MAYBE I SHOULD'VE GONE TO MY USUAL BARBER...
FIDGET
A BOY HAS BEEN LOITERING IN FRONT OF THE SHOP FOR A WHILE NOW, BOSS.
HE MUST BE A FIRST-TIME CUSTOMER~!
fu
Come on in~!

Chapter 28

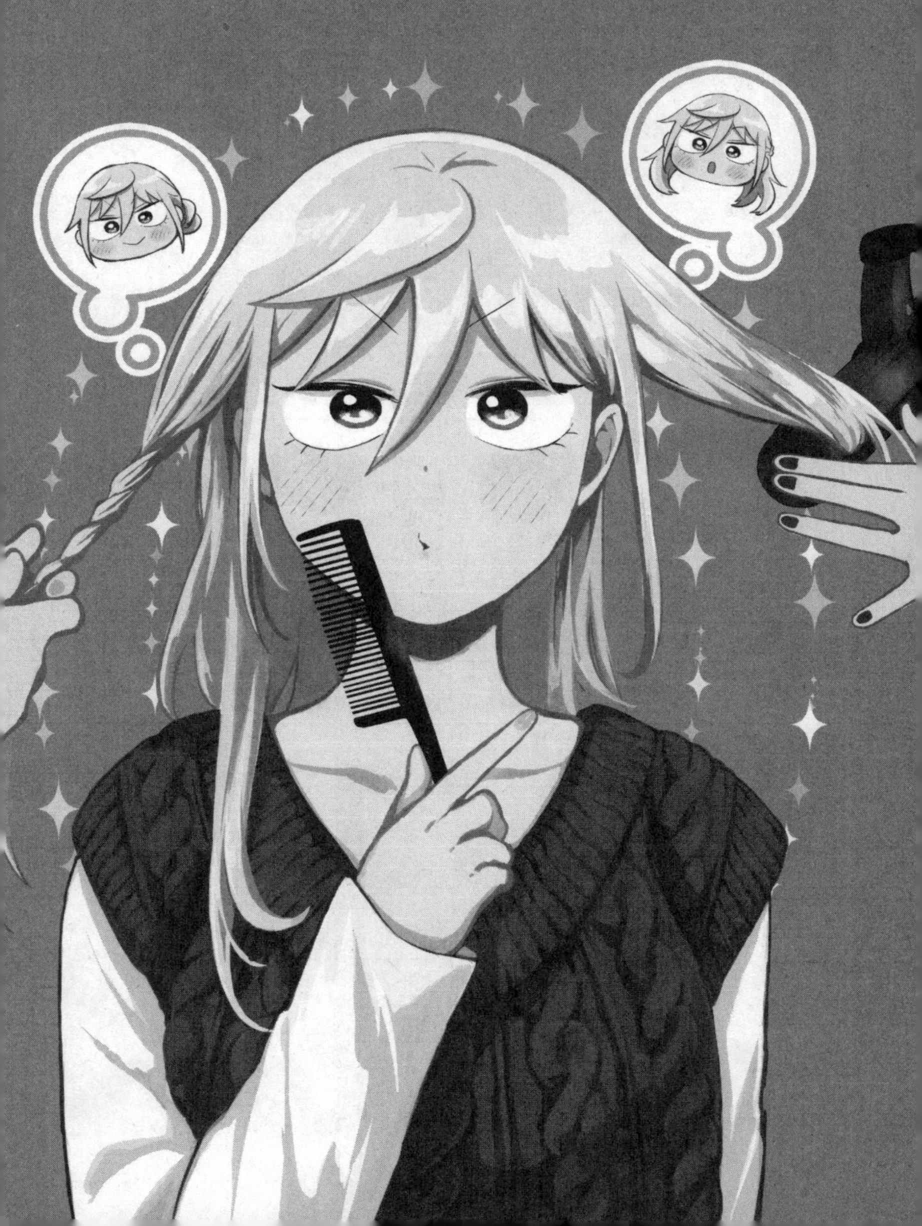

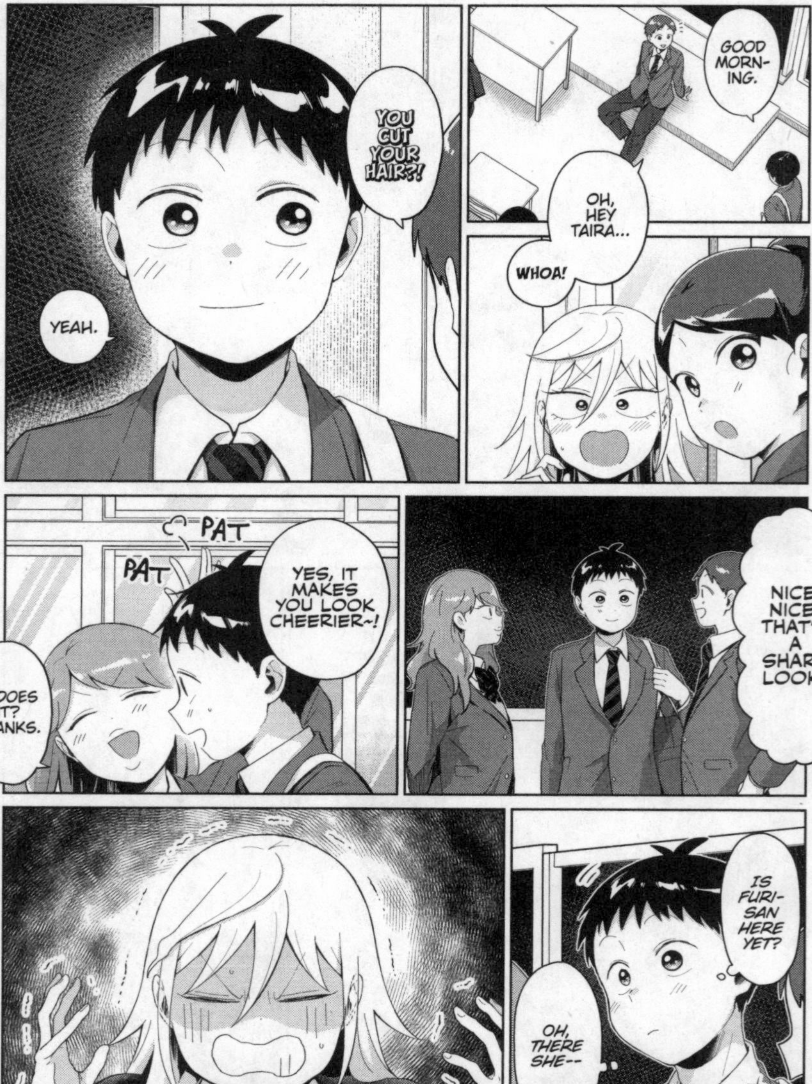
GOOD MORN-ING.
OH, HEY TAIRA...
WHOA!
YOU CUT YOUR HAIR?!
YEAH.
NICE, NICE! THAT'S A SHARP LOOK!
YES, IT MAKES YOU LOOK CHEERIER~!
PAT
PAT
D-DOES IT? THANKS.
IS FURI-SAN HERE YET?
OH, THERE SHE--

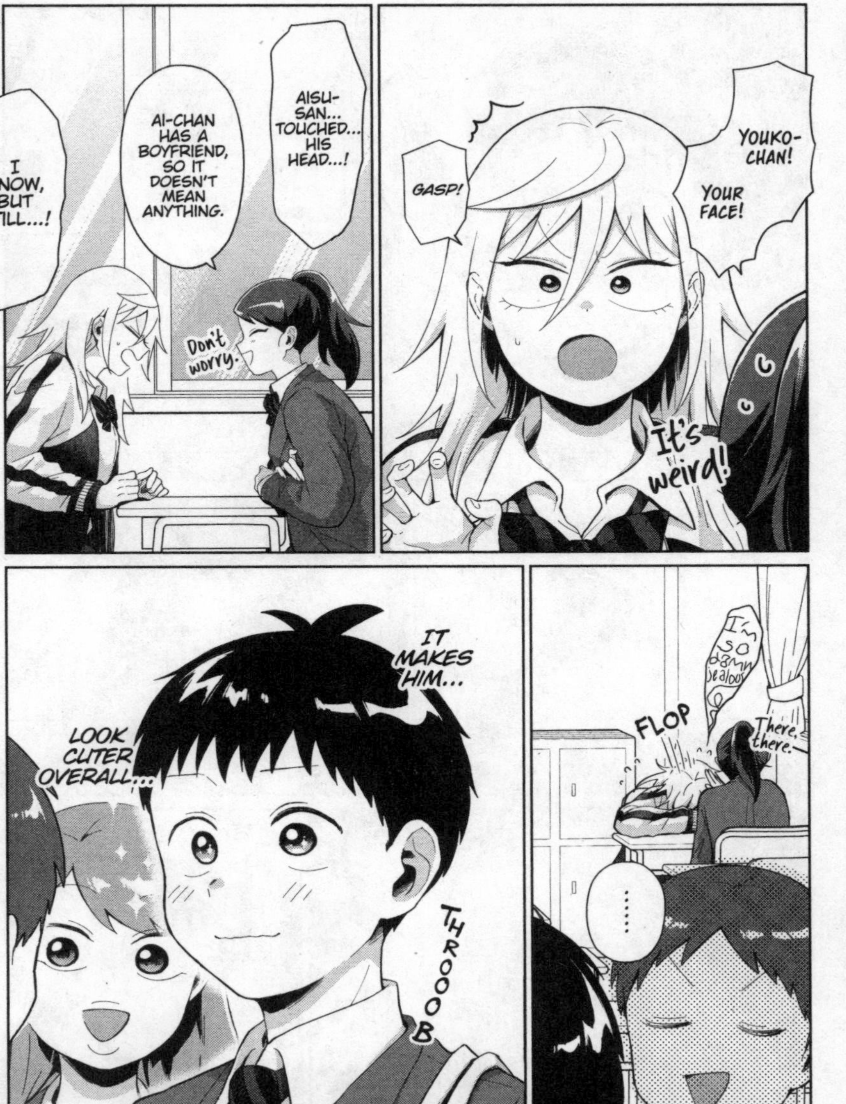
YOUKO-CHAN!
YOUR FACE!
GASP!
It's weird!
AISU-SAN... TOUCHED... HIS HEAD...!
AI-CHAN HAS A BOYFRIEND, SO IT DOESN'T MEAN ANYTHING.
I KNOW, BUT STILL...!
Don't worry.
I'm so damn jealous
FLOP
There, there.
......
IT MAKES HIM...
LOOK CUTER OVERALL...
THROOOOB

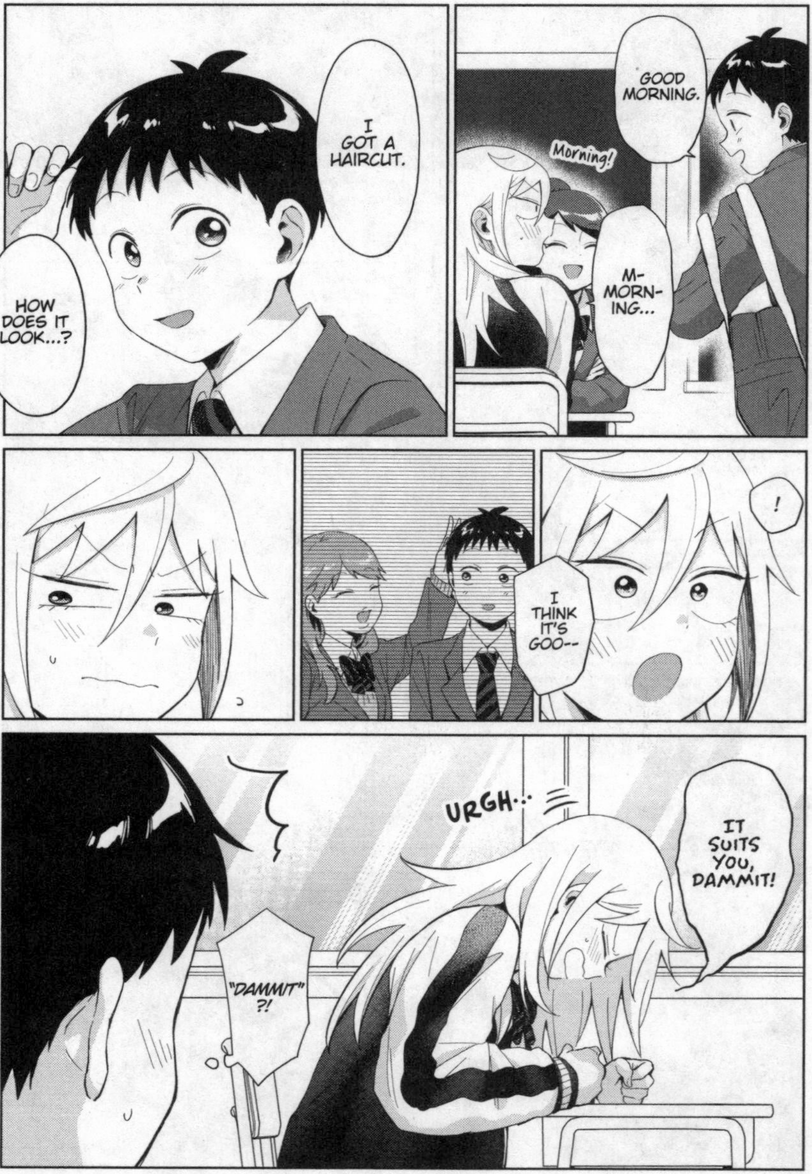
GOOD MORNING.
Morning!
M-MORNING...
I GOT A HAIRCUT.
HOW DOES IT LOOK...?
!
I THINK IT'S GOO--
IT SUITS YOU, DAMMIT!
URGH...
"DAMMIT"?!

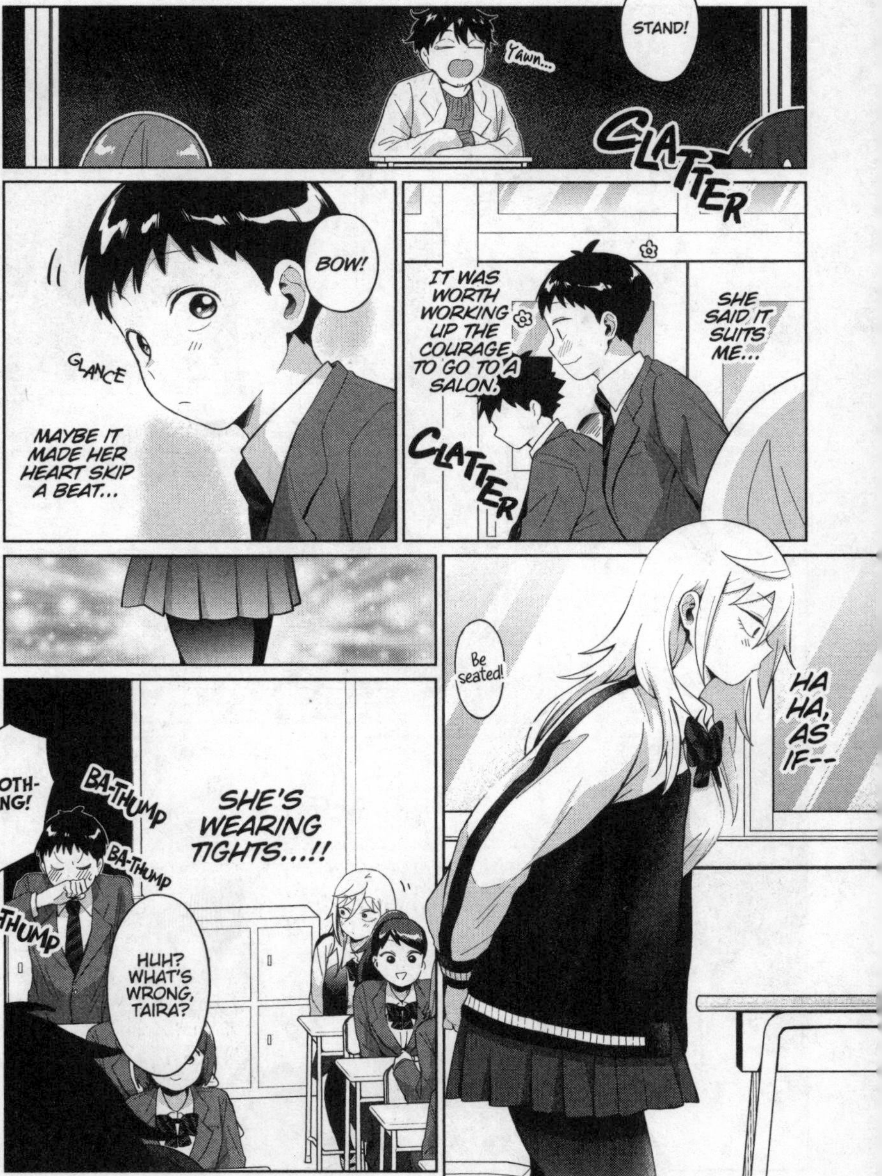
STAND!
Yawn...
CLATTER
SHE SAID IT SUITS ME...
IT WAS WORTH WORKING UP THE COURAGE TO GO TO A SALON!
CLATTER
BOW!
GLANCE
MAYBE IT MADE HER HEART SKIP A BEAT...
HA HA, AS IF--
Be seated!
SHE'S WEARING TIGHTS...!!
BA-THUMP
BA-THUMP
NOTHING!
BA-THUMP
HUH? WHAT'S WRONG, TAIRA?

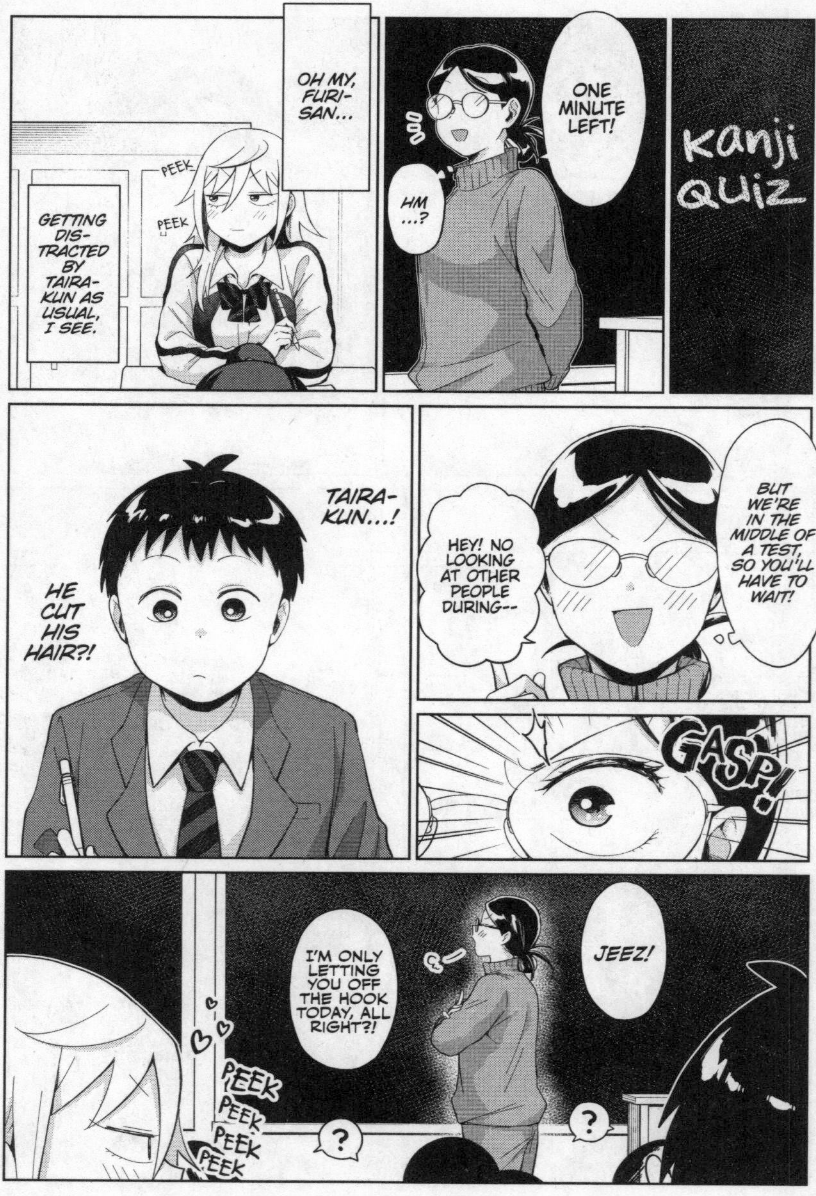
Kanji Quiz
ONE MINUTE LEFT!
HM ...?
OH MY, FURI-SAN...
PEEK
PEEK
GETTING DISTRACTED BY TAIRA-KUN AS USUAL, I SEE.
BUT WE'RE IN THE MIDDLE OF A TEST, SO YOU'LL HAVE TO WAIT!
HEY! NO LOOKING AT OTHER PEOPLE DURING--
GASP!
TAIRA-KUN...!
HE CUT HIS HAIR?!
JEEZ!
I'M ONLY LETTING YOU OFF THE HOOK TODAY, ALL RIGHT?!
?
?
PEEK
PEEK
PEEK
PEEK

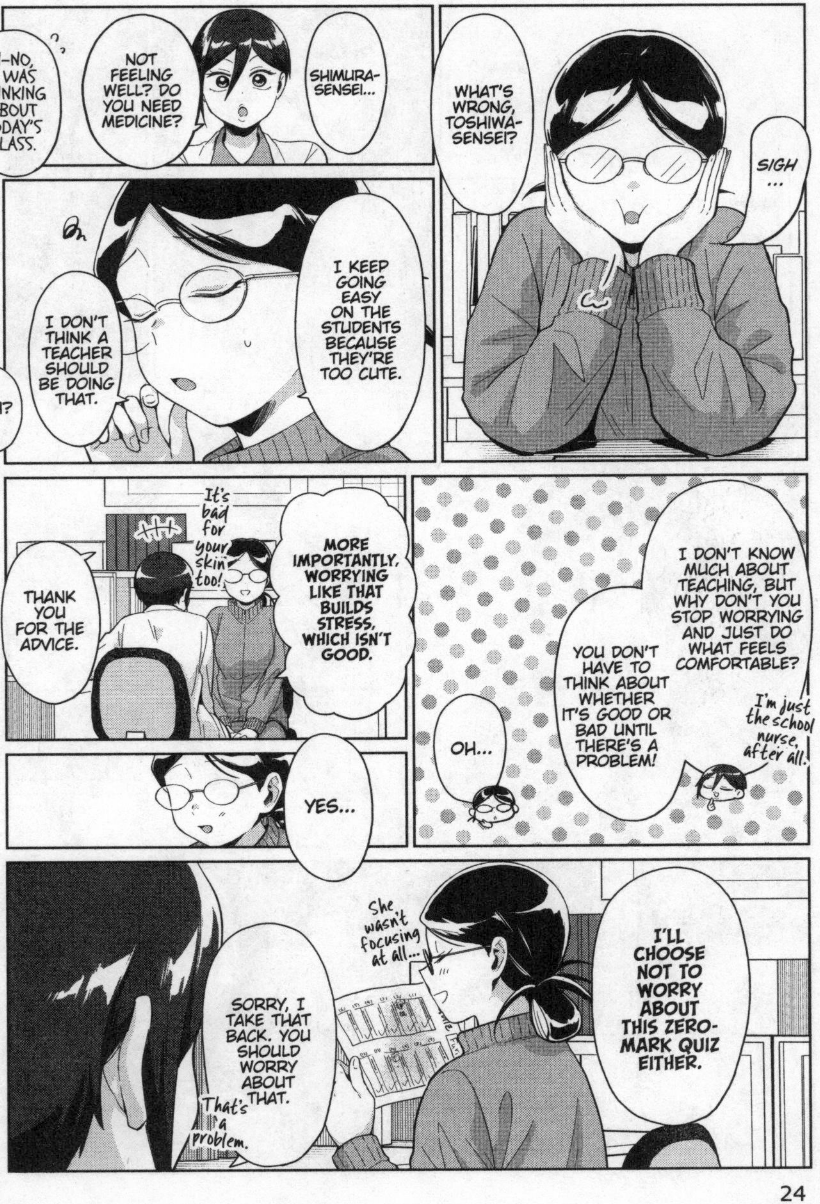
SIGH...
WHAT'S WRONG, TOSHIWA-SENSEI?
SHIMURA-SENSEI...
NOT FEELING WELL? DO YOU NEED MEDICINE?
N-NO, I WAS THINKING ABOUT TODAY'S CLASS.
I KEEP GOING EASY ON THE STUDENTS BECAUSE THEY'RE TOO CUTE.
I DON'T THINK A TEACHER SHOULD BE DOING THAT.
OH?
I DON'T KNOW MUCH ABOUT TEACHING, BUT WHY DON'T YOU STOP WORRYING AND JUST DO WHAT FEELS COMFORTABLE?
YOU DON'T HAVE TO THINK ABOUT WHETHER IT'S GOOD OR BAD UNTIL THERE'S A PROBLEM!
I'm just the school nurse, after all!
OH...
MORE IMPORTANTLY, WORRYING LIKE THAT BUILDS STRESS, WHICH ISN'T GOOD.
It's bad for your skin too!
THANK YOU FOR THE ADVICE.
YES...
I'LL CHOOSE NOT TO WORRY ABOUT THIS ZERO-MARK QUIZ EITHER.
She wasn't focusing at all...
SORRY, I TAKE THAT BACK. YOU SHOULD WORRY ABOUT THAT.
That's a problem.

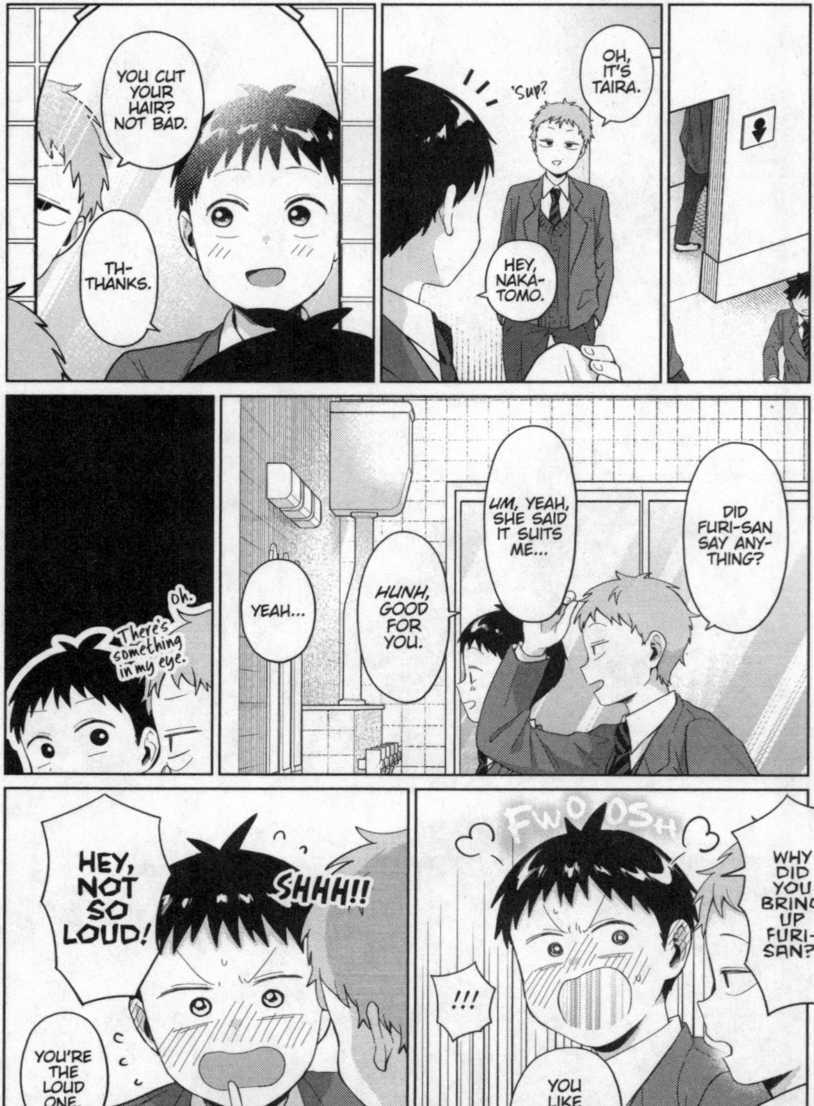
OH, IT'S TAIRA.
'Sup?
HEY, NAKA-TOMO.
YOU CUT YOUR HAIR? NOT BAD.
TH-THANKS.
DID FURI-SAN SAY ANY-THING?
UM, YEAH, SHE SAID IT SUITS ME...
HUNH, GOOD FOR YOU.
YEAH...
Oh.
There's something in my eye.
FWOOSH
WHY DID YOU BRING UP FURI-SAN?!
!!!
YOU LIKE HER, DON'T YOU?
HEY, NOT SO LOUD!
SHHH!!
YOU'RE THE LOUD ONE.

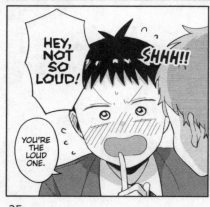

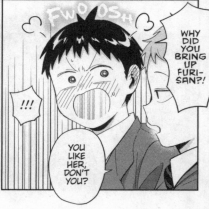

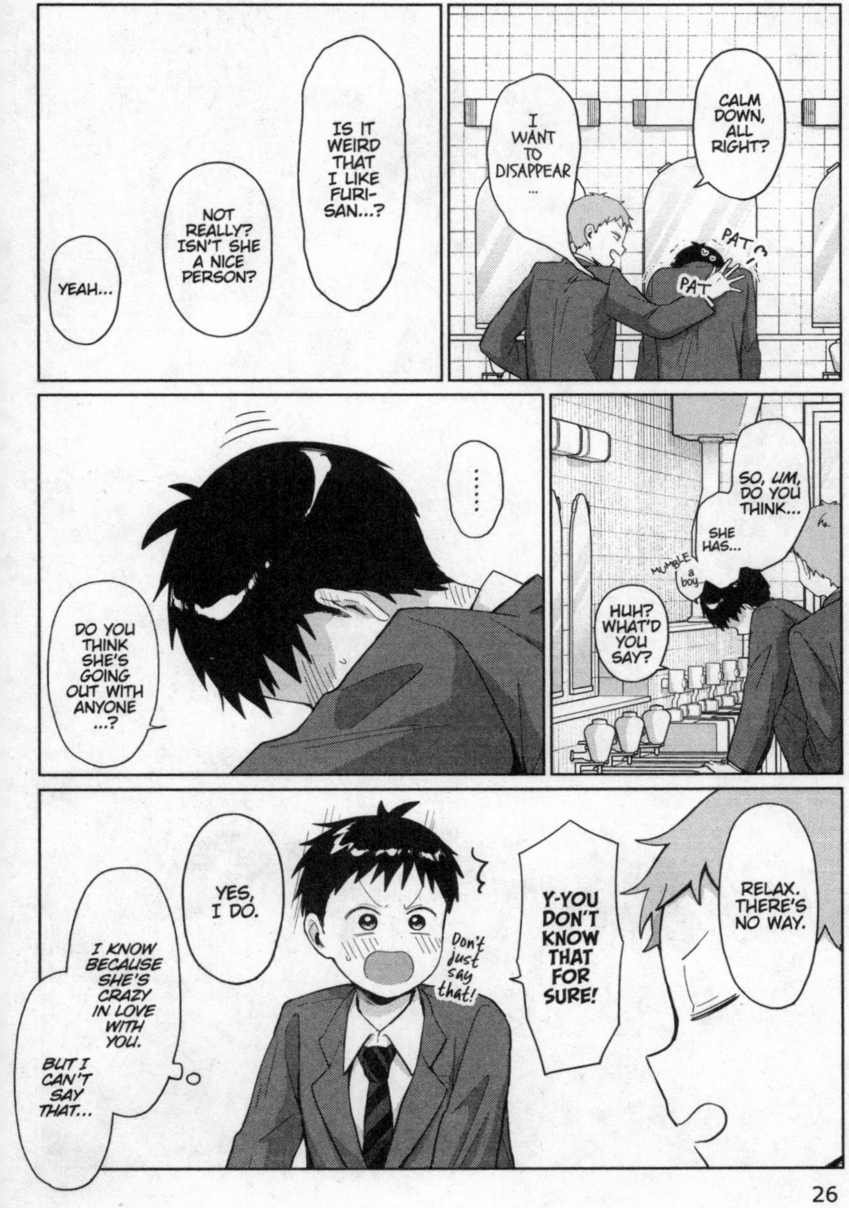
CALM DOWN, ALL RIGHT?
I WANT TO DISAPPEAR...
PAT
PAT
IS IT WEIRD THAT I LIKE FURI-SAN...?
NOT REALLY? ISN'T SHE A NICE PERSON?
YEAH...
SO, UM, DO YOU THINK...
SHE HAS...
MUMBLE
a boy...
HUH? WHAT'D YOU SAY?
......
DO YOU THINK SHE'S GOING OUT WITH ANYONE...?
RELAX. THERE'S NO WAY.
Y-YOU DON'T KNOW THAT FOR SURE!
Don't just say that!
YES, I DO.
I KNOW BECAUSE SHE'S CRAZY IN LOVE WITH YOU.
BUT I CAN'T SAY THAT...

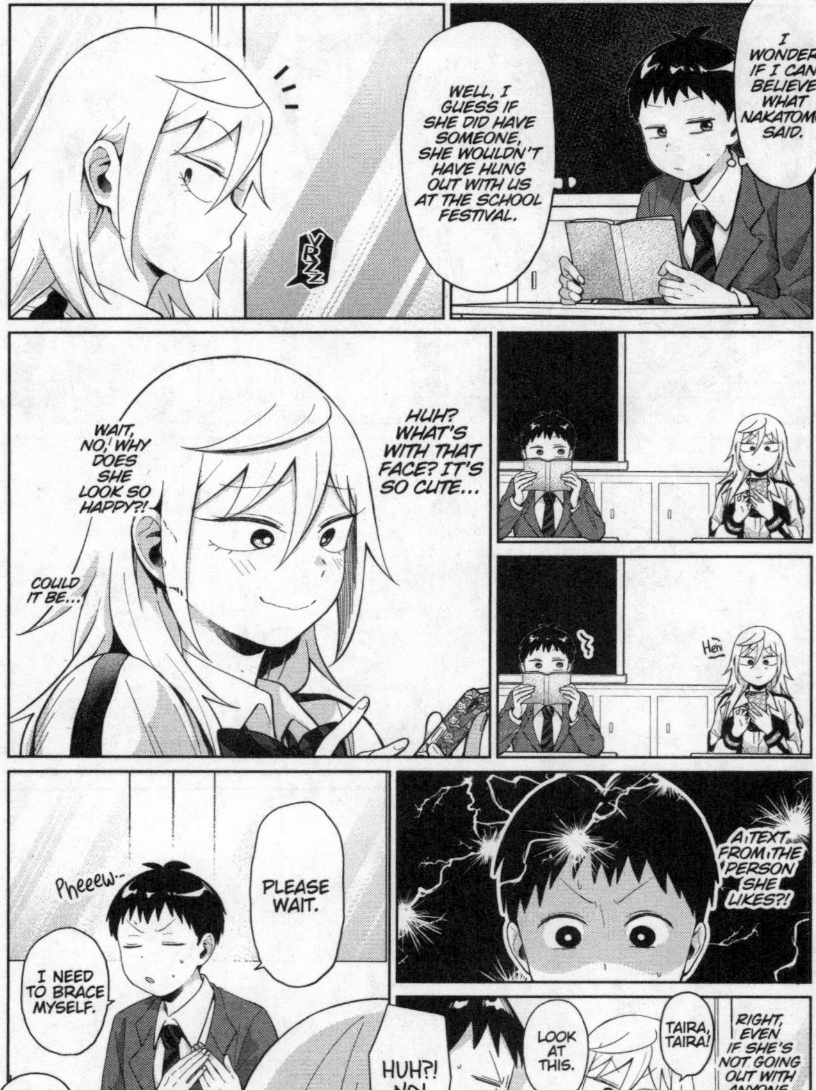
I WONDER IF I CAN BELIEVE WHAT NAKATOMO SAID.
WELL, I GUESS IF SHE DID HAVE SOMEONE, SHE WOULDN'T HAVE HUNG OUT WITH US AT THE SCHOOL FESTIVAL.
VRZZ
Heh
HUH? WHAT'S WITH THAT FACE? IT'S SO CUTE...
WAIT, NO, WHY DOES SHE LOOK SO HAPPY?!
COULD IT BE...
A TEXT FROM THE PERSON SHE LIKES?!
RIGHT, EVEN IF SHE'S NOT GOING OUT WITH ANYONE, SHE MIGHT HAVE A CRUSH ON SOMEONE.
TAIRA, TAIRA!
LOOK AT THIS.
HUH?! NO!
PLEASE WAIT.
Pheeew...
I NEED TO BRACE MYSELF.
HUH? WHY?

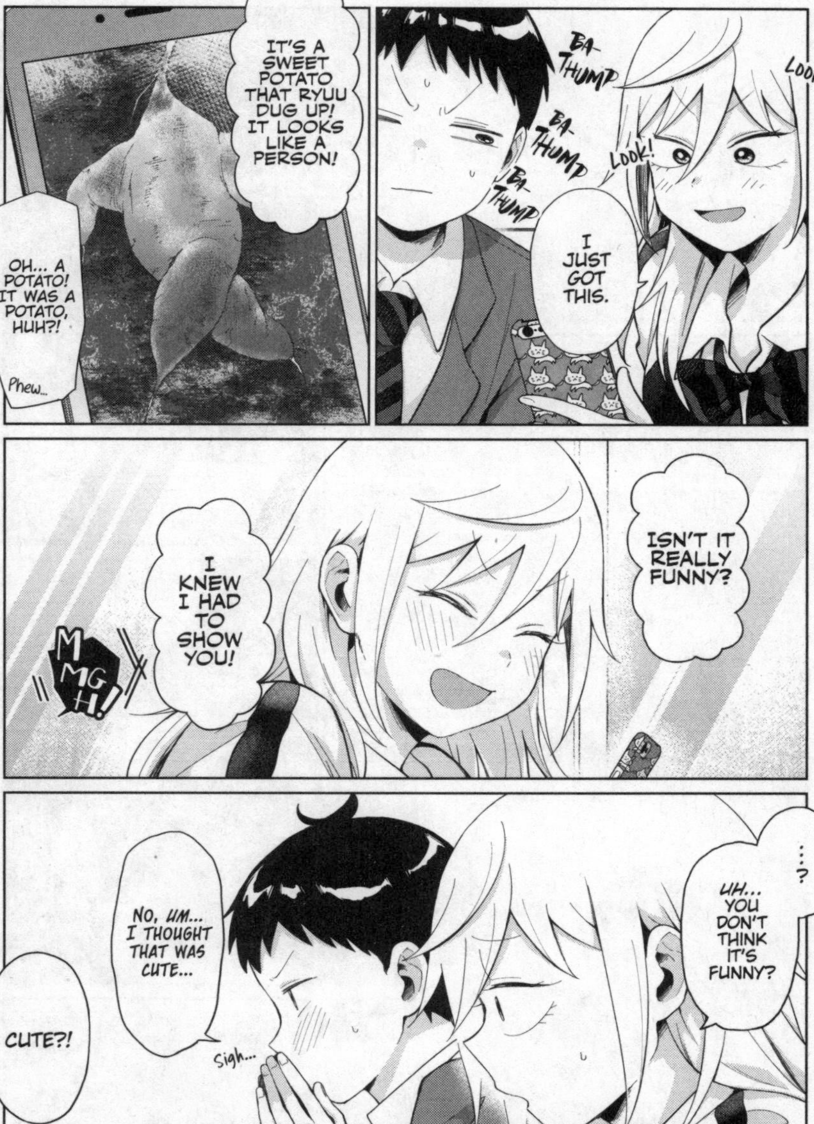
LOOK!
BA-THUMP
BA-THUMP
BA-THUMP
LOOK!
I JUST GOT THIS.
IT'S A SWEET POTATO THAT RYUU DUG UP! IT LOOKS LIKE A PERSON!
OH... A POTATO! IT WAS A POTATO, HUH?!
Phew...
ISN'T IT REALLY FUNNY?
I KNEW I HAD TO SHOW YOU!
MMGH!
...?
UH... YOU DON'T THINK IT'S FUNNY?
NO, UM... I THOUGHT THAT WAS CUTE...
Sigh...
CUTE?!

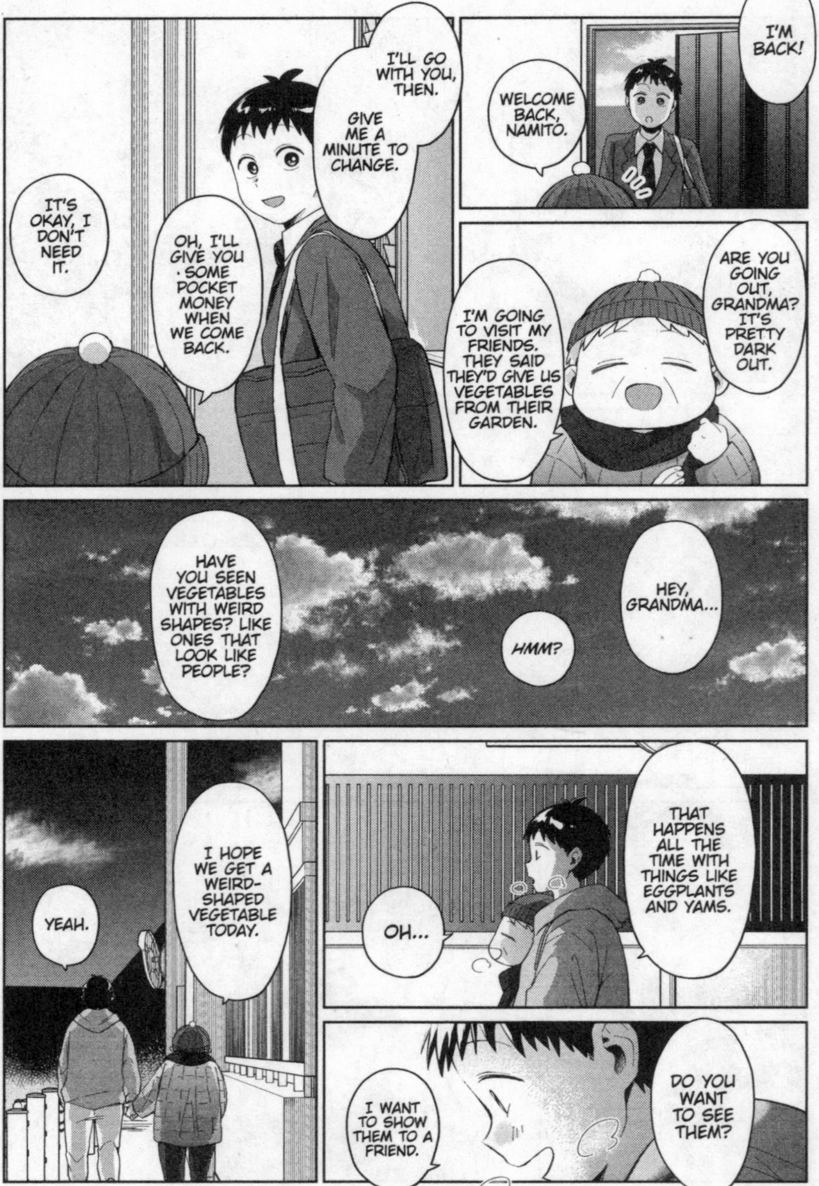
I'M BACK!
WELCOME BACK, NAMITO.
ARE YOU GOING OUT, GRANDMA? IT'S PRETTY DARK OUT.
I'M GOING TO VISIT MY FRIENDS. THEY SAID THEY'D GIVE US VEGETABLES FROM THEIR GARDEN.
I'LL GO WITH YOU, THEN.
GIVE ME A MINUTE TO CHANGE.
OH, I'LL GIVE YOU SOME POCKET MONEY WHEN WE COME BACK.
IT'S OKAY, I DON'T NEED IT.
HEY, GRANDMA...
HMM?
HAVE YOU SEEN VEGETABLES WITH WEIRD SHAPES? LIKE ONES THAT LOOK LIKE PEOPLE?
THAT HAPPENS ALL THE TIME WITH THINGS LIKE EGGPLANTS AND YAMS.
OH...
DO YOU WANT TO SEE THEM?
I WANT TO SHOW THEM TO A FRIEND.
I HOPE WE GET A WEIRD-SHAPED VEGETABLE TODAY.
YEAH.

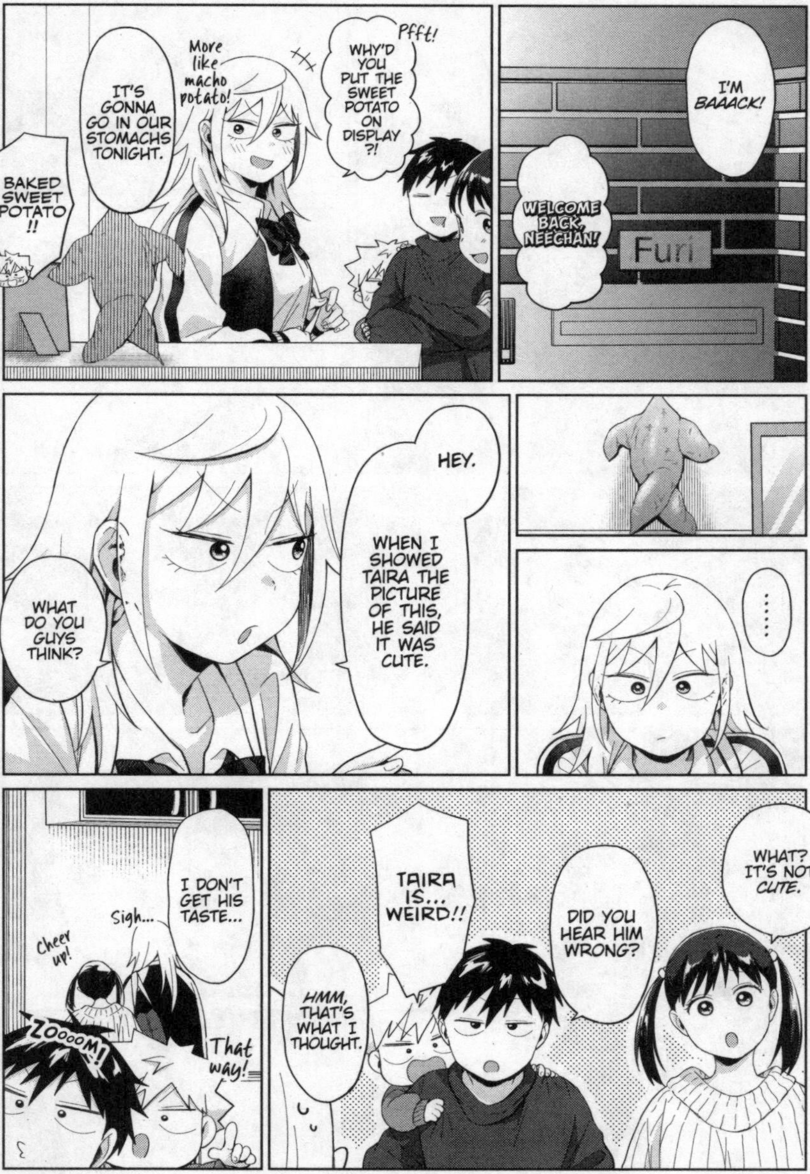
I'M BAAACK!
WELCOME BACK, NEECHAN!
Furi
Pfft!
WHY'D YOU PUT THE SWEET POTATO ON DISPLAY?!
More like macho potato!
IT'S GONNA GO IN OUR STOMACHS TONIGHT.
BAKED SWEET POTATO!!
......
HEY.
WHEN I SHOWED TAIRA THE PICTURE OF THIS, HE SAID IT WAS CUTE.
WHAT DO YOU GUYS THINK?
WHAT? IT'S NOT CUTE.
DID YOU HEAR HIM WRONG?
TAIRA IS... WEIRD!!
HMM, THAT'S WHAT I THOUGHT.
I DON'T GET HIS TASTE...
Sigh...
Cheer up!
That way!
ZOOOOM!

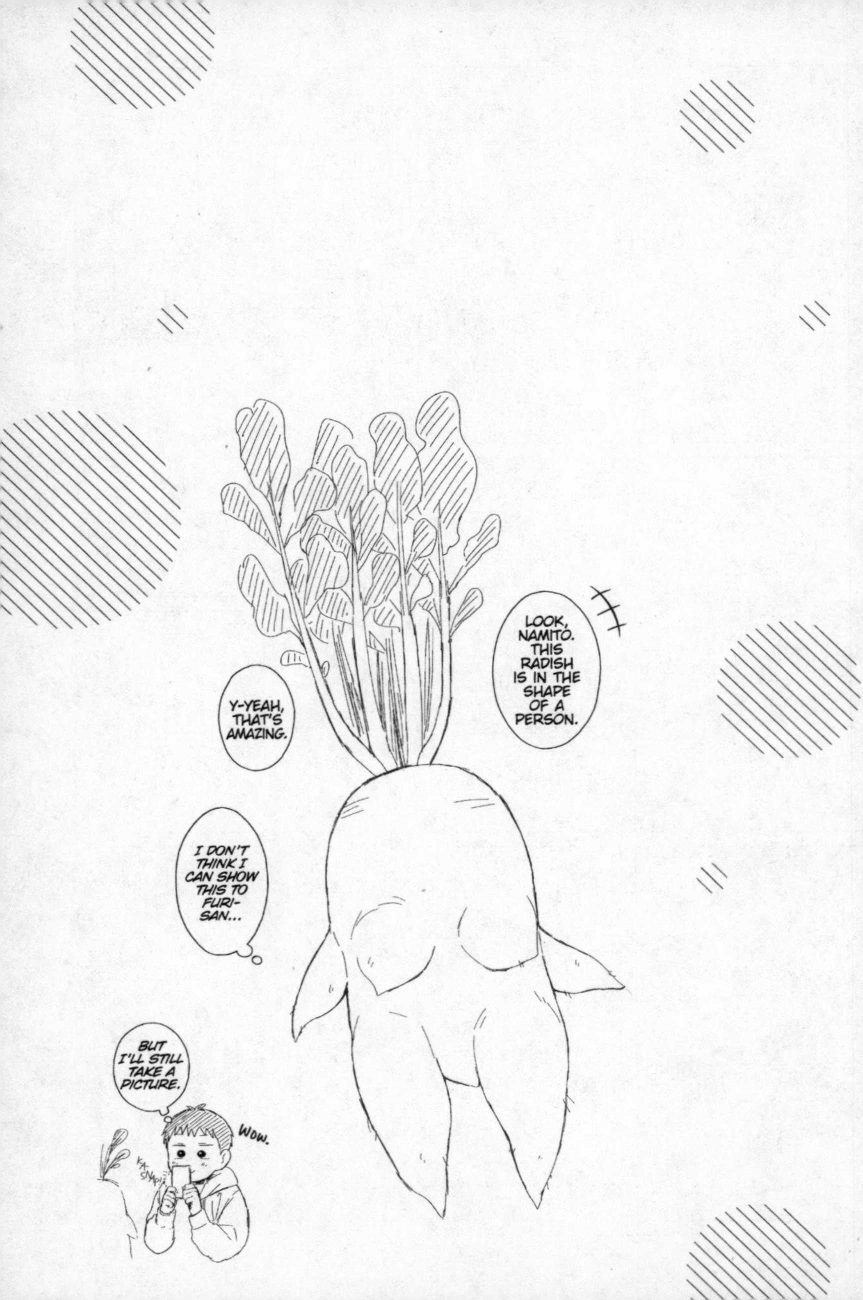
LOOK, NAMITO. THIS RADISH IS IN THE SHAPE OF A PERSON.
Y-YEAH, THAT'S AMAZING.
I DON'T THINK I CAN SHOW THIS TO FURI-SAN...
WOW.
BUT I'LL STILL TAKE A PICTURE.
KA-SNAP!

Chapter 29

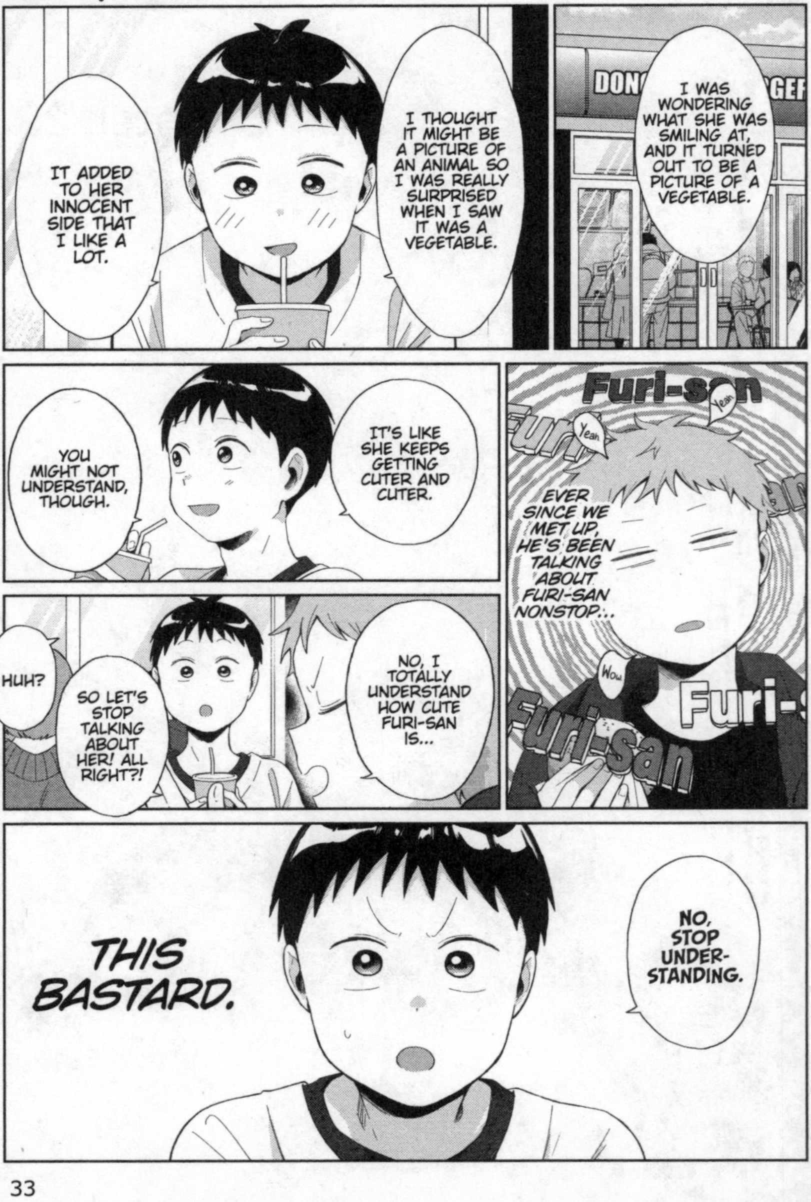
I WAS WONDERING WHAT SHE WAS SMILING AT, AND IT TURNED OUT TO BE A PICTURE OF A VEGETABLE.
I THOUGHT IT MIGHT BE A PICTURE OF AN ANIMAL SO I WAS REALLY SURPRISED WHEN I SAW IT WAS A VEGETABLE.
IT ADDED TO HER INNOCENT SIDE THAT I LIKE A LOT.
Furi-san
Yeah
Yeah
EVER SINCE WE MET UP, HE'S BEEN TALKING ABOUT FURI-SAN NONSTOP...
Wow
Furi-san
Furi-san
IT'S LIKE SHE KEEPS GETTING CUTER AND CUTER.
YOU MIGHT NOT UNDERSTAND, THOUGH.
NO, I TOTALLY UNDERSTAND HOW CUTE FURI-SAN IS...
SO LET'S STOP TALKING ABOUT HER! ALL RIGHT?!
HUH?
NO, STOP UNDER-STANDING.
THIS BASTARD.

Chapter 29

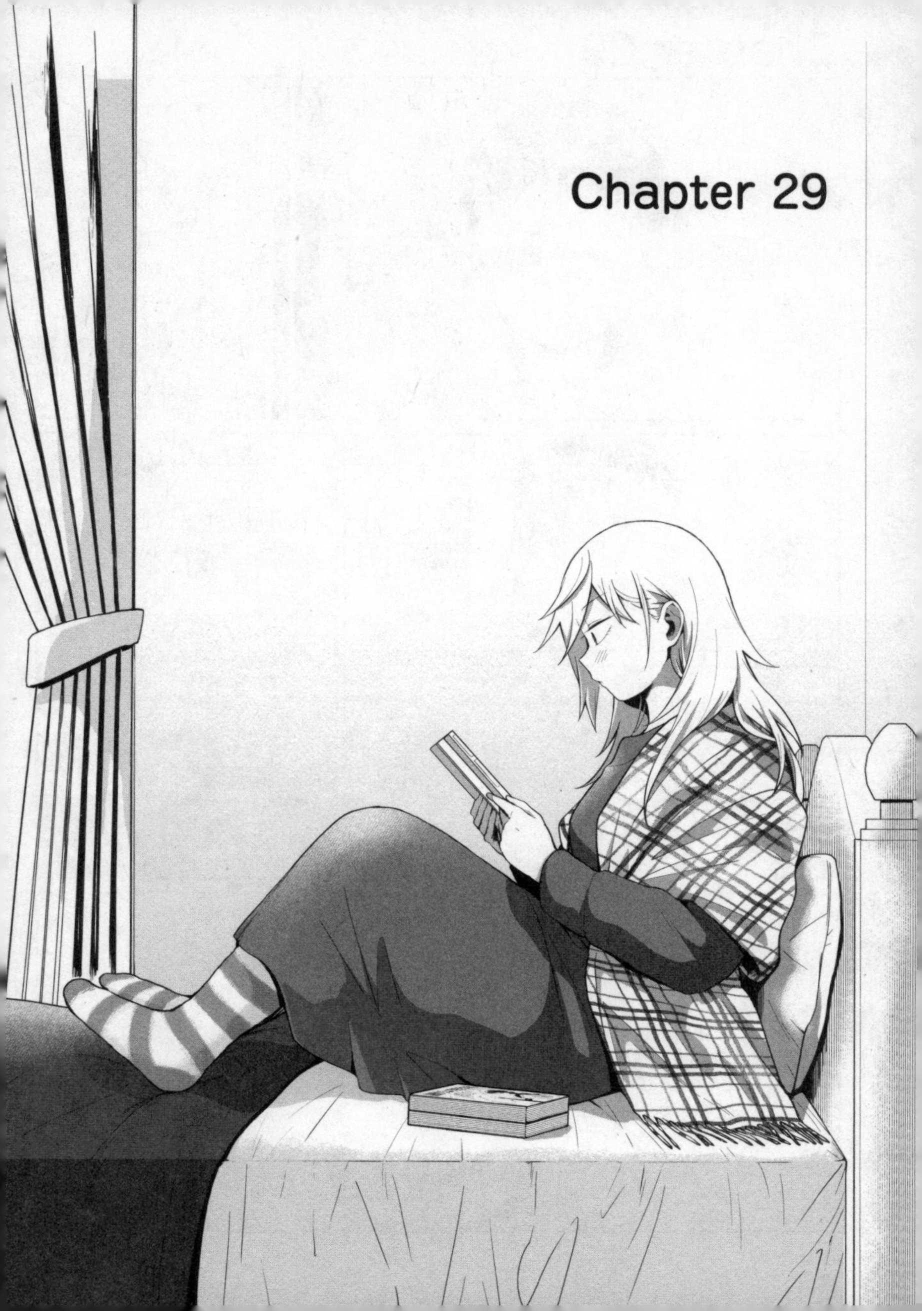

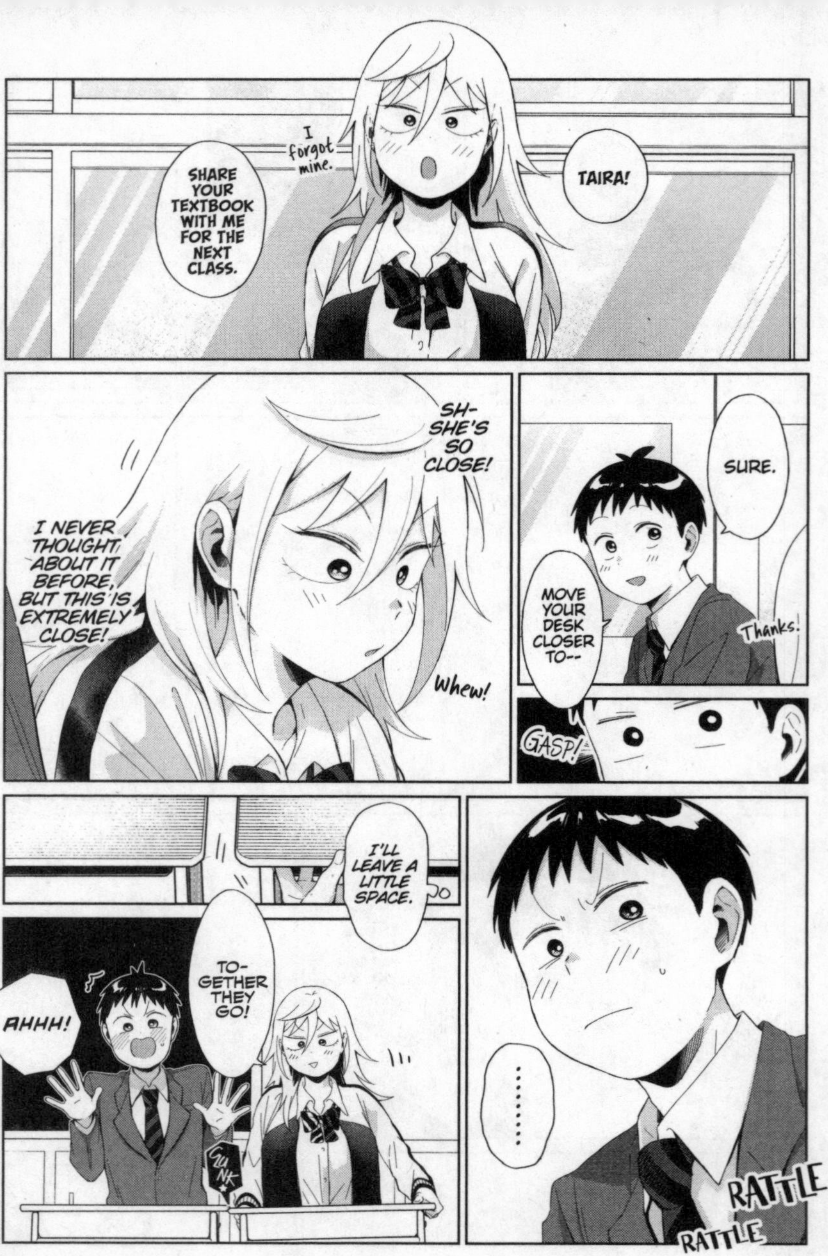
TAIRA!
I forgot mine.
SHARE YOUR TEXTBOOK WITH ME FOR THE NEXT CLASS.
SURE.
MOVE YOUR DESK CLOSER TO--
Thanks!
GASP!
SH-SHE'S SO CLOSE!
I NEVER THOUGHT ABOUT IT BEFORE, BUT THIS IS EXTREMELY CLOSE!
Whew!
......
RATTLE
RATTLE
I'LL LEAVE A LITTLE SPACE.
TO-GETHER THEY GO!
AHHH!
CLUNK

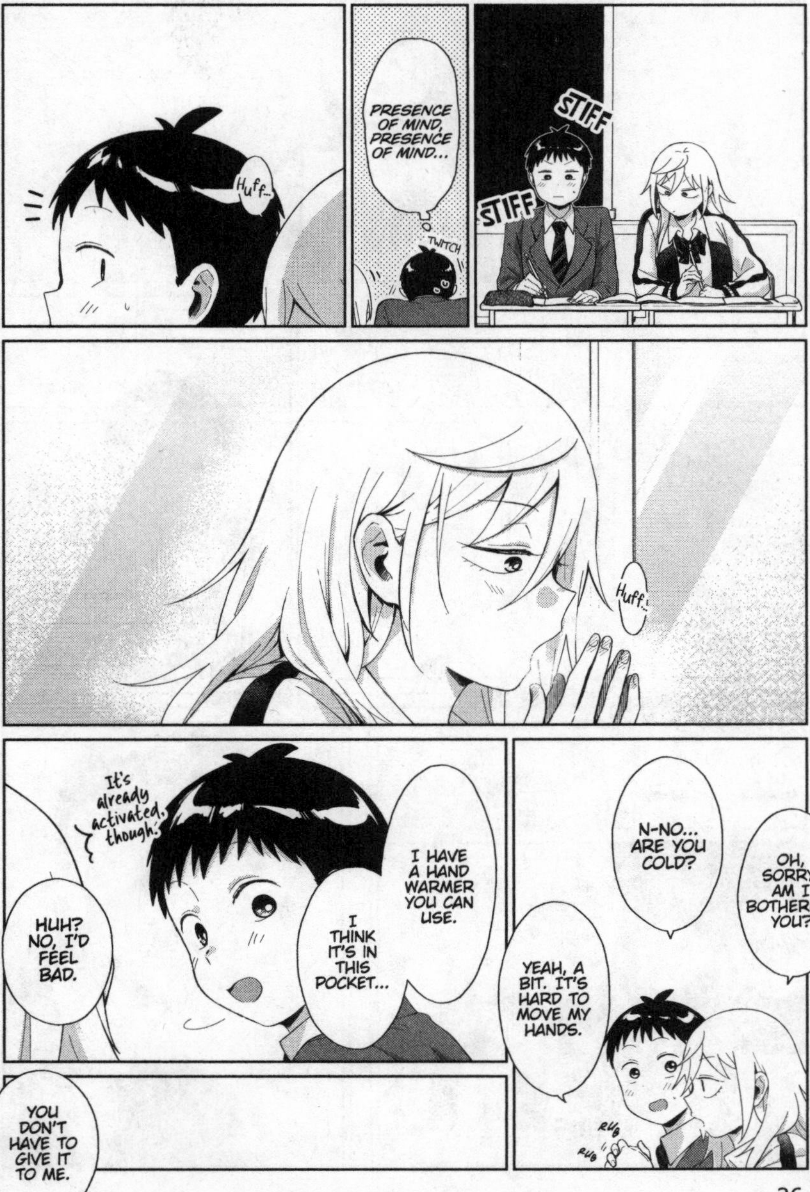
STIFF
STIFF
PRESENCE OF MIND, PRESENCE OF MIND...
TWITCH
Huff...
Huff...
OH, SORRY. AM I BOTHERING YOU?
N-NO... ARE YOU COLD?
YEAH, A BIT. IT'S HARD TO MOVE MY HANDS.
RUB
RUB
I HAVE A HAND WARMER YOU CAN USE.
I THINK IT'S IN THIS POCKET...
It's already activated, though.
HUH? NO, I'D FEEL BAD.
YOU DON'T HAVE TO GIVE IT TO ME.

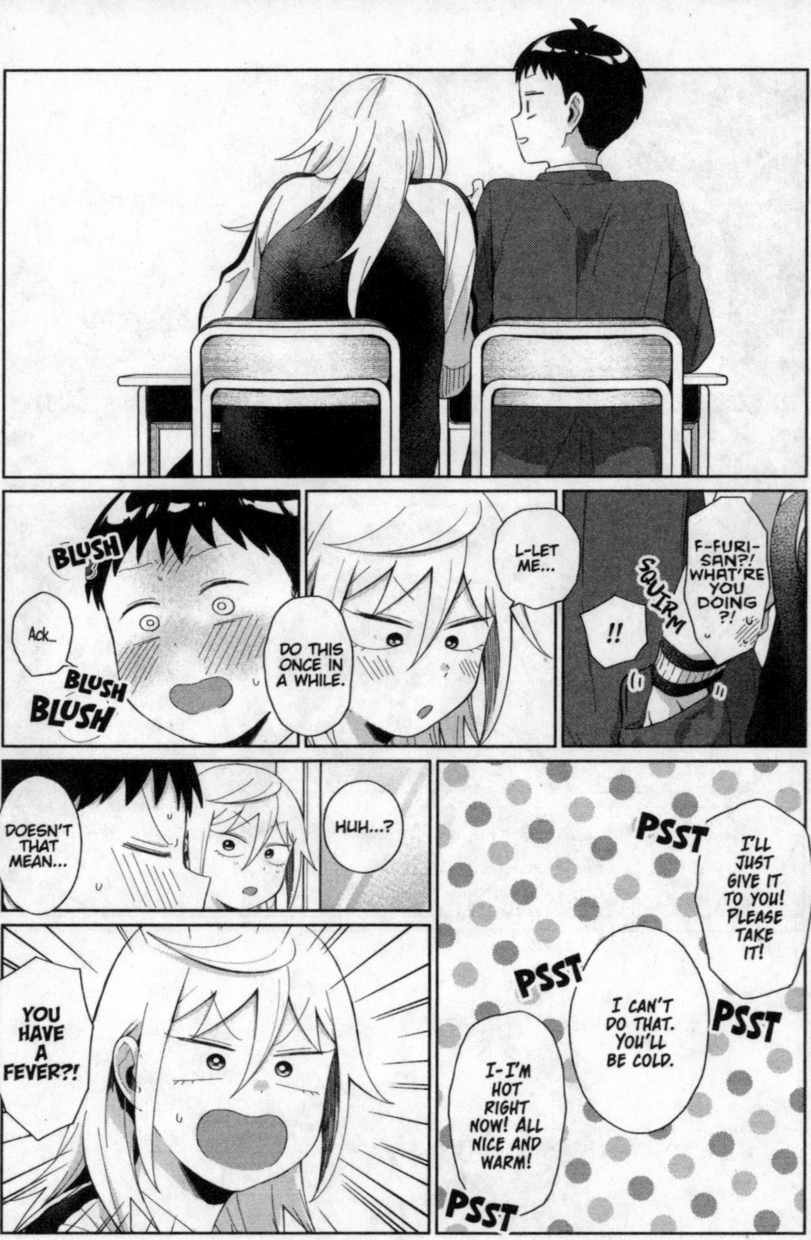
F-FURI-SAN?! WHAT'RE YOU DOING?!
SQUIRM
!!
L-LET ME...
DO THIS ONCE IN A WHILE.
BLUSH
Ack...
BLUSH
BLUSH
PSST
I'LL JUST GIVE IT TO YOU! PLEASE TAKE IT!
PSST
I CAN'T DO THAT. YOU'LL BE COLD.
PSST
I-I'M HOT RIGHT NOW! ALL NICE AND WARM!
PSST
HUH...?
DOESN'T THAT MEAN...
YOU HAVE A FEVER?!

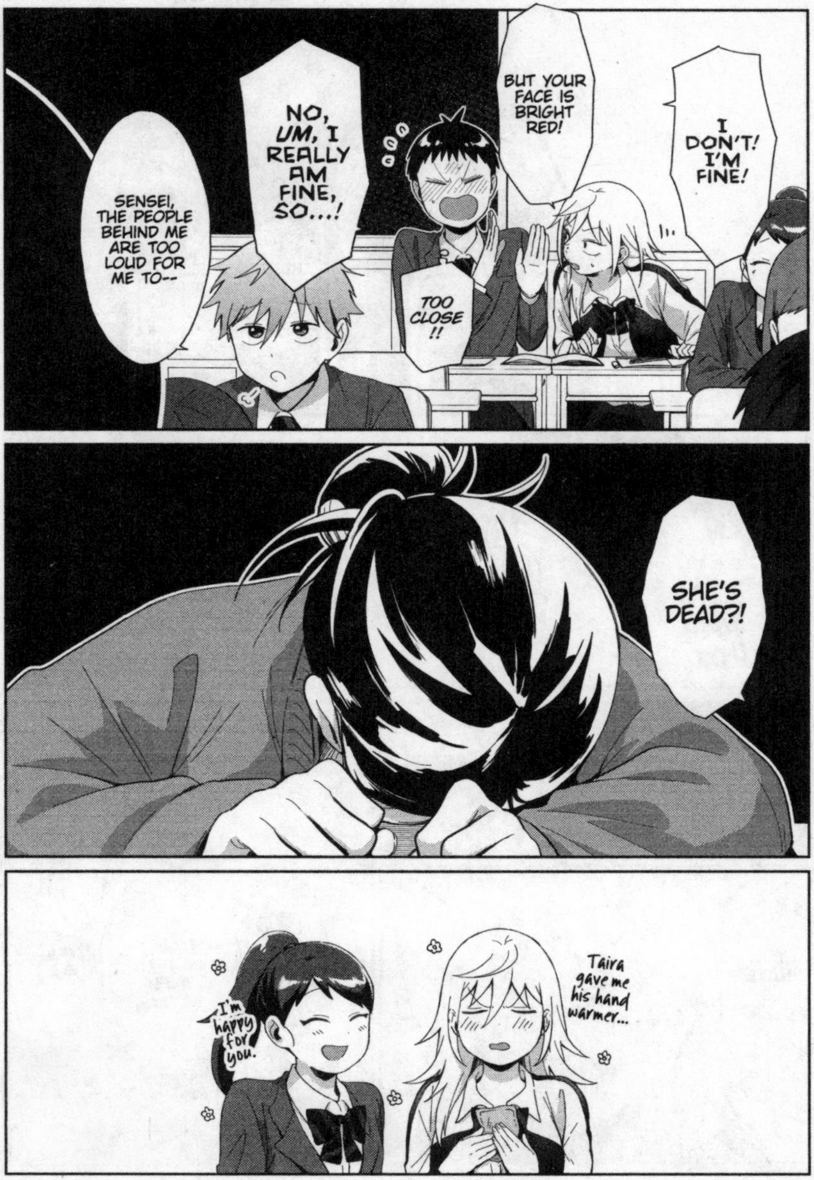
I DON'T! I'M FINE!
BUT YOUR FACE IS BRIGHT RED!
NO, UM, I REALLY AM FINE, SO...!
TOO CLOSE!!
SENSEI, THE PEOPLE BEHIND ME ARE TOO LOUD FOR ME TO--
SHE'S DEAD?!
Taira gave me his hand warmer...
I'm happy for you.

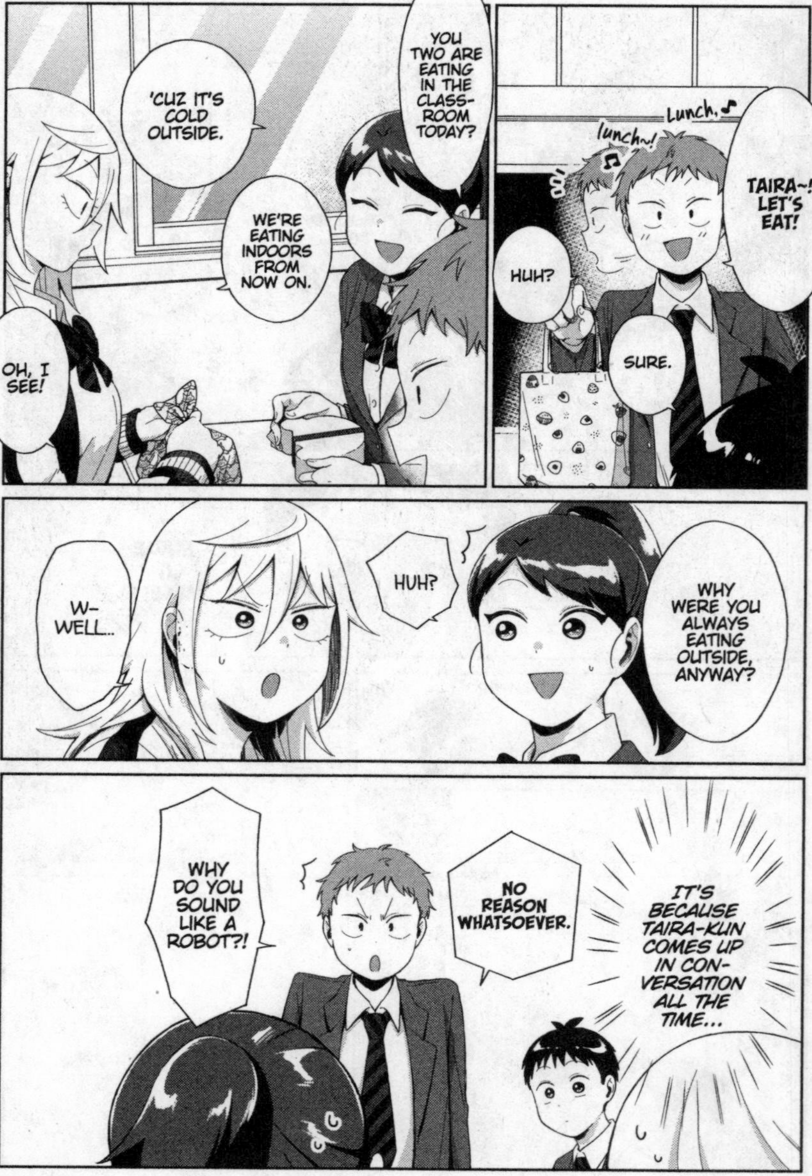
Lunch,♪
lunch~!♪
TAIRA~! LET'S EAT!
HUH?
SURE.
YOU TWO ARE EATING IN THE CLASSROOM TODAY?
'CUZ IT'S COLD OUTSIDE.
WE'RE EATING INDOORS FROM NOW ON.
OH, I SEE!
WHY WERE YOU ALWAYS EATING OUTSIDE, ANYWAY?
HUH?
W-WELL...
IT'S BECAUSE TAIRA-KUN COMES UP IN CON-VERSATION ALL THE TIME...
NO REASON WHATSOEVER.
WHY DO YOU SOUND LIKE A ROBOT?!

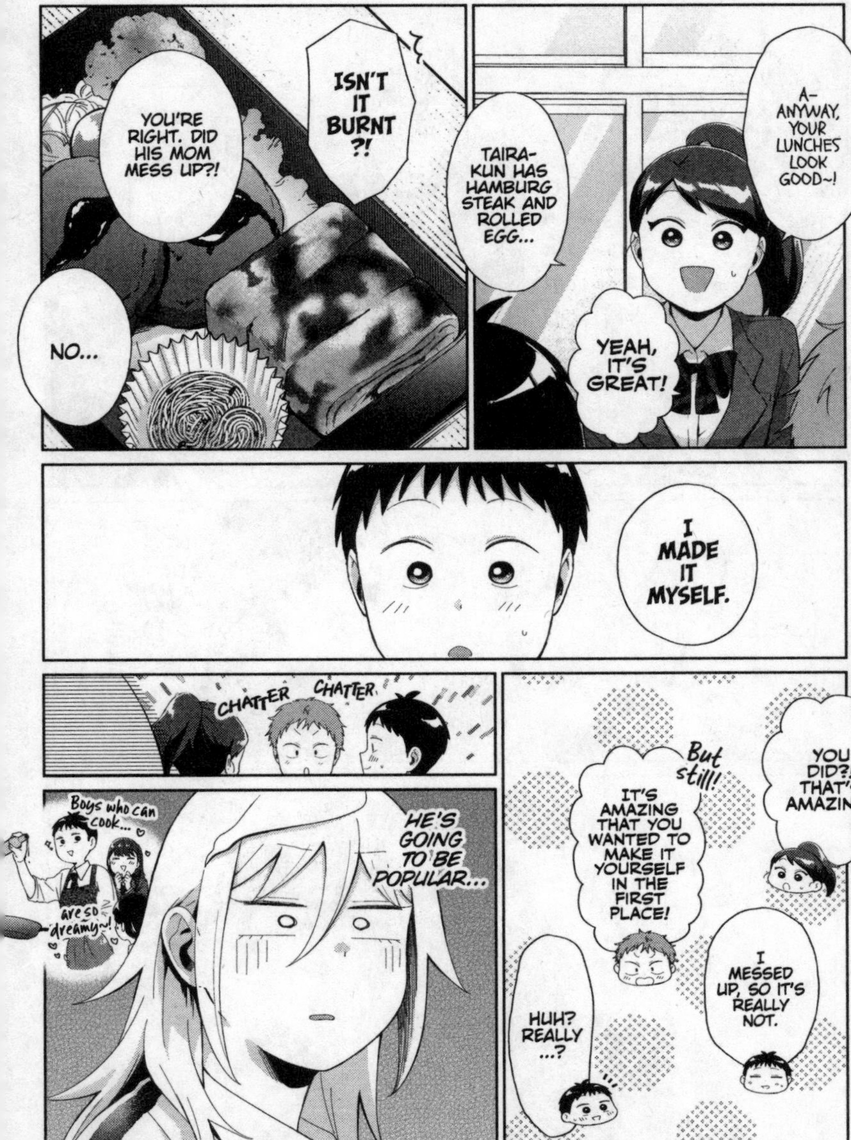
A-ANYWAY, YOUR LUNCHES LOOK GOOD~!
TAIRA-KUN HAS HAMBURG STEAK AND ROLLED EGG...
YEAH, IT'S GREAT!
ISN'T IT BURNT?!
YOU'RE RIGHT. DID HIS MOM MESS UP?!
NO...
I MADE IT MYSELF.
YOU DID?! THAT'S AMAZING!
But still!
IT'S AMAZING THAT YOU WANTED TO MAKE IT YOURSELF IN THE FIRST PLACE!
I MESSED UP, SO IT'S REALLY NOT.
HUH? REALLY ...?
CHATTER CHATTER
HE'S GOING TO BE POPULAR...
Boys who can cook... are so dreamy~!

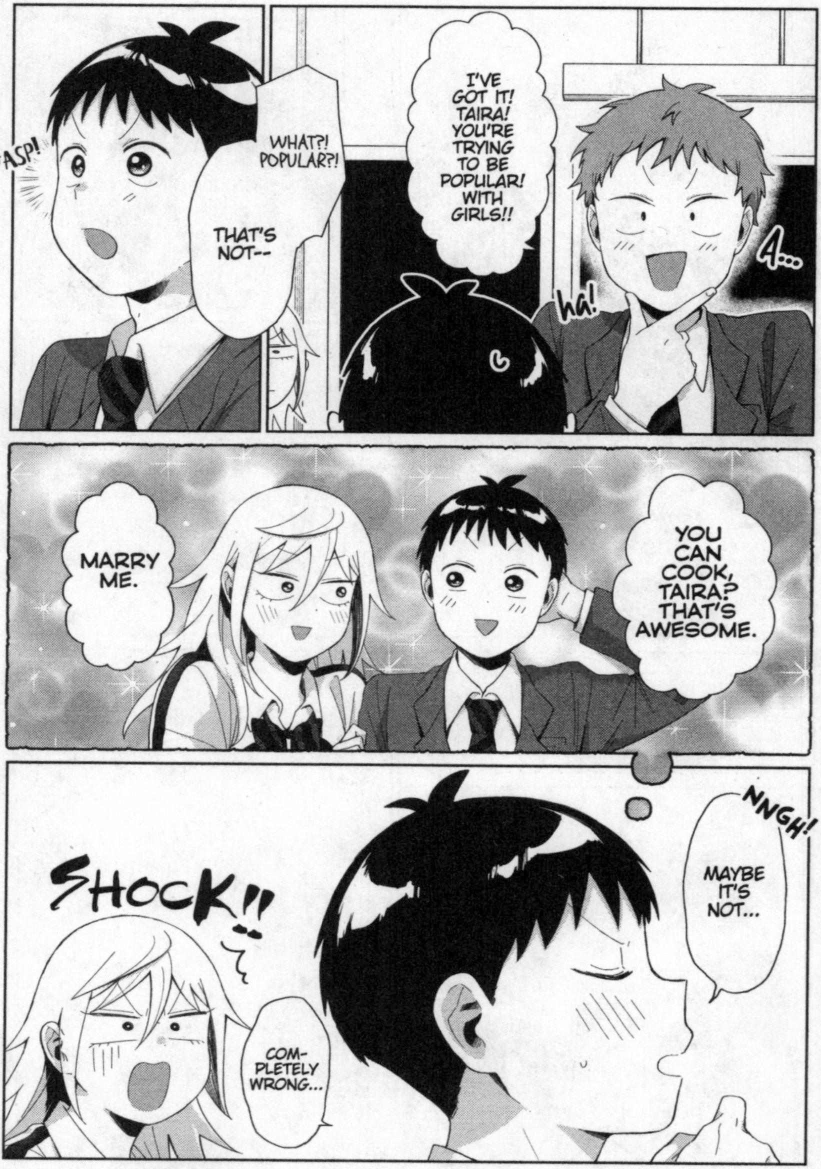
I'VE GOT IT! TAIRA! YOU'RE TRYING TO BE POPULAR! WITH GIRLS!!
A...
ha!
WHAT?! POPULAR?!
THAT'S NOT--
GASP!
YOU CAN COOK, TAIRA? THAT'S AWESOME.
MARRY ME.
NNGH!
MAYBE IT'S NOT...
SHOCK!!
COM-PLETELY WRONG...

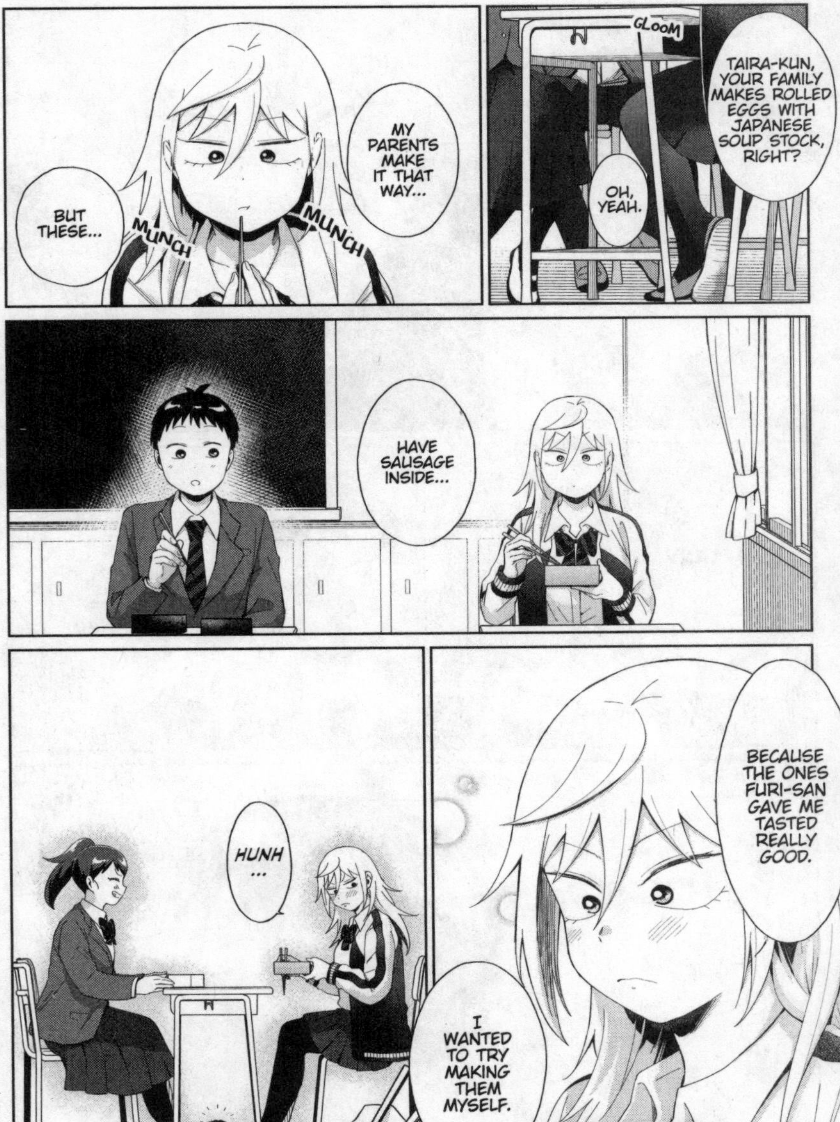
GLOOM
TAIRA-KUN, YOUR FAMILY MAKES ROLLED EGGS WITH JAPANESE SOUP STOCK, RIGHT?
OH, YEAH.
MY PARENTS MAKE IT THAT WAY...
MUNCH
MUNCH
BUT THESE...
HAVE SAUSAGE INSIDE...
BECAUSE THE ONES FURI-SAN GAVE ME TASTED REALLY GOOD.
I WANTED TO TRY MAKING THEM MYSELF.
HUNH ...

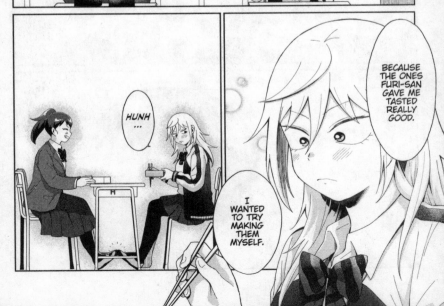

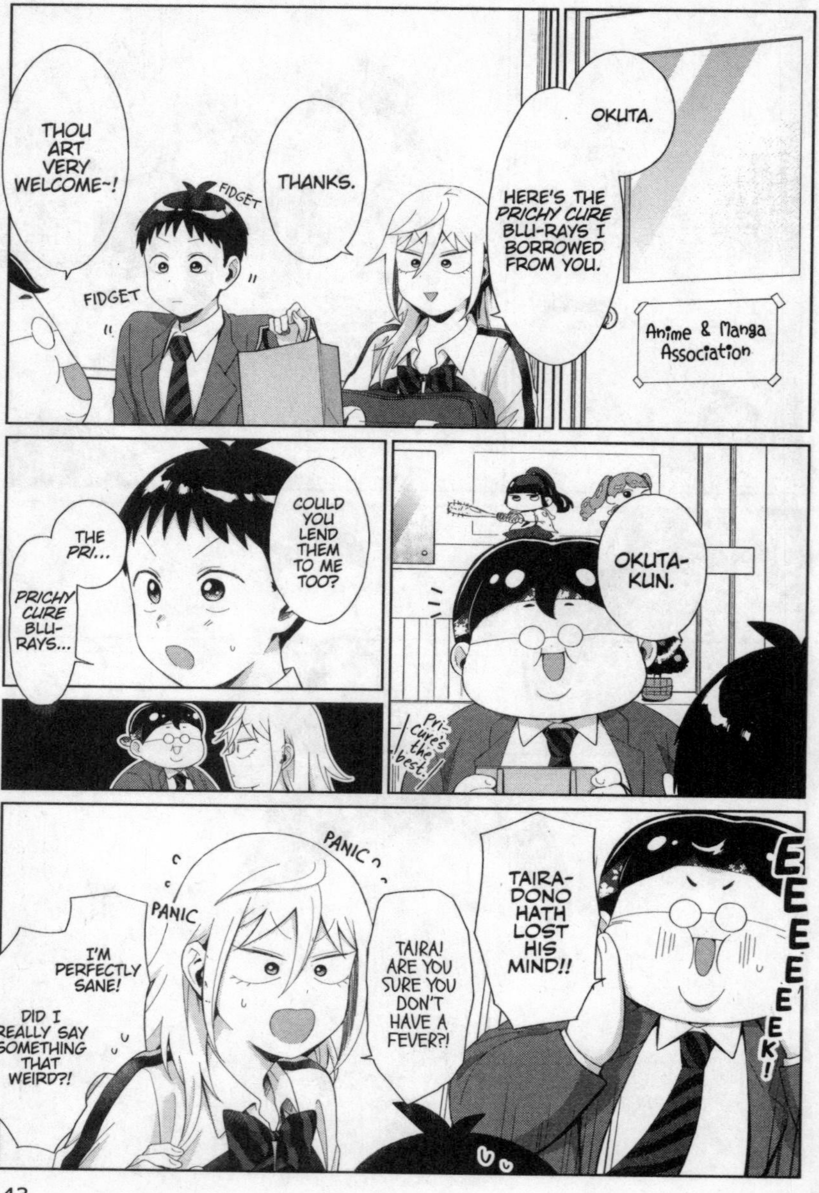
OKUTA.
HERE'S THE *PRICHY CURE* BLU-RAYS I BORROWED FROM YOU.
Anime & Manga Association
THANKS.
FIDGET
FIDGET
THOU ART VERY WELCOME~!
OKUTA-KUN.
Pri-Cure's the best.
COULD YOU LEND THEM TO ME TOO?
THE *PRI*...
PRICHY CURE BLU-RAYS...
EEEEEEEK!
TAIRA-DONO HATH LOST HIS MIND!!
TAIRA! ARE YOU SURE YOU DON'T HAVE A FEVER?!
PANIC
PANIC
I'M PERFECTLY SANE!
DID I REALLY SAY SOMETHING THAT WEIRD?!

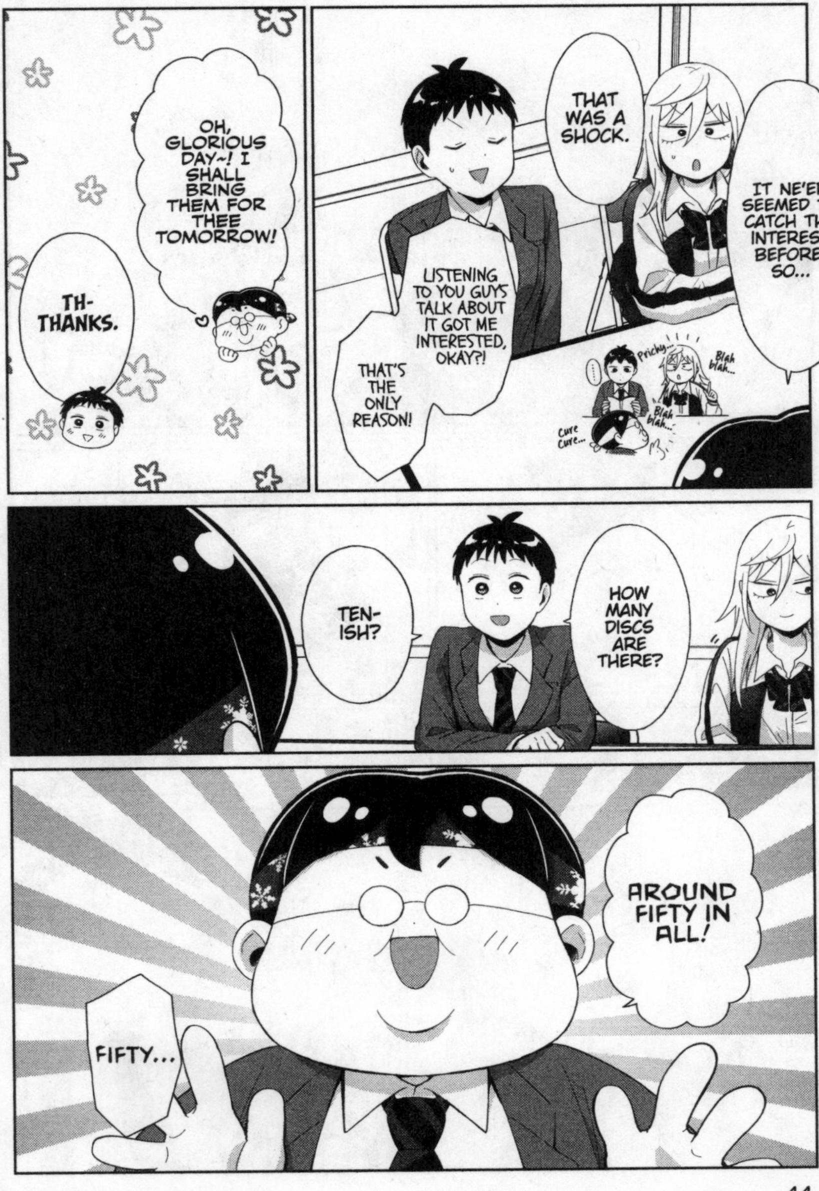
THAT WAS A SHOCK.
IT NE'ER SEEMED TO CATCH THY INTEREST BEFORE, SO...
LISTENING TO YOU GUYS TALK ABOUT IT GOT ME INTERESTED, OKAY?!
THAT'S THE ONLY REASON!
Prichy...
Blah blah...
Blah blah...
Cure Cure...
OH, GLORIOUS DAY~! I SHALL BRING THEM FOR THEE TOMORROW!
TH-THANKS.
HOW MANY DISCS ARE THERE?
TEN-ISH?
AROUND FIFTY IN ALL!
FIFTY...

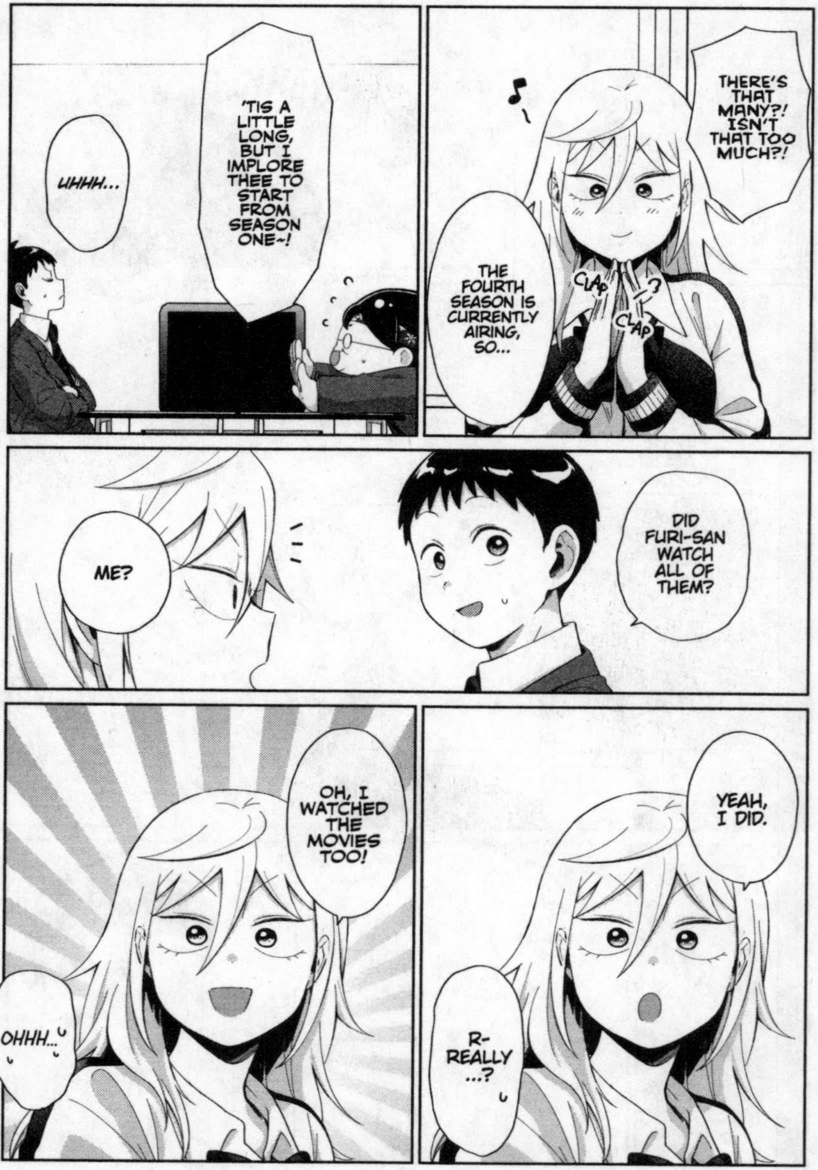
THERE'S THAT MANY?! ISN'T THAT TOO MUCH?!
CLAP CLAP
THE FOURTH SEASON IS CURRENTLY AIRING, SO...
'TIS A LITTLE LONG, BUT I IMPLORE THEE TO START FROM SEASON ONE~!
UHHH...
DID FURI-SAN WATCH ALL OF THEM?
ME?
YEAH, I DID.
R-REALLY ...?
OH, I WATCHED THE MOVIES TOO!
OHHH...

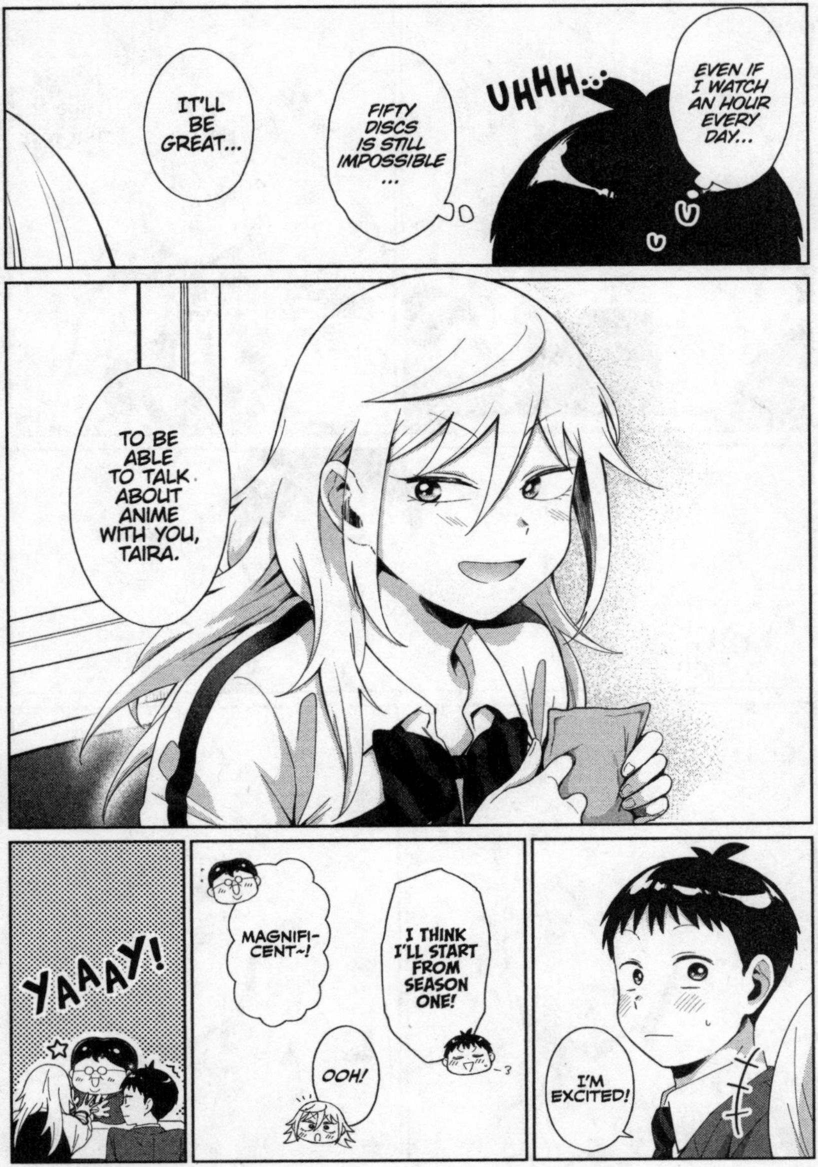
EVEN IF I WATCH AN HOUR EVERY DAY...
UHHH...
FIFTY DISCS IS STILL IMPOSSIBLE...
IT'LL BE GREAT...
TO BE ABLE TO TALK ABOUT ANIME WITH YOU, TAIRA.
I'M EXCITED!
I THINK I'LL START FROM SEASON ONE!
MAGNIFI-CENT~!
OOH!
YAAAY!

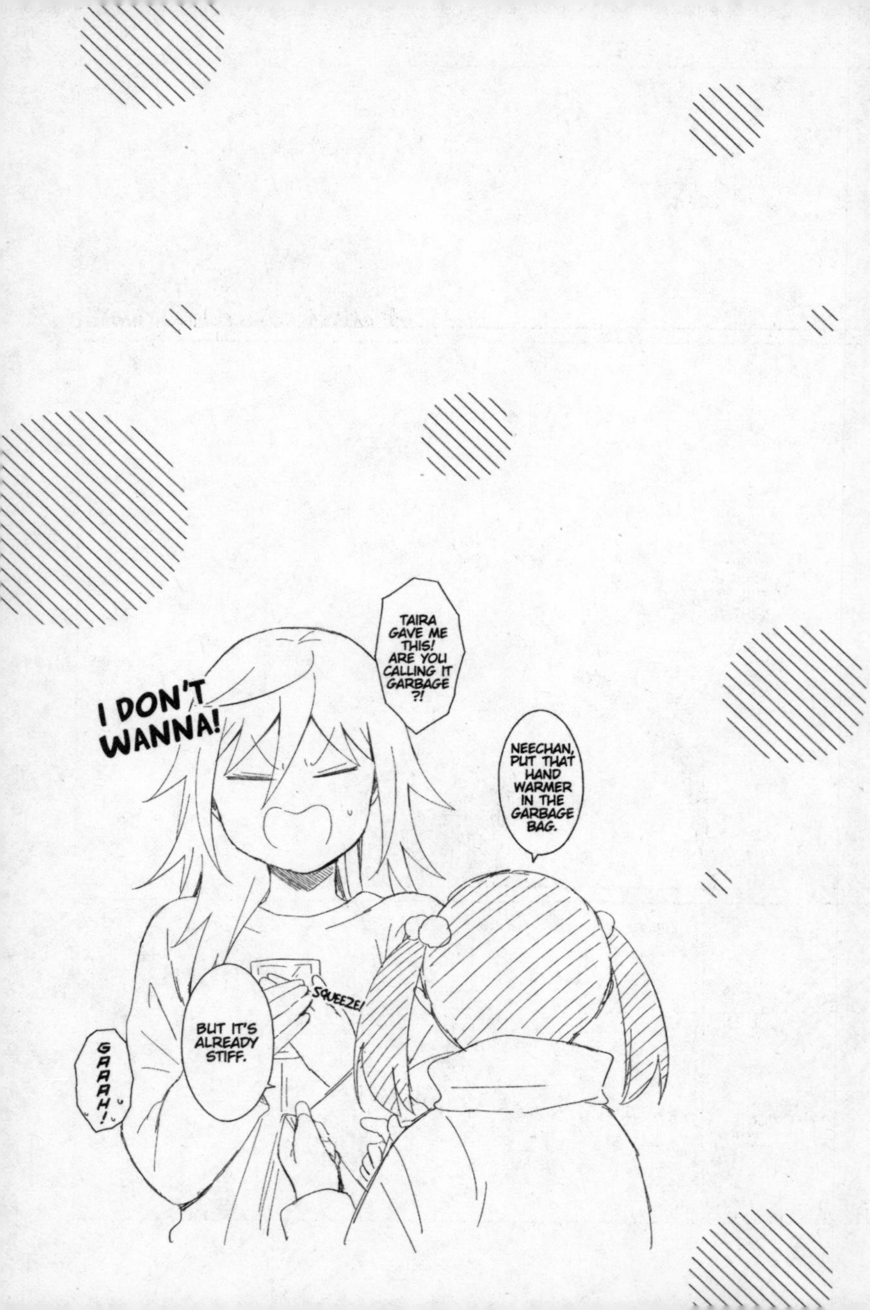
NEECHAN, PUT THAT HAND WARMER IN THE GARBAGE BAG.
I DON'T WANNA!
TAIRA GAVE ME THIS! ARE YOU CALLING IT GARBAGE?!
SQUEEZE!
BUT IT'S ALREADY STIFF.
GAAAH!

Chapter 30

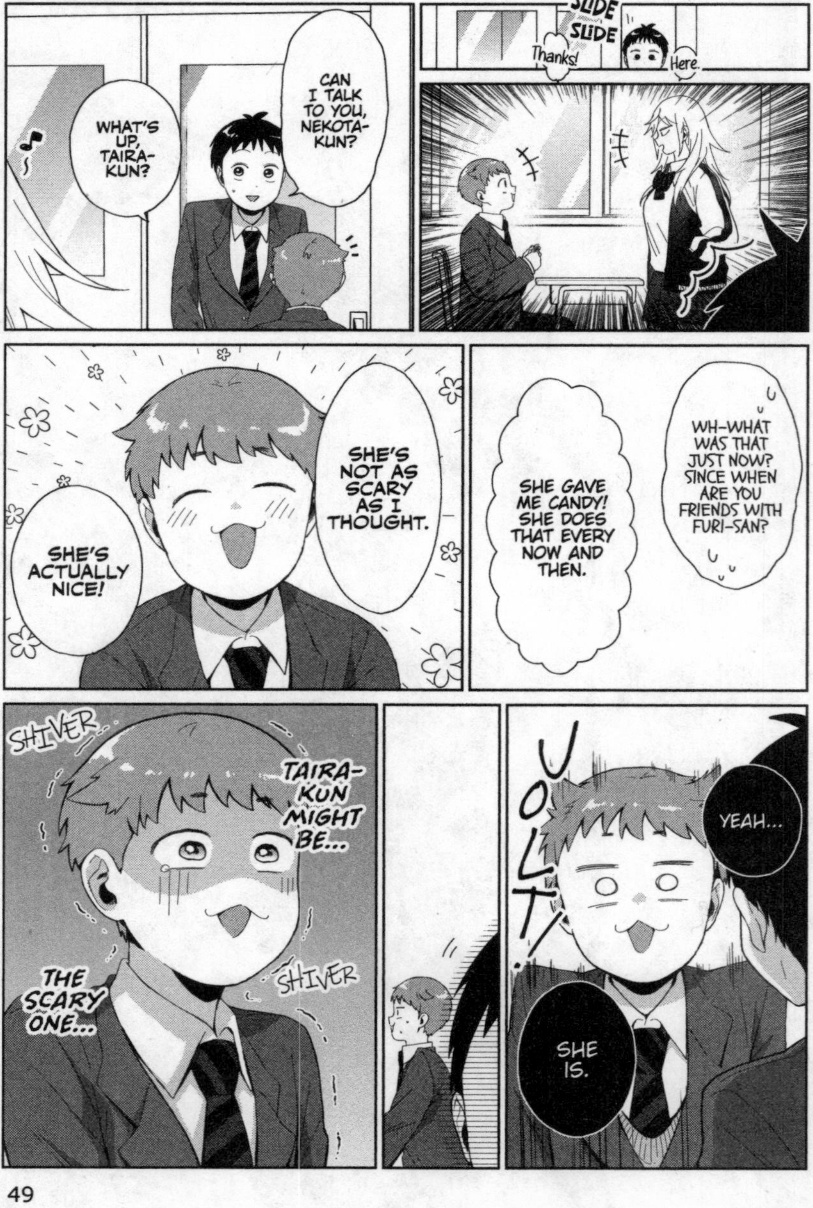
SLIDE
SLIDE
Here.
Thanks!
CAN I TALK TO YOU, NEKOTA-KUN?
WHAT'S UP, TAIRA-KUN?
WH-WHAT WAS THAT JUST NOW? SINCE WHEN ARE YOU FRIENDS WITH FURI-SAN?
SHE GAVE ME CANDY! SHE DOES THAT EVERY NOW AND THEN.
SHE'S NOT AS SCARY AS I THOUGHT.
SHE'S ACTUALLY NICE!
YEAH...
JOLT!
SHE IS.
SHIVER
TAIRA-KUN MIGHT BE...
THE SCARY ONE...
SHIVER

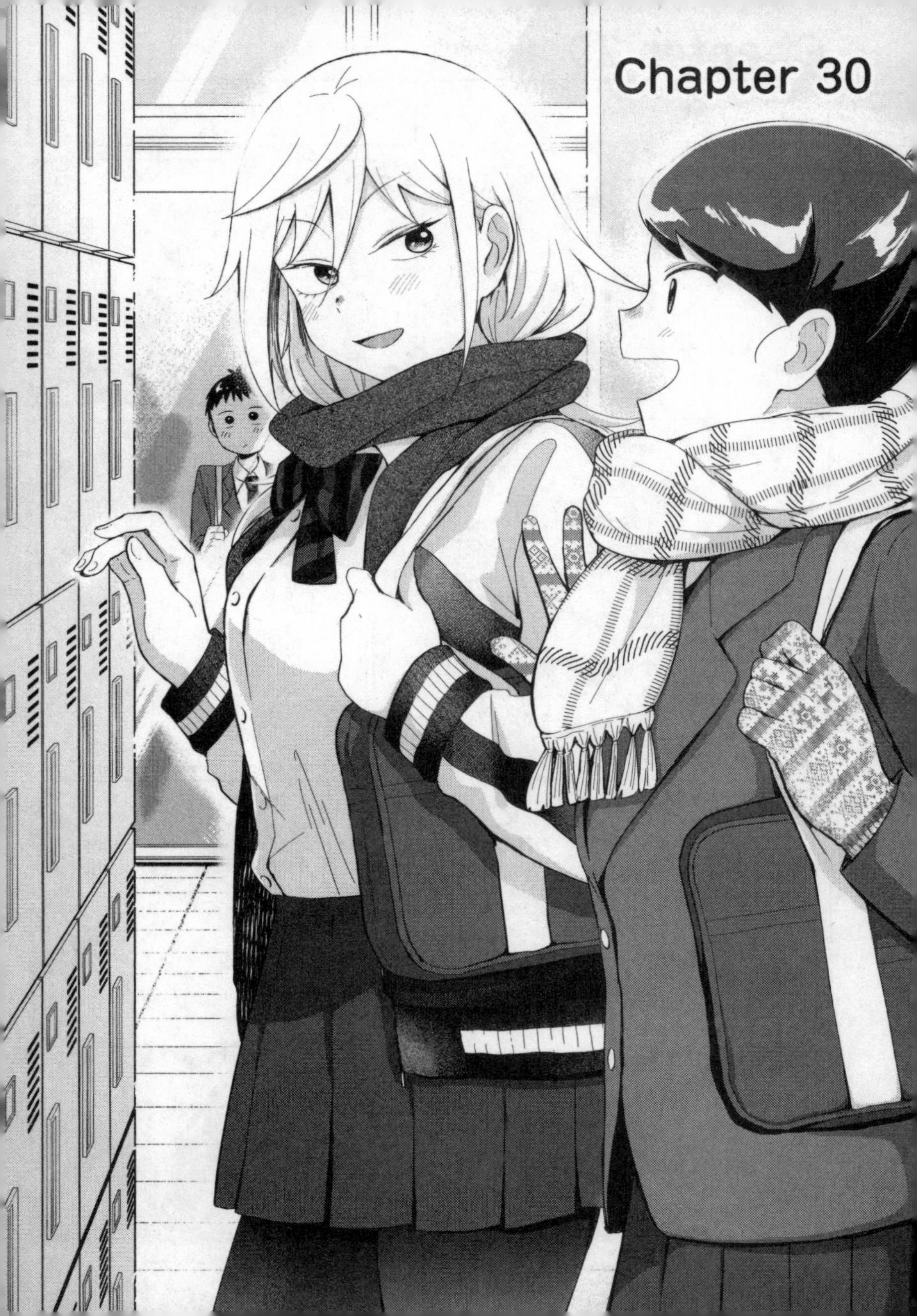
Chapter 30

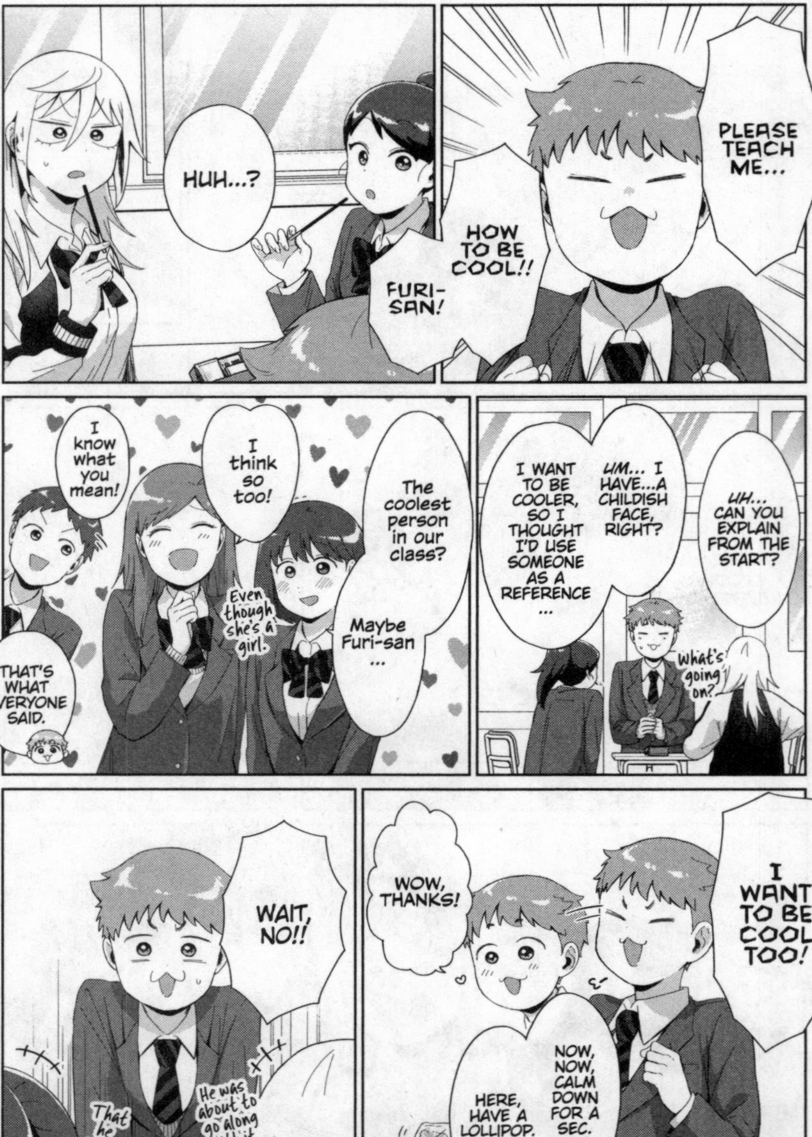

PLEASE TEACH ME...
HOW TO BE COOL!!
FURI-SAN!
HUH...?
UH... CAN YOU EXPLAIN FROM THE START?
UM... I HAVE...A CHILDISH FACE, RIGHT?
I WANT TO BE COOLER, SO I THOUGHT I'D USE SOMEONE AS A REFERENCE ...
What's going on?
The coolest person in our class?
I think so too!
I know what you mean!
Maybe Furi-san ...
Even though she's a girl.
THAT'S WHAT EVERYONE SAID.
I WANT TO BE COOL TOO!
WOW, THANKS!
NOW, NOW, CALM DOWN FOR A SEC.
HERE, HAVE A LOLLIPOP.
WAIT, NO!!
He was about to go along with it.
That he was.

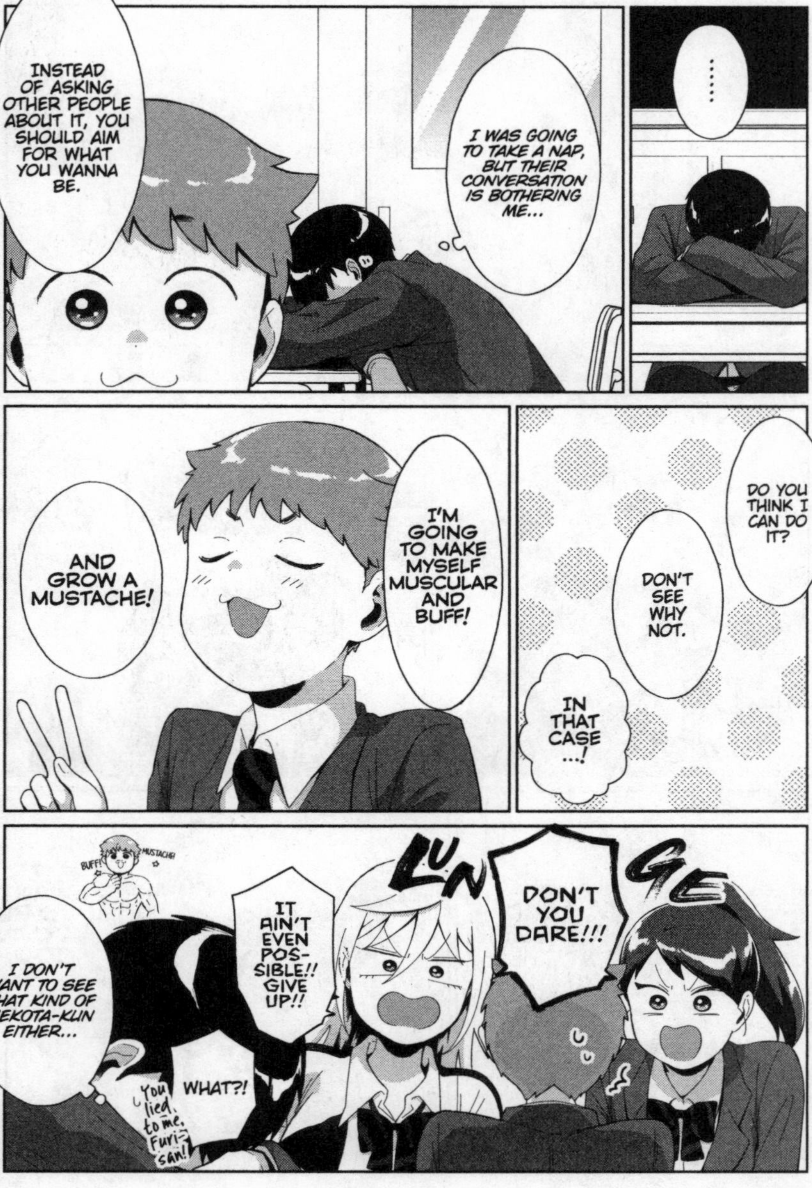
......
I WAS GOING TO TAKE A NAP, BUT THEIR CONVERSATION IS BOTHERING ME...
INSTEAD OF ASKING OTHER PEOPLE ABOUT IT, YOU SHOULD AIM FOR WHAT YOU WANNA BE.
DO YOU THINK I CAN DO IT?
DON'T SEE WHY NOT.
IN THAT CASE ...!
I'M GOING TO MAKE MYSELF MUSCULAR AND BUFF!
AND GROW A MUSTACHE!
LUNGE
DON'T YOU DARE!!!
IT AIN'T EVEN POS-SIBLE!! GIVE UP!!
WHAT?!
You lied to me, Furi-san!
MUSTACHE!
BUFF!
I DON'T WANT TO SEE THAT KIND OF NEKOTA-KUN EITHER...

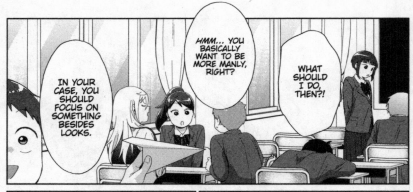

WHAT SHOULD I DO, THEN?!
HMM... YOU BASICALLY WANT TO BE MORE MANLY, RIGHT?
IN YOUR CASE, YOU SHOULD FOCUS ON SOMETHING BESIDES LOOKS.
WHY DON'T YOU TRY CHANGING THE WAY YOU TALK?
YEAH, YOU MIGHT SEEM MANLIER IF YOU TALK IN A GRUFF WAY.
OOH, I SEE!
HMM...
THAT DEFINITELY SOUNDS LIKE SOMETHING I CAN DO!
WELL, YOU AREN'T OFF TO A GREAT START~!
HEH HEH HEH!
OH!
AH HA HA HA!
HE CAN'T CHANGE SO QUICKLY.
I CAN'T SEE THEM, BUT THEY SOUND LIKE THEY'RE HAVING FUN!!
FIDGET
I'M SO JEALOUS!
FIDGET

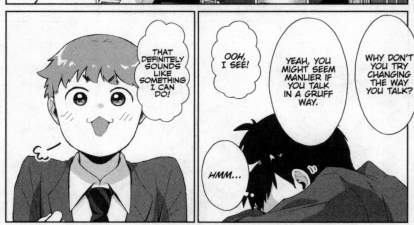

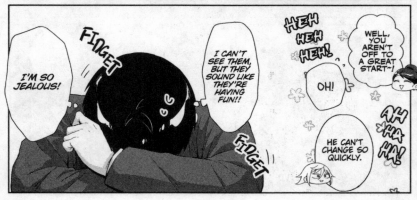

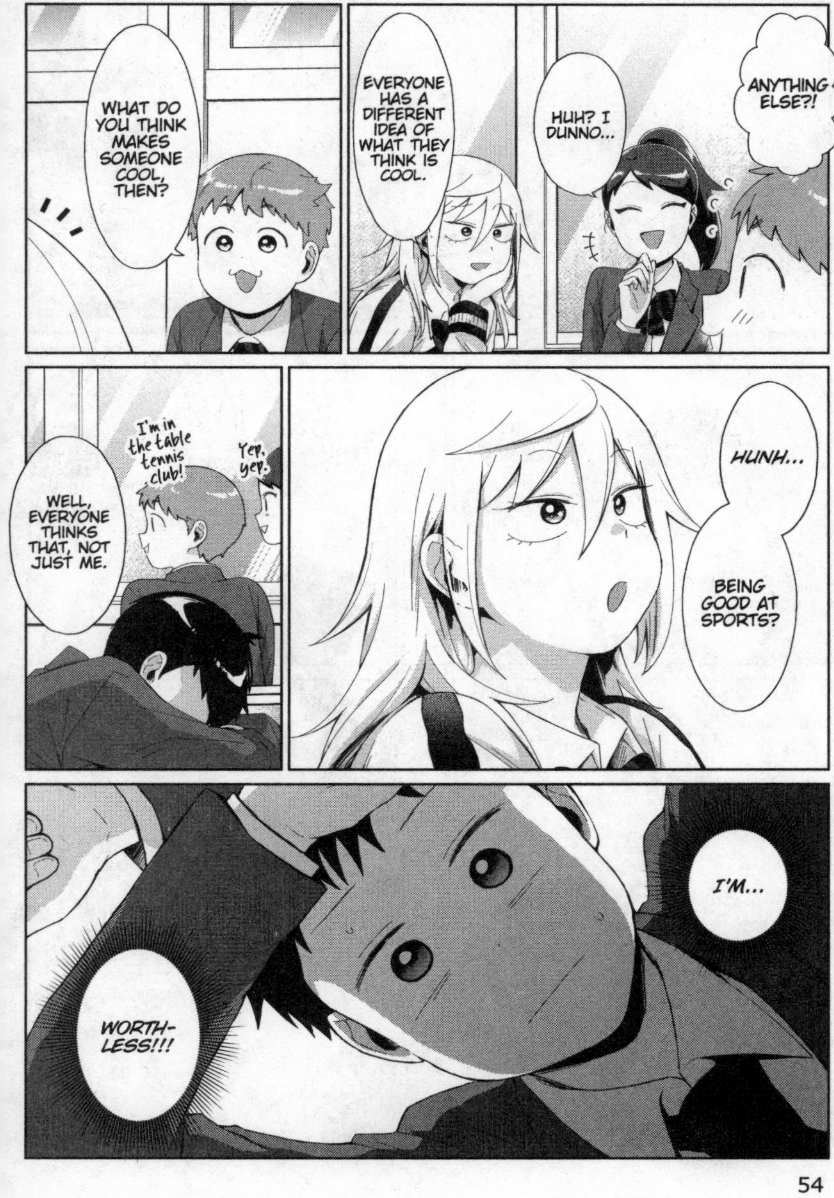
ANYTHING ELSE?!
HUH? I DUNNO...
EVERYONE HAS A DIFFERENT IDEA OF WHAT THEY THINK IS COOL.
WHAT DO YOU THINK MAKES SOMEONE COOL, THEN?
HUNH...
BEING GOOD AT SPORTS?
Yep, yep.
I'm in the table tennis club!
WELL, EVERYONE THINKS THAT, NOT JUST ME.
I'M...
WORTH-LESS!!!

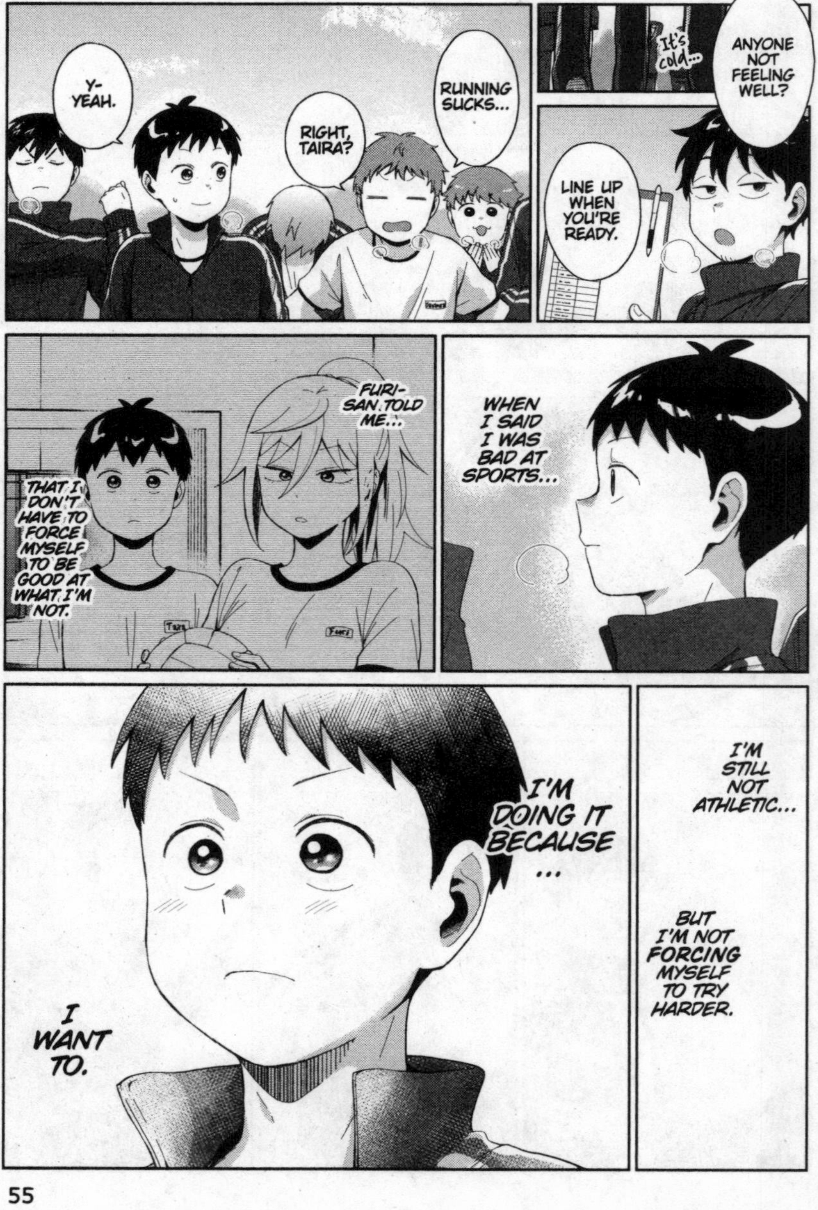
It's cold...
ANYONE NOT FEELING WELL?
LINE UP WHEN YOU'RE READY.
RUNNING SUCKS...
RIGHT, TAIRA?
Y-YEAH.
WHEN I SAID I WAS BAD AT SPORTS...
FURI-SAN TOLD ME...
THAT I DON'T HAVE TO FORCE MYSELF TO BE GOOD AT WHAT I'M NOT.
I'M STILL NOT ATHLETIC...
BUT I'M NOT FORCING MYSELF TO TRY HARDER.
I'M DOING IT BECAUSE...
I WANT TO.

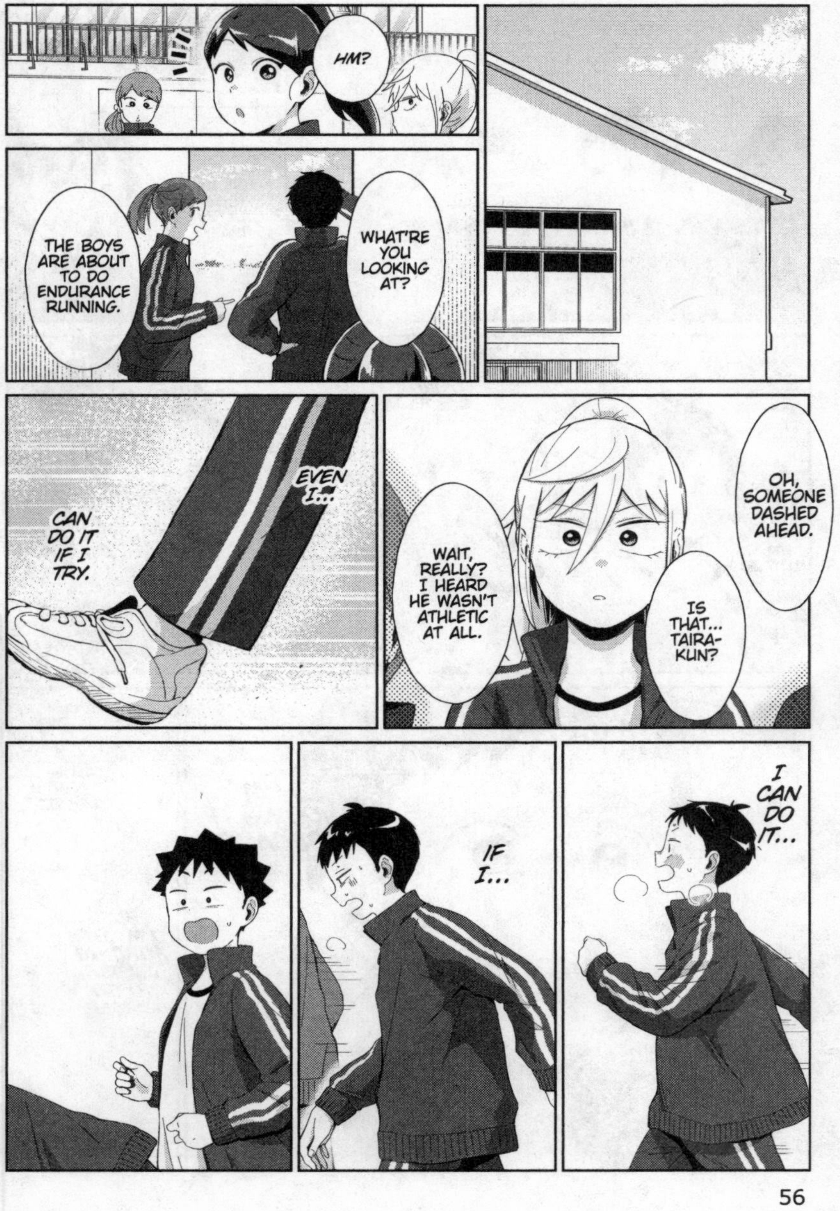
HM?
WHAT'RE YOU LOOKING AT?
THE BOYS ARE ABOUT TO DO ENDURANCE RUNNING.
OH, SOMEONE DASHED AHEAD.
IS THAT... TAIRA-KUN?
WAIT, REALLY? I HEARD HE WASN'T ATHLETIC AT ALL.
EVEN I...
CAN DO IT IF I TRY.
I CAN DO IT...
IF I...

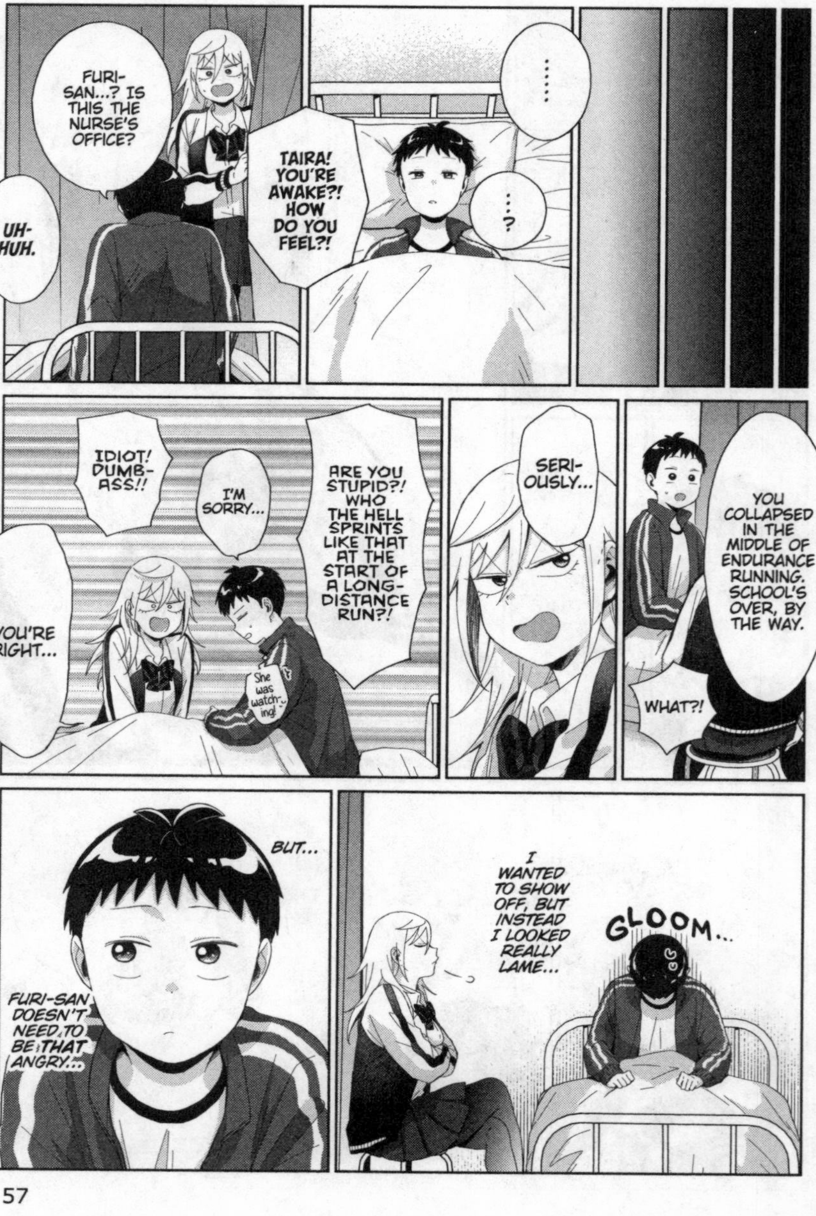

……
TAIRA! YOU'RE AWAKE?! HOW DO YOU FEEL?!
…?
FURI-SAN…? IS THIS THE NURSE'S OFFICE?
UH-HUH.
YOU COLLAPSED IN THE MIDDLE OF ENDURANCE RUNNING. SCHOOL'S OVER, BY THE WAY.
WHAT?!
SERI-OUSLY…
ARE YOU STUPID?! WHO THE HELL SPRINTS LIKE THAT AT THE START OF A LONG-DISTANCE RUN?!
I'M SORRY…
IDIOT! DUMB-ASS!!
YOU'RE RIGHT…
She was watch-ing!
GLOOM…
I WANTED TO SHOW OFF, BUT INSTEAD I LOOKED REALLY LAME…
BUT…
FURI-SAN DOESN'T NEED TO BE THAT ANGRY…

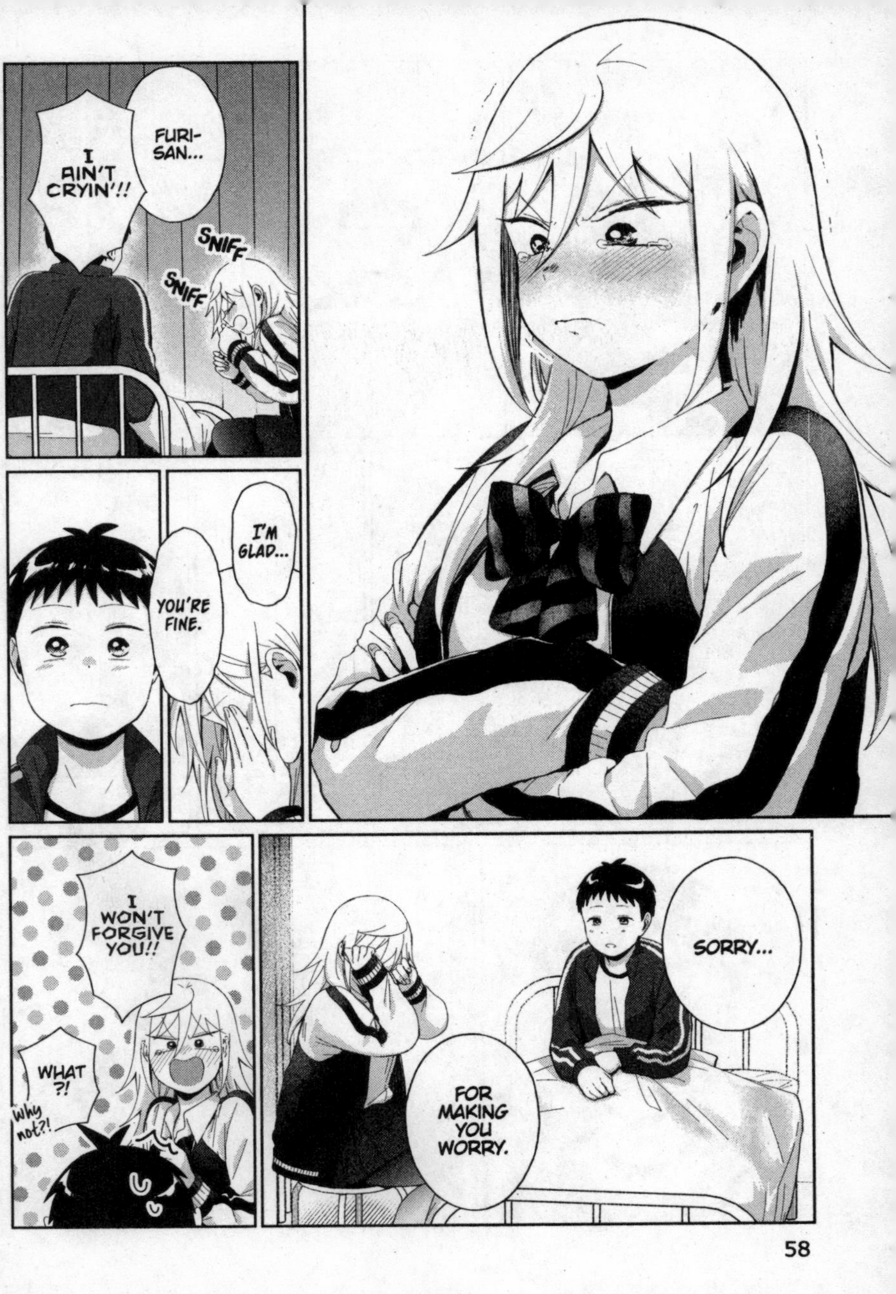
FURI-SAN...
I AIN'T CRYIN'!!
SNIFF
SNIFF
I'M GLAD...
YOU'RE FINE.
SORRY...
FOR MAKING YOU WORRY.
I WON'T FORGIVE YOU!!
WHAT ?!
Why not?!

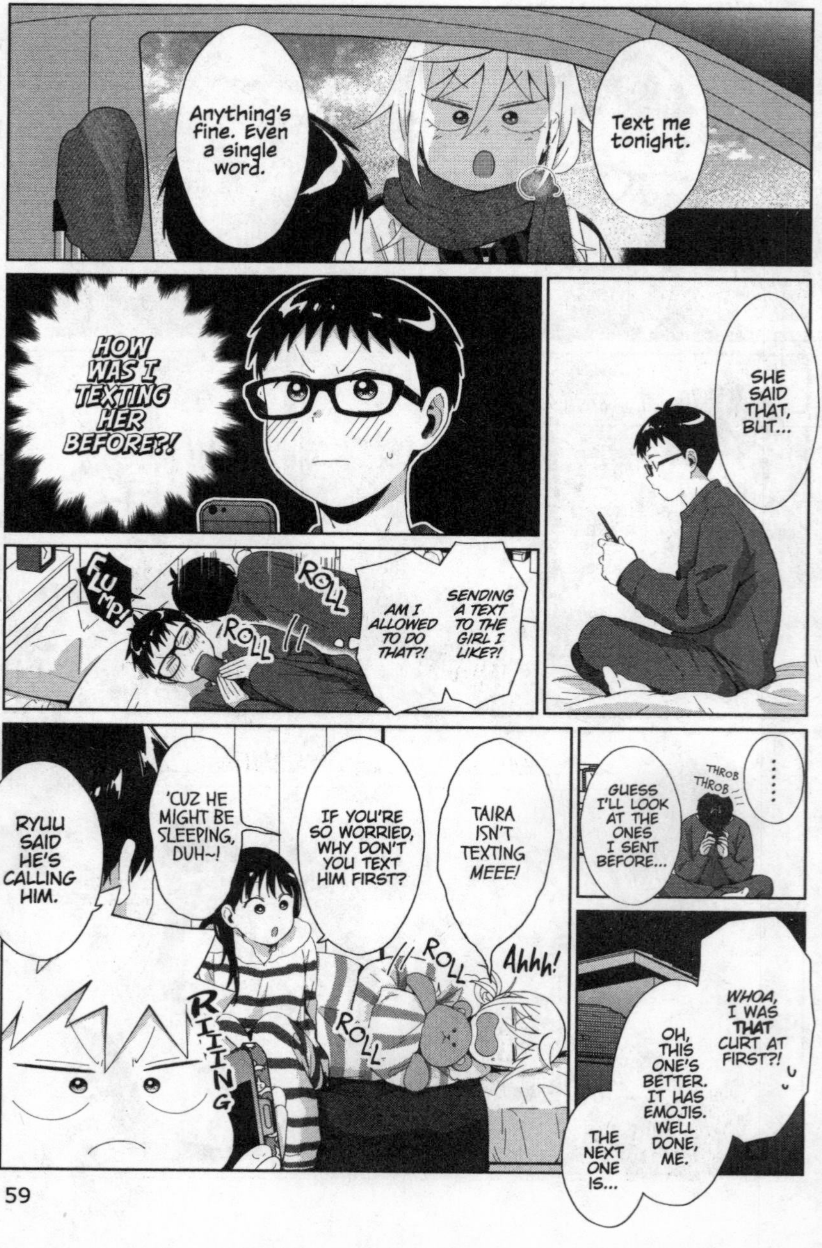
Text me tonight.
Anything's fine. Even a single word.
SHE SAID THAT, BUT...
HOW WAS I TEXTING HER BEFORE?!
SENDING A TEXT TO THE GIRL I LIKE?!
AM I ALLOWED TO DO THAT?!
ROLL
ROLL
FLUMP!
......
THROB THROB
GUESS I'LL LOOK AT THE ONES I SENT BEFORE...
WHOA, I WAS THAT CURT AT FIRST?!
OH, THIS ONE'S BETTER. IT HAS EMOJIS. WELL DONE, ME.
THE NEXT ONE IS...
TAIRA ISN'T TEXTING MEEE!
Ahhh!
ROLL
ROLL
IF YOU'RE SO WORRIED, WHY DON'T YOU TEXT HIM FIRST?
'CUZ HE MIGHT BE SLEEPING, DUH~!
RYUU SAID HE'S CALLING HIM.
RIIING

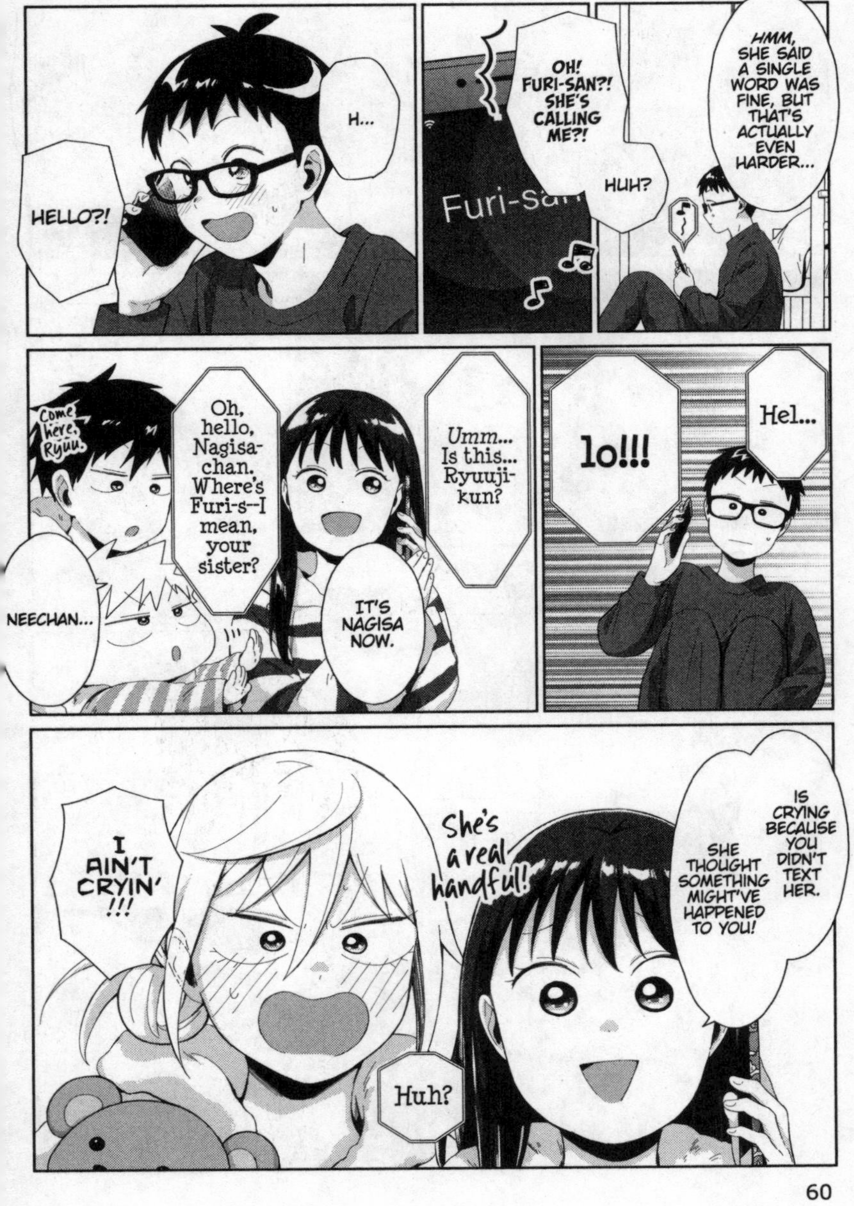
HMM, SHE SAID A SINGLE WORD WAS FINE, BUT THAT'S ACTUALLY EVEN HARDER...
OH! FURI-SAN?! SHE'S CALLING ME?!
HUH?
Furi-San
H...
HELLO?!
Hel...
lo!!!
Umm... Is this... Ryuuji-kun?
IT'S NAGISA NOW.
Oh, hello, Nagisa-chan. Where's Furi-s--I mean, your sister?
Come here, Ryuu.
NEECHAN...
IS CRYING BECAUSE YOU DIDN'T TEXT HER.
SHE THOUGHT SOMETHING MIGHT'VE HAPPENED TO YOU!
She's a real handful!
Huh?
I AIN'T CRYIN'!!!

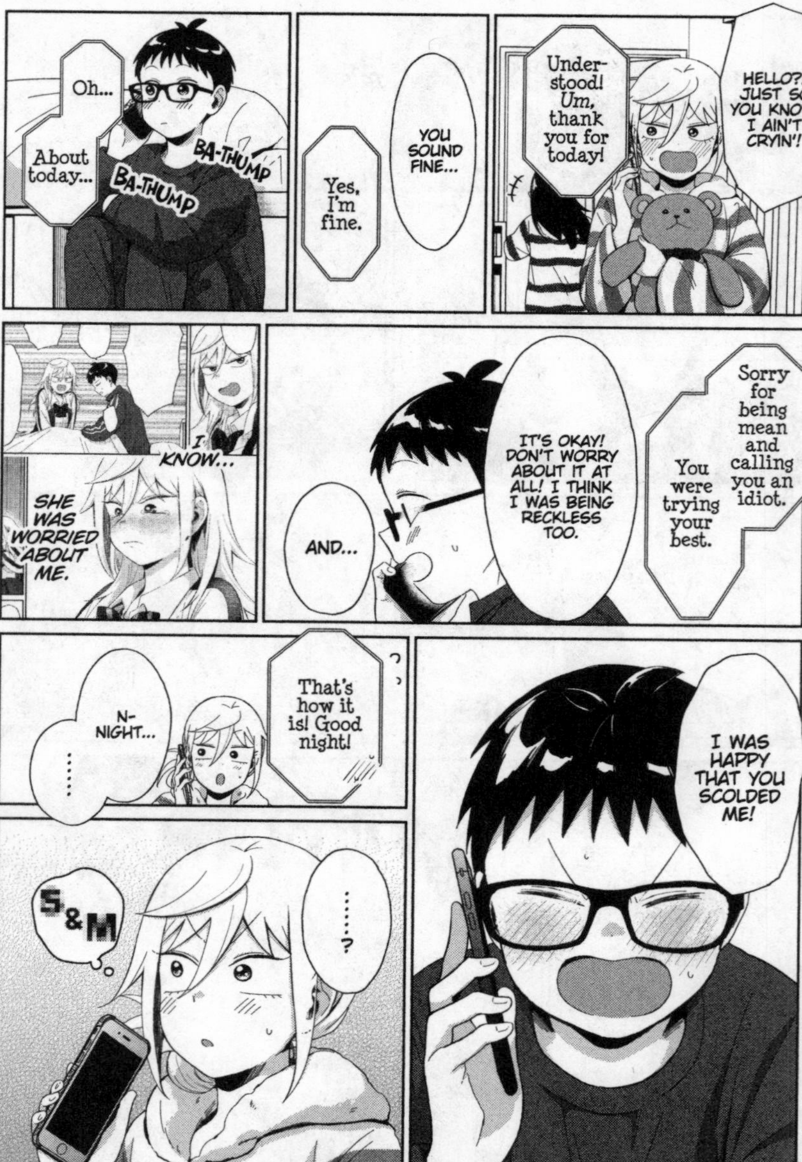
HELLO?! JUST SO YOU KNOW, I AIN'T CRYIN'!
Under-stood! Um, thank you for today!
YOU SOUND FINE...
Yes, I'm fine.
Oh...
About today...
BA-THUMP
BA-THUMP
Sorry for being mean and calling you an idiot.
You were trying your best.
IT'S OKAY! DON'T WORRY ABOUT IT AT ALL! I THINK I WAS BEING RECKLESS TOO.
AND...
I KNOW...
SHE WAS WORRIED ABOUT ME.
I WAS HAPPY THAT YOU SCOLDED ME!
That's how it is! Good night!
N-NIGHT...
......
......?
S&M

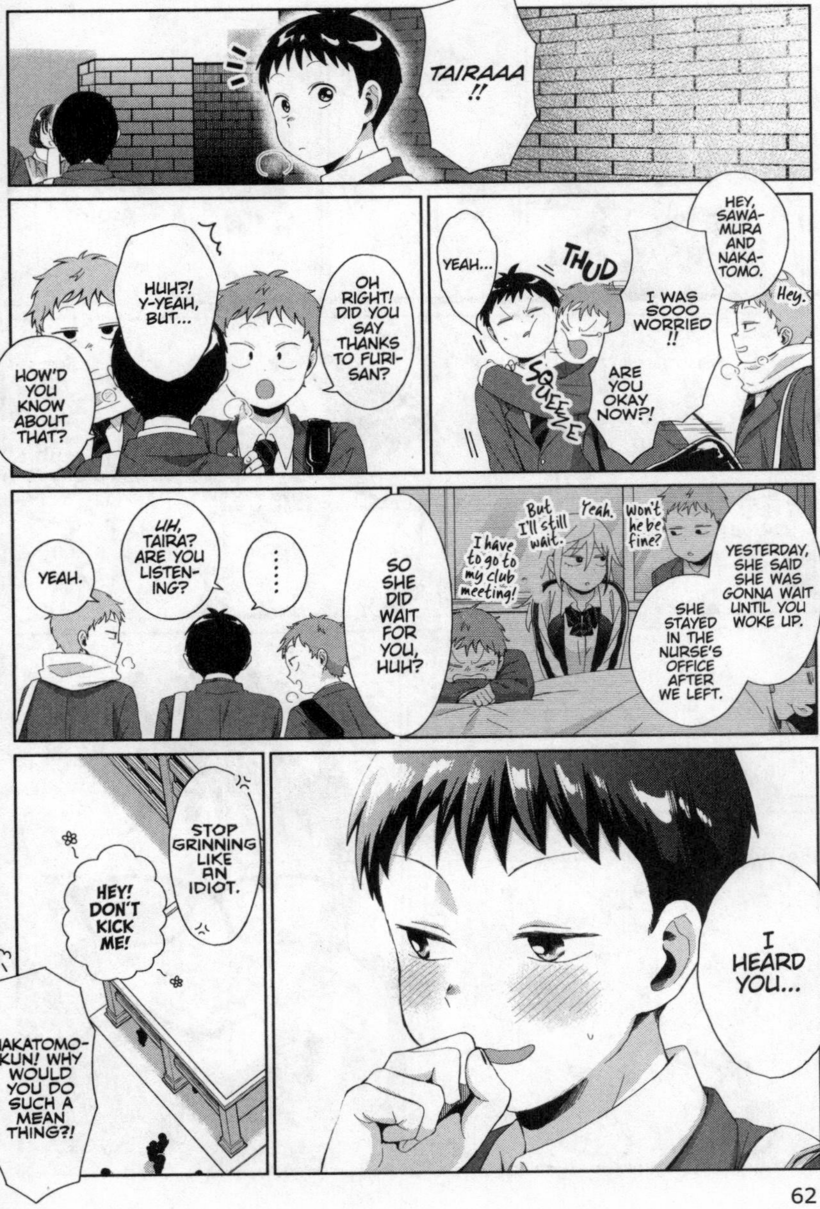
TAIRAAA !!
HEY, SAWAMURA AND NAKATOMO.
Hey.
I WAS SOOO WORRIED !!
ARE YOU OKAY NOW?!
THUD
YEAH...
SQUEEZE
OH RIGHT! DID YOU SAY THANKS TO FURI-SAN?
HUH?! Y-YEAH, BUT...
HOW'D YOU KNOW ABOUT THAT?
YESTERDAY, SHE SAID SHE WAS GONNA WAIT UNTIL YOU WOKE UP.
Won't he be fine?
Yeah.
But I'll still wait.
I have to go to my club meeting!
SHE STAYED IN THE NURSE'S OFFICE AFTER WE LEFT.
SO SHE DID WAIT FOR YOU, HUH?
......
UH, TAIRA? ARE YOU LISTENING?
YEAH.
I HEARD YOU...
STOP GRINNING LIKE AN IDIOT.
HEY! DON'T KICK ME!
NAKATOMO-KUN! WHY WOULD YOU DO SUCH A MEAN THING?!

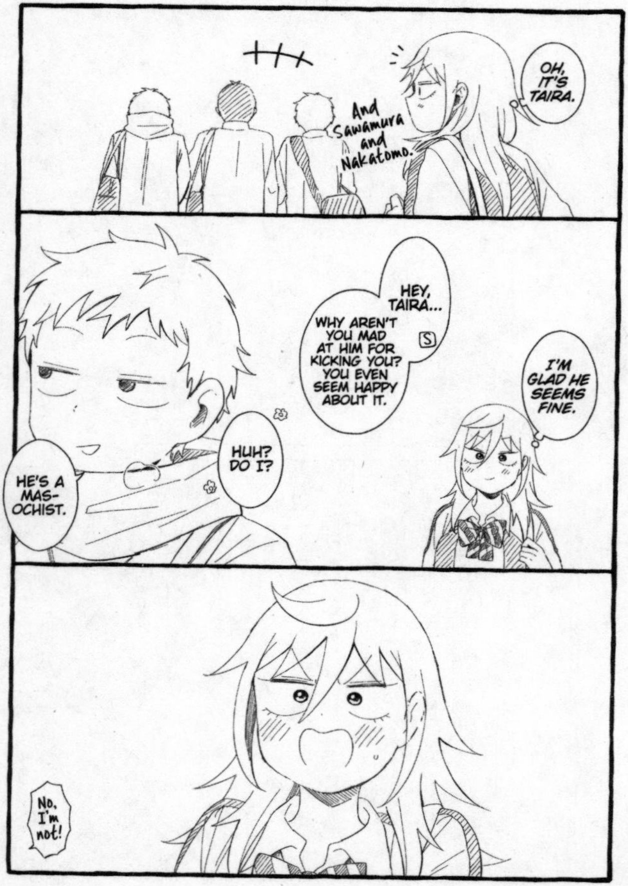
OH, IT'S TAIRA.
And Sawamura and Nakatomo.
I'M GLAD HE SEEMS FINE.
HEY, TAIRA...
WHY AREN'T YOU MAD AT HIM FOR KICKING YOU? YOU EVEN SEEM HAPPY ABOUT IT.
HUH? DO I?
HE'S A MAS-OCHIST.
No, I'm not!

Chapter 31

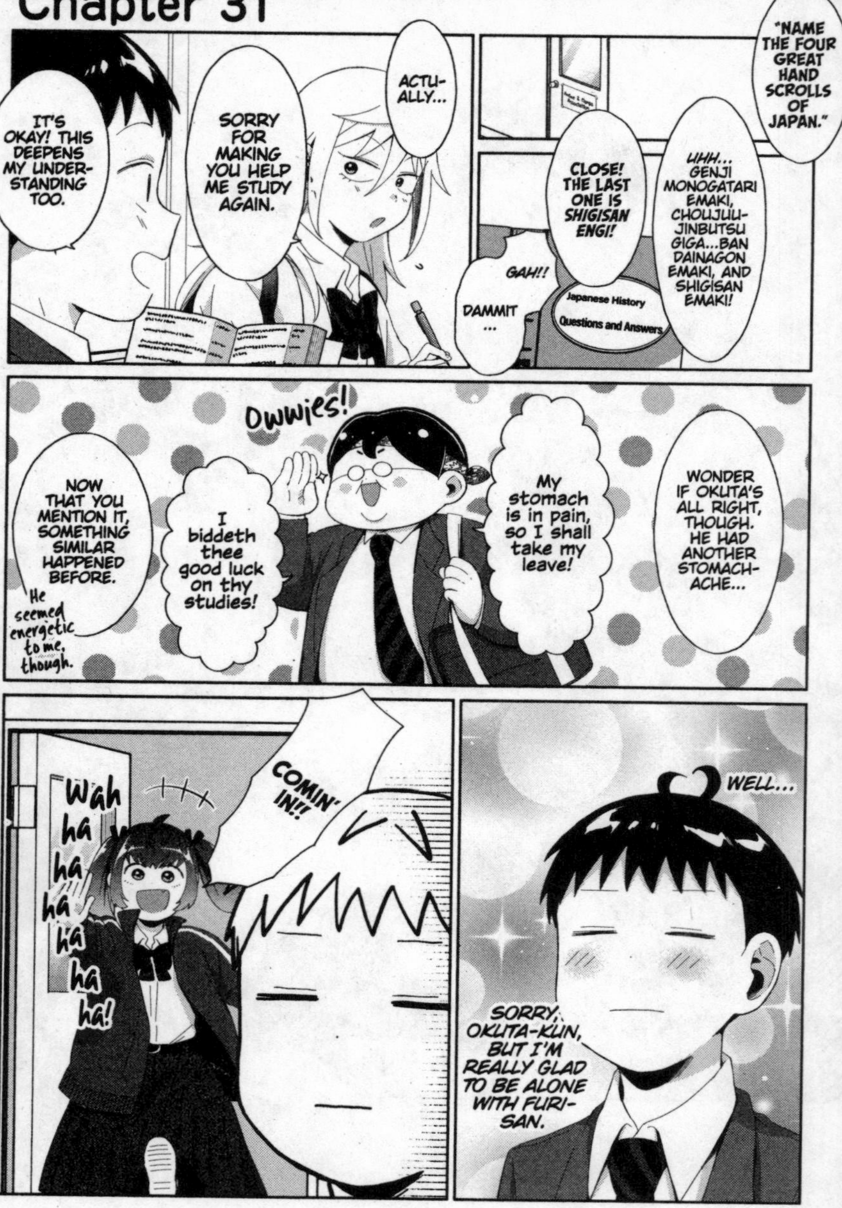
"NAME THE FOUR GREAT HAND SCROLLS OF JAPAN."
UHH... GENJI MONOGATARI EMAKI, CHOUJUU-JINBUTSU GIGA...BAN DAINAGON EMAKI, AND SHIGISAN EMAKI!
CLOSE! THE LAST ONE IS SHIGISAN ENGI!
GAH!!
DAMMIT ...
Japanese History
Questions and Answers
ACTU-ALLY...
SORRY FOR MAKING YOU HELP ME STUDY AGAIN.
IT'S OKAY! THIS DEEPENS MY UNDER-STANDING TOO.
WONDER IF OKUTA'S ALL RIGHT, THOUGH. HE HAD ANOTHER STOMACH-ACHE...
My stomach is in pain, so I shall take my leave!
Owwies!
I biddeth thee good luck on thy studies!
NOW THAT YOU MENTION IT, SOMETHING SIMILAR HAPPENED BEFORE.
He seemed energetic to me, though.
WELL...
SORRY, OKUTA-KUN, BUT I'M REALLY GLAD TO BE ALONE WITH FURI-SAN.
COMIN' IN!!
Wah ha ha ha ha ha ha ha!

Chapter 31

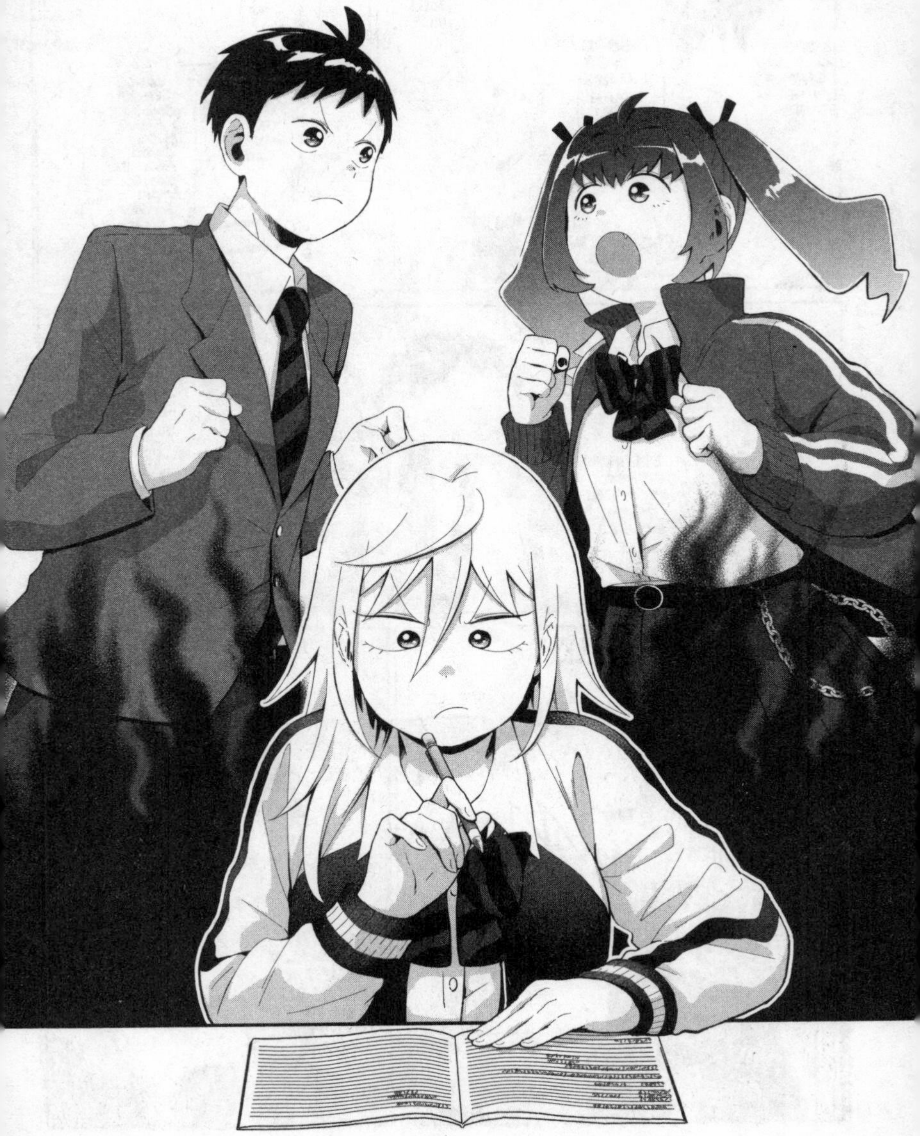

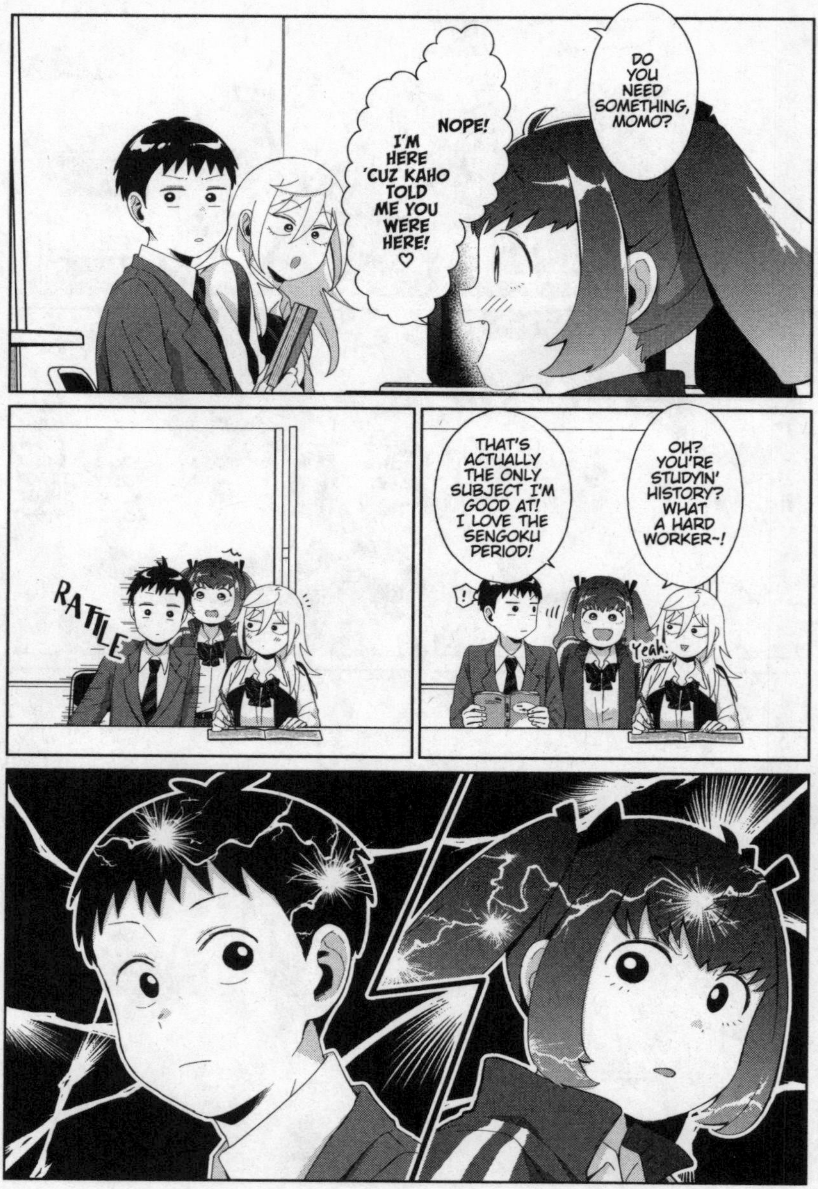
DO YOU NEED SOMETHING, MOMO?
NOPE! I'M HERE 'CUZ KAHO TOLD ME YOU WERE HERE! ♡
OH? YOU'RE STUDYIN' HISTORY? WHAT A HARD WORKER~!
THAT'S ACTUALLY THE ONLY SUBJECT I'M GOOD AT! I LOVE THE SENGOKU PERIOD!
Yeah.
RATTLE

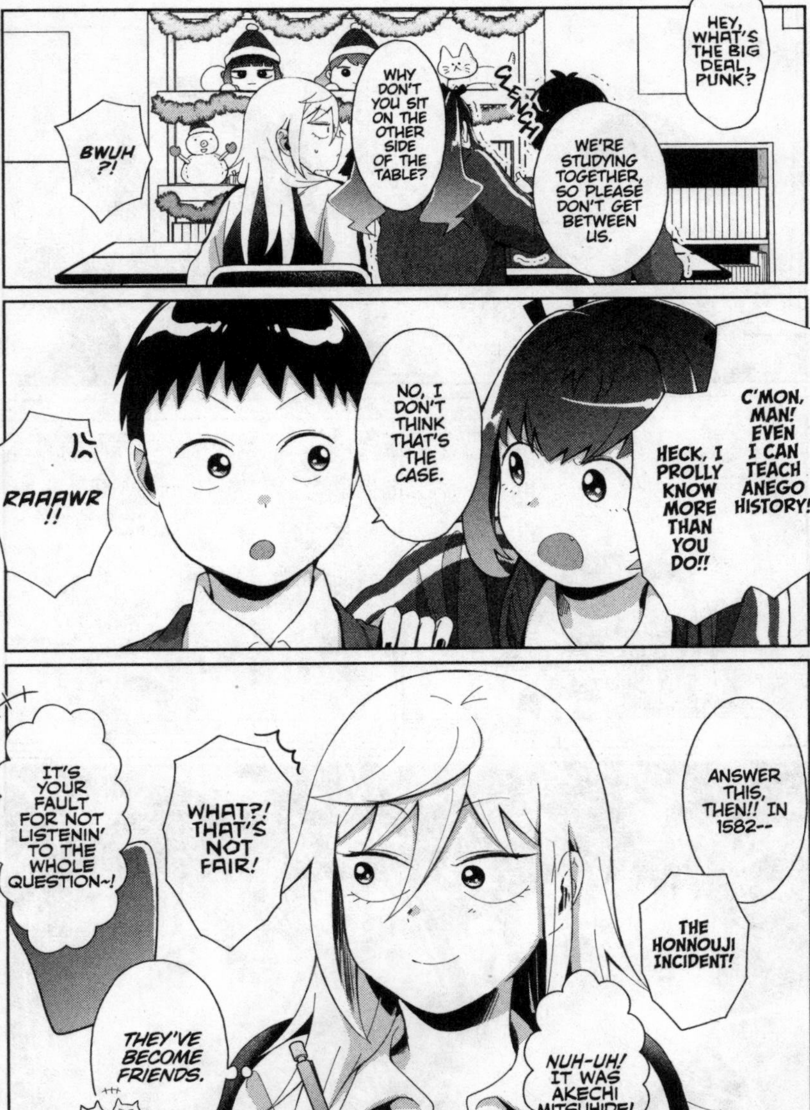
HEY, WHAT'S THE BIG DEAL, PUNK?
CLENCH
WE'RE STUDYING TOGETHER, SO PLEASE DON'T GET BETWEEN US.
WHY DON'T YOU SIT ON THE OTHER SIDE OF THE TABLE?
BWUH ?!
C'MON, MAN! EVEN I CAN TEACH ANEGO HISTORY!
HECK, I PROLLY KNOW MORE THAN YOU DO!!
NO, I DON'T THINK THAT'S THE CASE.
RAAAWR !!
ANSWER THIS, THEN!! IN 1582--
THE HONNOUJI INCIDENT!
NUH-UH! IT WAS AKECHI MITSUHIDE!
WHAT?! THAT'S NOT FAIR!
IT'S YOUR FAULT FOR NOT LISTENIN' TO THE WHOLE QUESTION~!
THEY'VE BECOME FRIENDS.
Meow!
Meow!

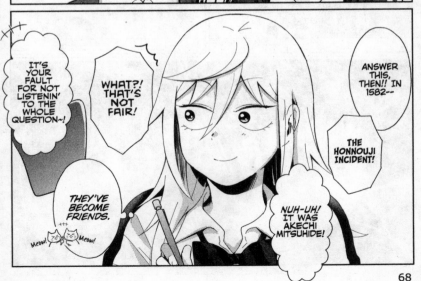

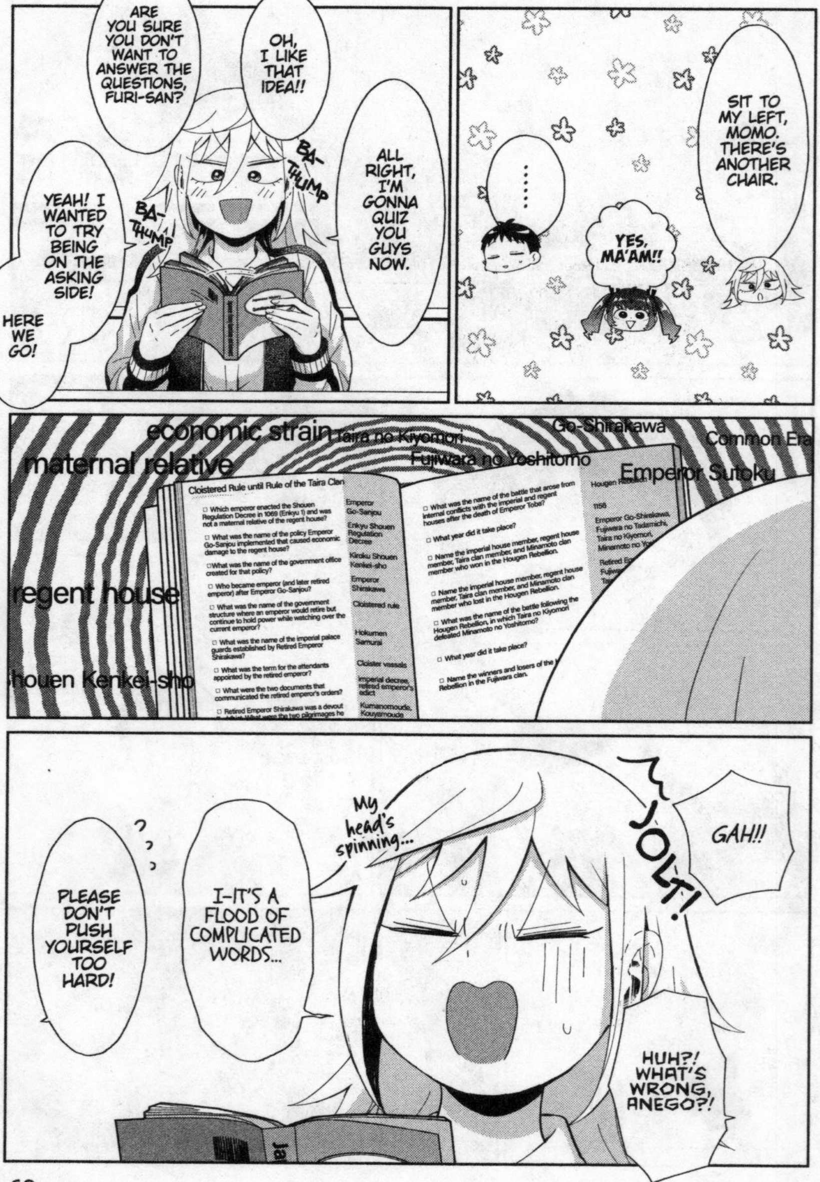
SIT TO MY LEFT, MOMO. THERE'S ANOTHER CHAIR.
YES, MA'AM!!
……
ALL RIGHT, I'M GONNA QUIZ YOU GUYS NOW.
BA-THUMP
BA-THUMP
OH, I LIKE THAT IDEA!!
ARE YOU SURE YOU DON'T WANT TO ANSWER THE QUESTIONS, FURI-SAN?
YEAH! I WANTED TO TRY BEING ON THE ASKING SIDE!
HERE WE GO!
Common Era
Go-Shirakawa
Emperor Sutoku
Fujiwara no Yoshitomo
Taira no Kiyomori
economic strain
maternal relative
regent house
houen Kenkei-sho
Hougen Rebellion
1156
Emperor Go-Shirakawa, Fujiwara no Tadamichi, Taira no Kiyomori,
□ What was the name of the battle that arose from internal conflicts with the imperial and regent houses after the death of Emperor Toba?
□ What year did it take place?
□ Name the imperial house member, regent house member, Taira clan member, and Minamoto clan member who won in the Hougen Rebellion.
□ Name the imperial house member, regent house member, Taira clan member, and Minamoto clan member who lost in the Hougen Rebellion.
□ What was the name of the battle following the Hougen Rebellion, in which Taira no Kiyomori defeated Minamoto no Yoshitomo?
□ What year did it take place?
□ Name the winners and losers of the
Rebellion in the Fujiwara clan.
Cloistered Rule until Rule of the Taira Clan
□ Which emperor enacted the Shouen Regulation Decree in 1069 (Enkyu 1) and was not a maternal relative of the regent house?
Emperor Go-Sanjou
□ What was the name of the policy Emperor Go-Sanjou implemented that caused economic damage to the regent house?
Enkyu Shouen Regulation Decree
□What was the name of the government office created for that policy?
Kiroku Shouen Kenkei-sho
□ Who became emperor (and later retired emperor) after Emperor Go-Sanjou?
Emperor Shirakawa
□ What was the name of the government structure where an emperor would retire but continue to hold power while watching over the current emperor?
Cloistered rule
□ What was the name of the imperial palace guards established by Retired Emperor Shirakawa?
Hokumen Samurai
□ What was the term for the attendants appointed by the retired emperor?
Cloister vassals
□ What were the two documents that communicated the retired emperor's orders?
imperial decree, retired emperor's edict
□ Retired Emperor Shirakawa was a devout
Kumanomoude, Kouyamoude
GAH!!
JOLT!
HUH?! WHAT'S WRONG, ANEGO?!
My head's spinning...
I-IT'S A FLOOD OF COMPLICATED WORDS...
PLEASE DON'T PUSH YOURSELF TOO HARD!

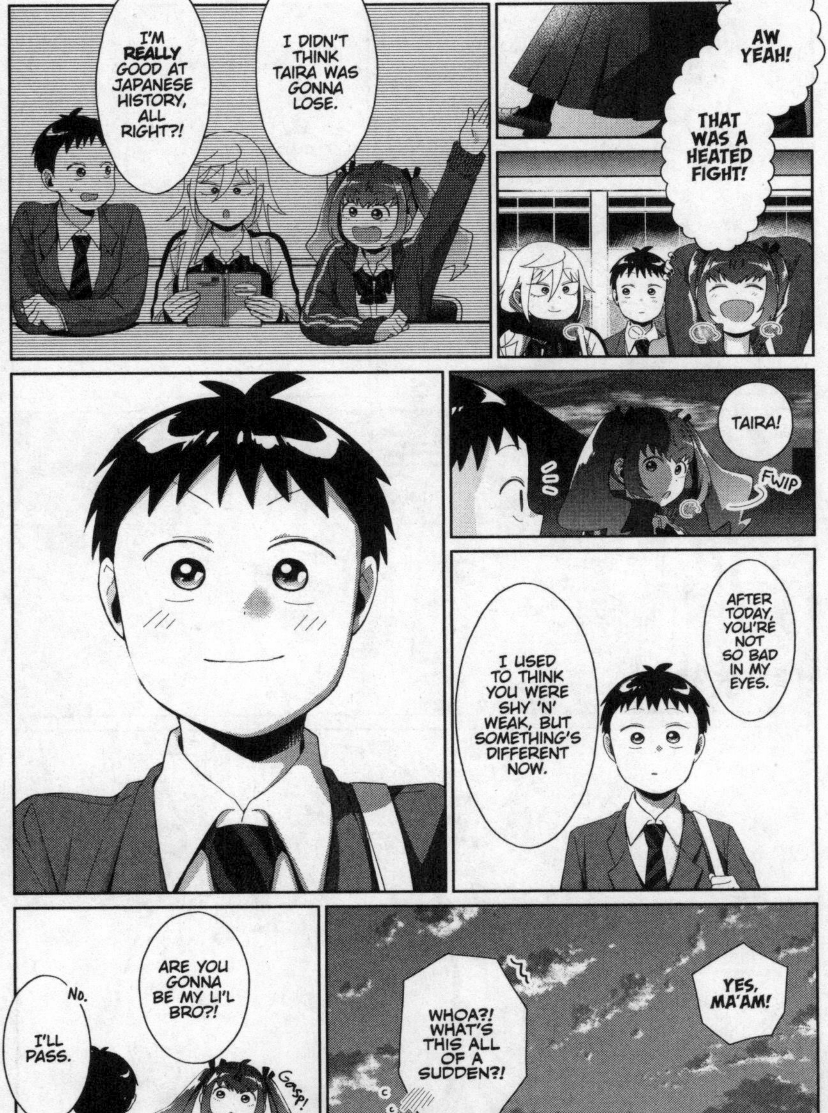
AW YEAH!
THAT WAS A HEATED FIGHT!
I DIDN'T THINK TAIRA WAS GONNA LOSE.
I'M **REALLY** GOOD AT JAPANESE HISTORY, ALL RIGHT?!
TAIRA!
FWIP
AFTER TODAY, YOU'RE NOT SO BAD IN MY EYES.
I USED TO THINK YOU WERE SHY 'N' WEAK, BUT SOMETHING'S DIFFERENT NOW.
YES, MA'AM!
WHOA?! WHAT'S THIS ALL OF A SUDDEN?!
ARE YOU GONNA BE MY LI'L BRO?!
No.
I'LL PASS.
Gasp!

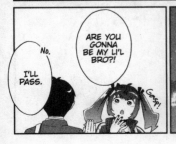

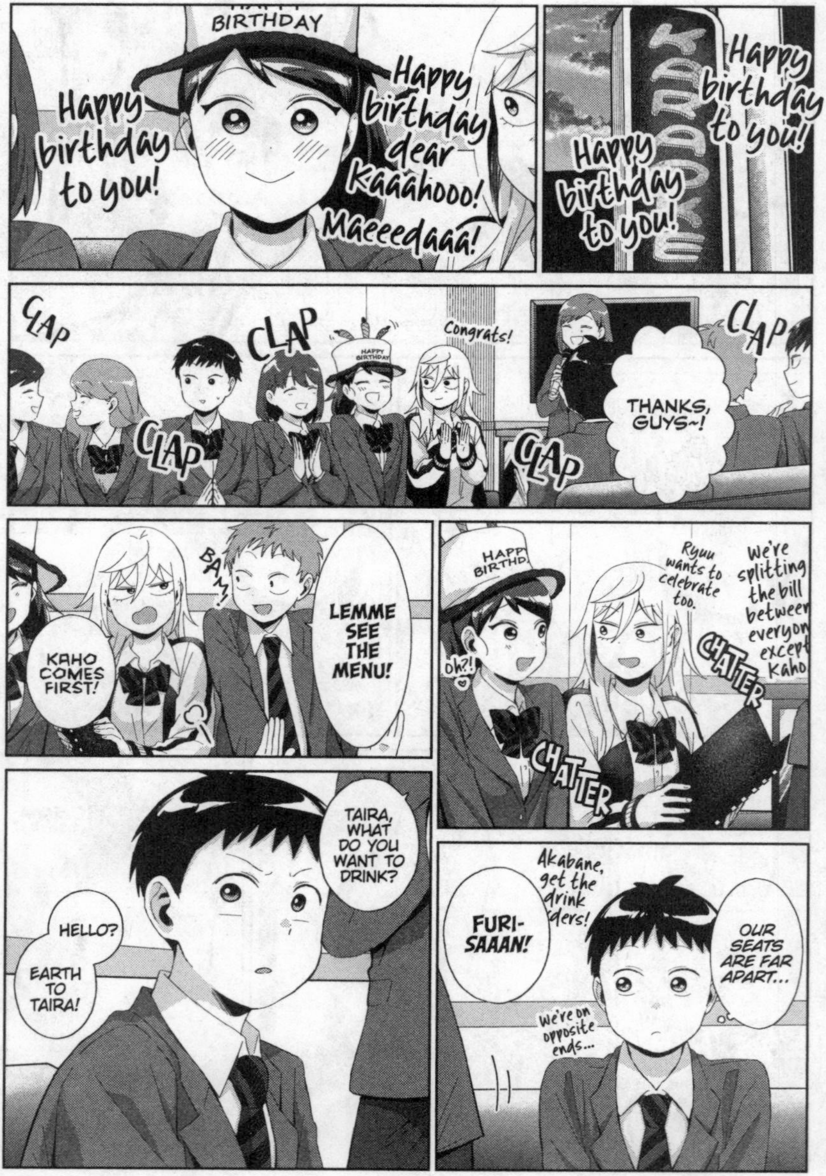
Happy birthday to you!
Happy birthday to you!
HAPPY BIRTHDAY
Happy birthday dear Kaaahooo!
Maeeedaaa!
Happy birthday to you!
CLAP
THANKS, GUYS~!
Congrats!
HAPPY BIRTHDAY
CLAP
CLAP
CLAP
CLAP
HAPPY BIRTHDAY
We're splitting the bill between everyon except Kaho
Ryuu wants to celebrate too.
CHATTER
Oh?!
CHATTER
LEMME SEE THE MENU!
BAM!
KAHO COMES FIRST!
Akabane, get the drink
ders!
OUR SEATS ARE FAR APART...
FURI-SAAAN!
We're on opposite ends...
TAIRA, WHAT DO YOU WANT TO DRINK?
HELLO?
EARTH TO TAIRA!

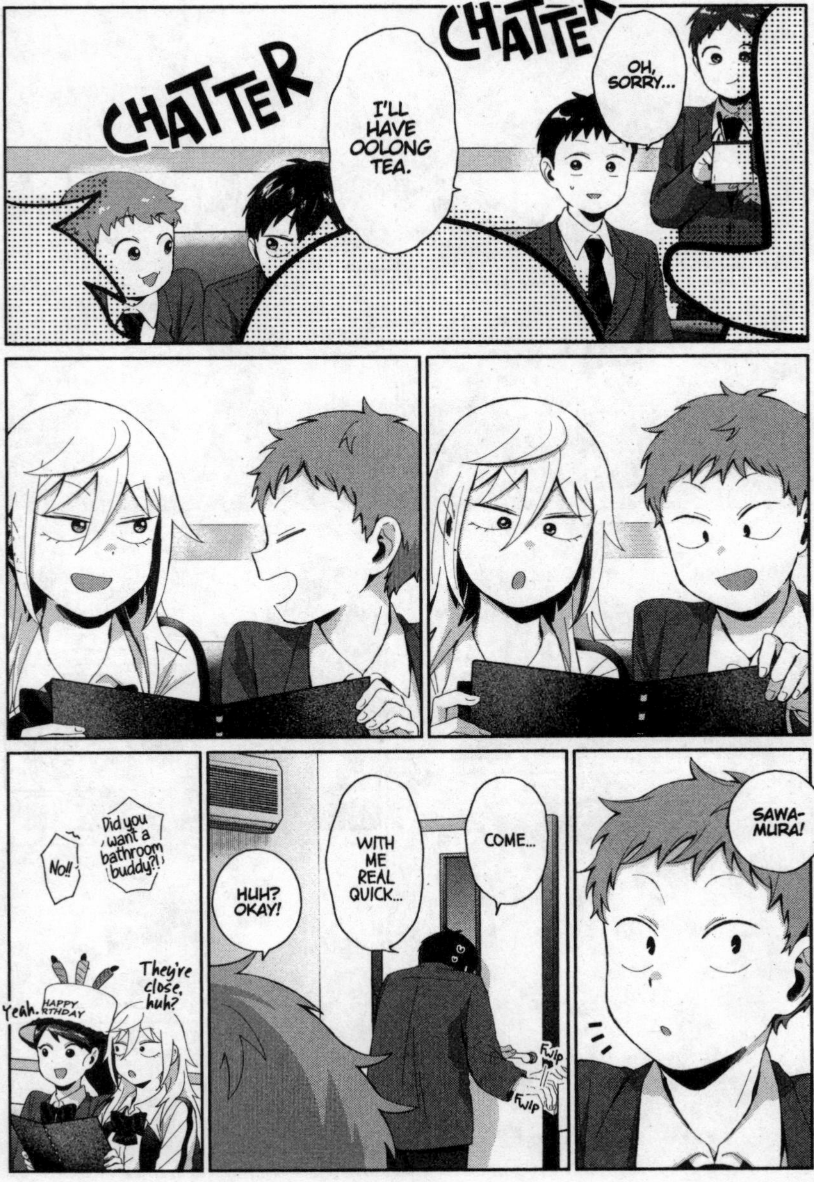
CHATTER
OH, SORRY...
I'LL HAVE OOLONG TEA.
CHATTER
SAWA-MURA!
COME...
WITH ME REAL QUICK...
HUH? OKAY!
Fwlp
Fwlp
Did you want a bathroom buddy?!
No!!
They're close, huh?
Yeah.
HAPPY
RTHDAY

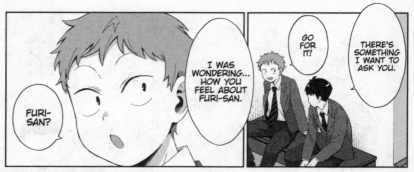

THERE'S SOMETHING I WANT TO ASK YOU.
GO FOR IT!
I WAS WONDERING... HOW YOU FEEL ABOUT FURI-SAN.
FURI-SAN?
YOU MEAN AS IN LIKE OR DISLIKE? OF COURSE I LIKE HER! SHE'S NOT SCARY AT ALL.
I was scared at first, though.
AS A FRIEND, YOU MEAN?
HUH? YEAH!
PHEW...
WHAT ABOUT IT?
I...LIKE FURI-SAN.
AS MORE THAN A FRIEND.
SO, UM, I WAS HOPING YOU COULD MAINTAIN MORE PHYSICAL DISTANCE FROM HER...
You're really close when you talk, and it bothers me...
BLUSH
WHY ARE YOU BLUSHING?!
BLUUUSH
BECAUSE I'VE NEVER HAD THIS HAPPEN BEFORE!!

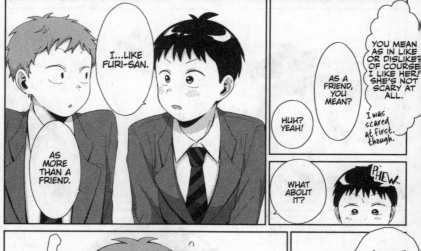

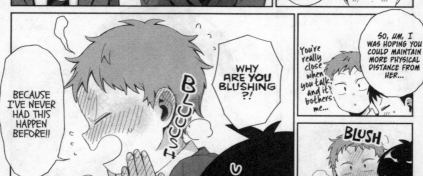

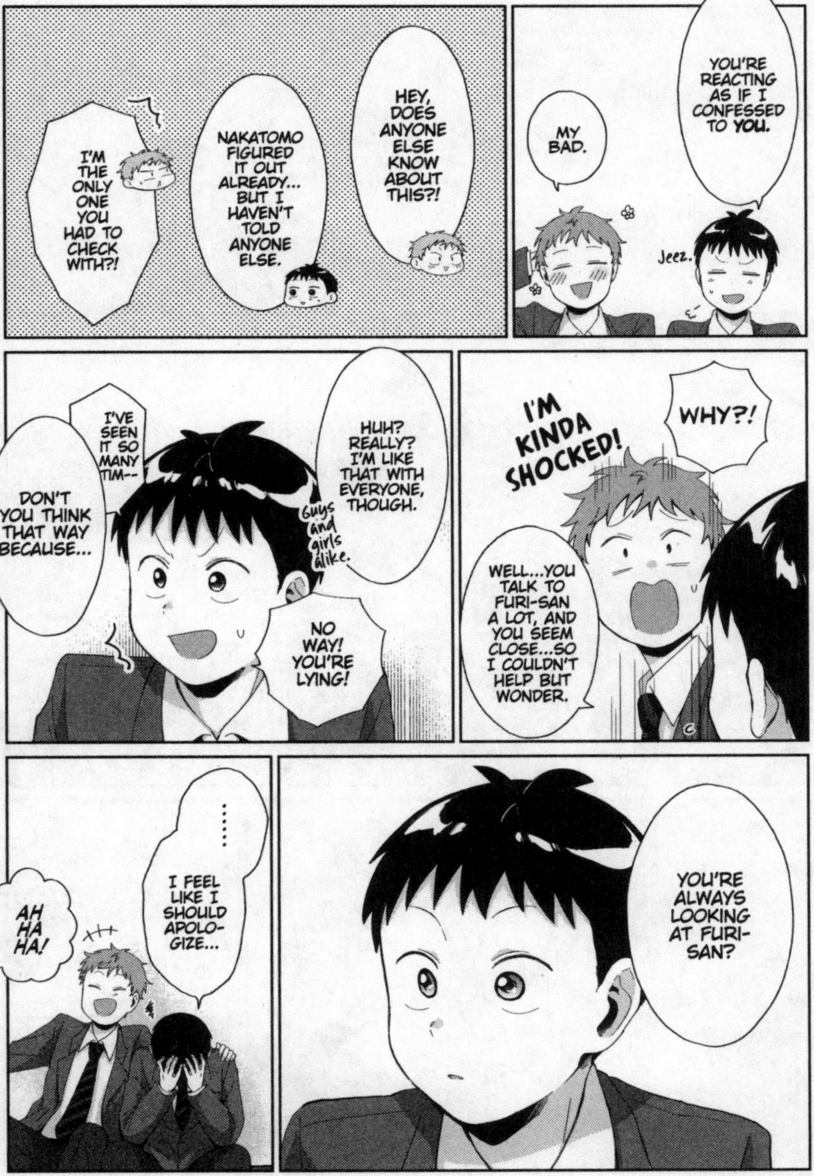
YOU'RE REACTING AS IF I CONFESSED TO **YOU.**
MY BAD.
Jeez.
HEY, DOES ANYONE ELSE KNOW ABOUT THIS?!
NAKATOMO FIGURED IT OUT ALREADY... BUT I HAVEN'T TOLD ANYONE ELSE.
I'M THE ONLY ONE YOU HAD TO CHECK WITH?!
WHY?!
I'M KINDA SHOCKED!
WELL...YOU TALK TO FURI-SAN A LOT, AND YOU SEEM CLOSE...SO I COULDN'T HELP BUT WONDER.
HUH? REALLY? I'M LIKE THAT WITH EVERYONE, THOUGH.
Guys and girls alike.
NO WAY! YOU'RE LYING!
I'VE SEEN IT SO MANY TIM--
DON'T YOU THINK THAT WAY BECAUSE...
YOU'RE ALWAYS LOOKING AT FURI-SAN?
......
I FEEL LIKE I SHOULD APOLOGIZE...
AH HA HA!

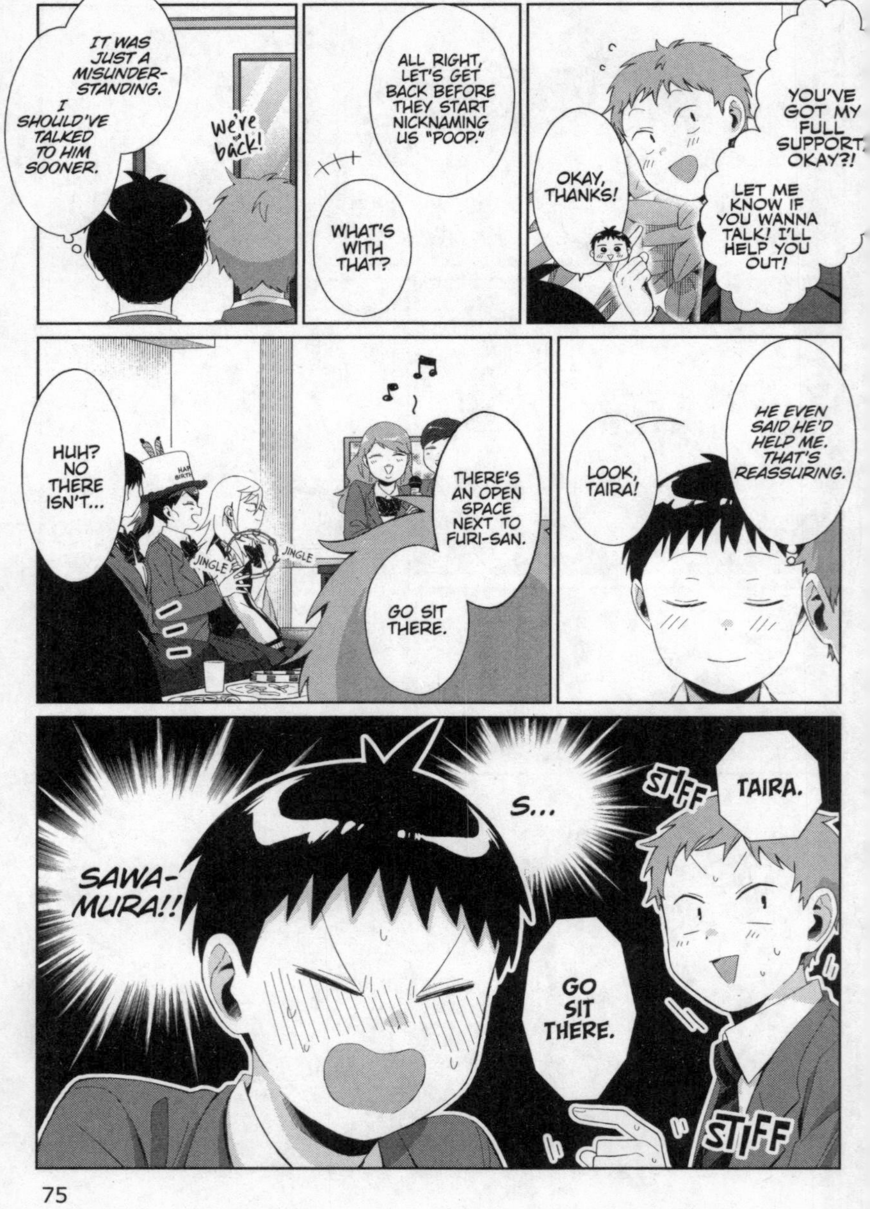
YOU'VE GOT MY FULL SUPPORT, OKAY?!
LET ME KNOW IF YOU WANNA TALK! I'LL HELP YOU OUT!
OKAY, THANKS!
ALL RIGHT, LET'S GET BACK BEFORE THEY START NICKNAMING US "POOP."
WHAT'S WITH THAT?
IT WAS JUST A MISUNDER-STANDING. I SHOULD'VE TALKED TO HIM SOONER.
We're back!
HE EVEN SAID HE'D HELP ME. THAT'S REASSURING.
LOOK, TAIRA!
THERE'S AN OPEN SPACE NEXT TO FURI-SAN.
GO SIT THERE.
JINGLE
JINGLE
HUH? NO THERE ISN'T...
TAIRA.
STIFF
S...
GO SIT THERE.
STIFF
SAWA-MURA!!

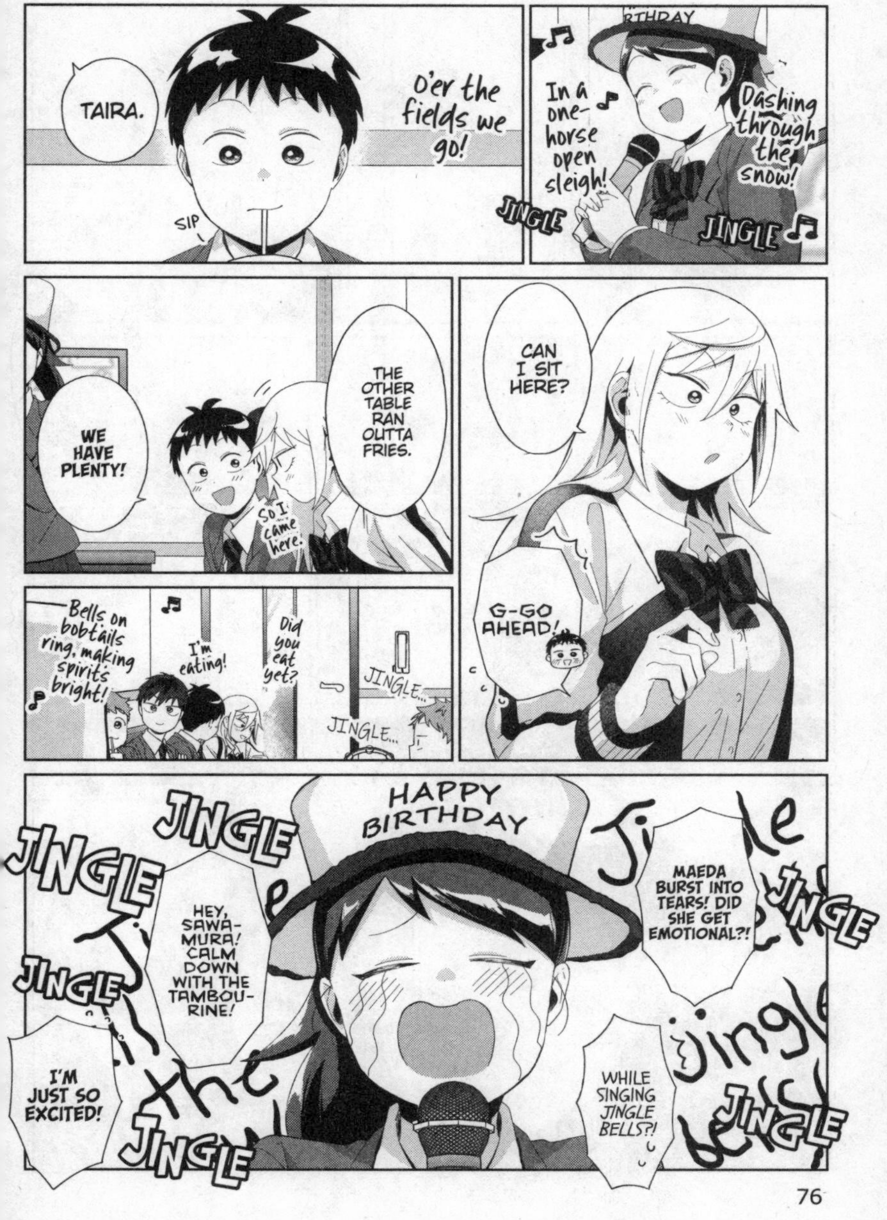
Dashing through the snow!
In a one-horse open sleigh!
JINGLE
JINGLE
O'er the fields we go!
TAIRA.
SIP
CAN I SIT HERE?
G-GO AHEAD!
THE OTHER TABLE RAN OUTTA FRIES.
So I came here.
WE HAVE PLENTY!
Did you eat yet?
I'm eating!
Bells on bobtails ring, making spirits bright!
JINGLE...
JINGLE...
HAPPY BIRTHDAY
JINGLE
MAEDA BURST INTO TEARS! DID SHE GET EMOTIONAL?!
WHILE SINGING JINGLE BELLS?!
JINGLE
JINGLE
HEY, SAWAMURA! CALM DOWN WITH THE TAMBOURINE!
JINGLE
I'M JUST SO EXCITED!
JINGLE
JINGLE

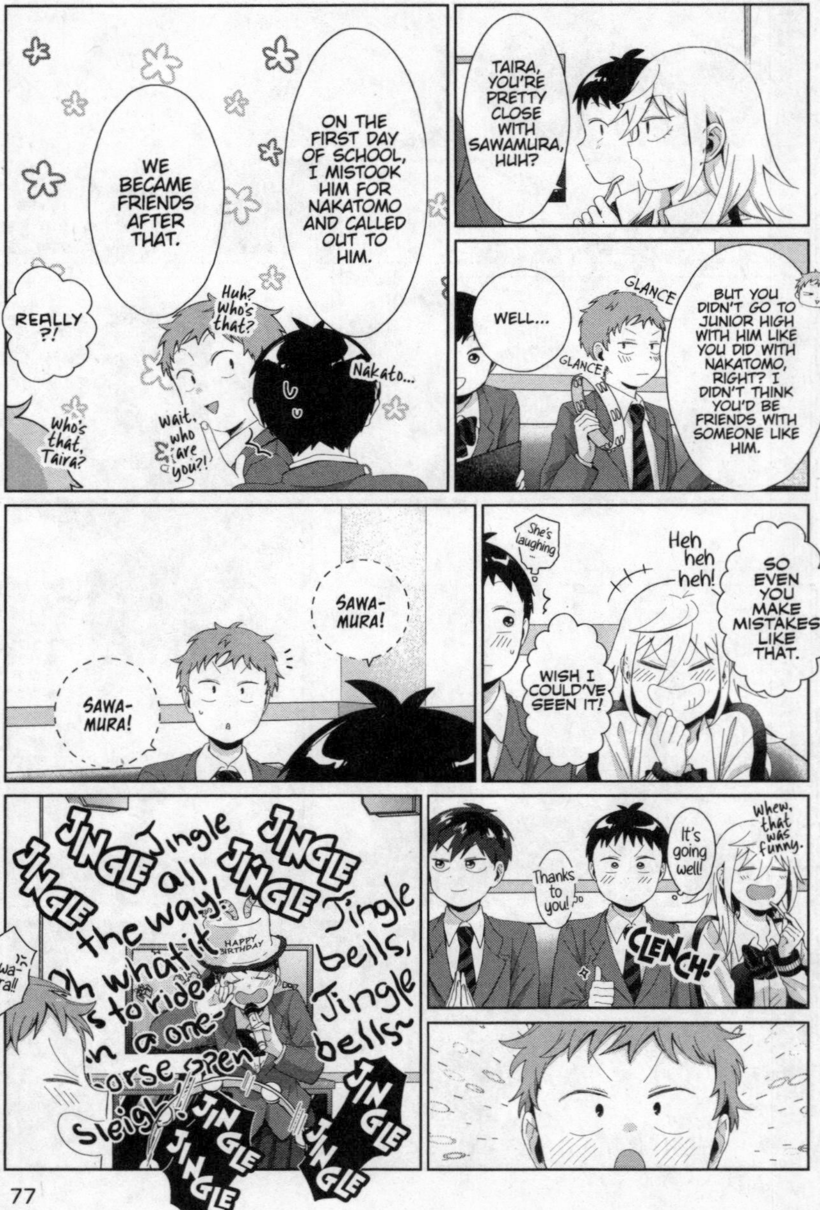
TAIRA, YOU'RE PRETTY CLOSE WITH SAWAMURA, HUH?
BUT YOU DIDN'T GO TO JUNIOR HIGH WITH HIM LIKE YOU DID WITH NAKATOMO, RIGHT? I DIDN'T THINK YOU'D BE FRIENDS WITH SOMEONE LIKE HIM.
GLANCE
WELL...
GLANCE
ON THE FIRST DAY OF SCHOOL, I MISTOOK HIM FOR NAKATOMO AND CALLED OUT TO HIM.
WE BECAME FRIENDS AFTER THAT.
Huh? Who's that?
Nakato...
REALLY?!
wait, who are you?!
Who's that, Taira?
SO EVEN YOU MAKE MISTAKES LIKE THAT.
Heh heh heh!
She's laughing...
WISH I COULD'VE SEEN IT!
SAWA-MURA!
SAWA-MURA!
whew, that was funny.
It's going well!
Thanks to you!
CLENCH!
JINGLE JINGLE
Jingle all the way!
JINGLE JINGLE
Jingle bells, Jingle bells~
HAPPY BIRTHDAY
Oh what it s to ride in a one-orse open sleigh!
Sawa-mura!!
JINGLE JINGLE
JINGLE JINGLE

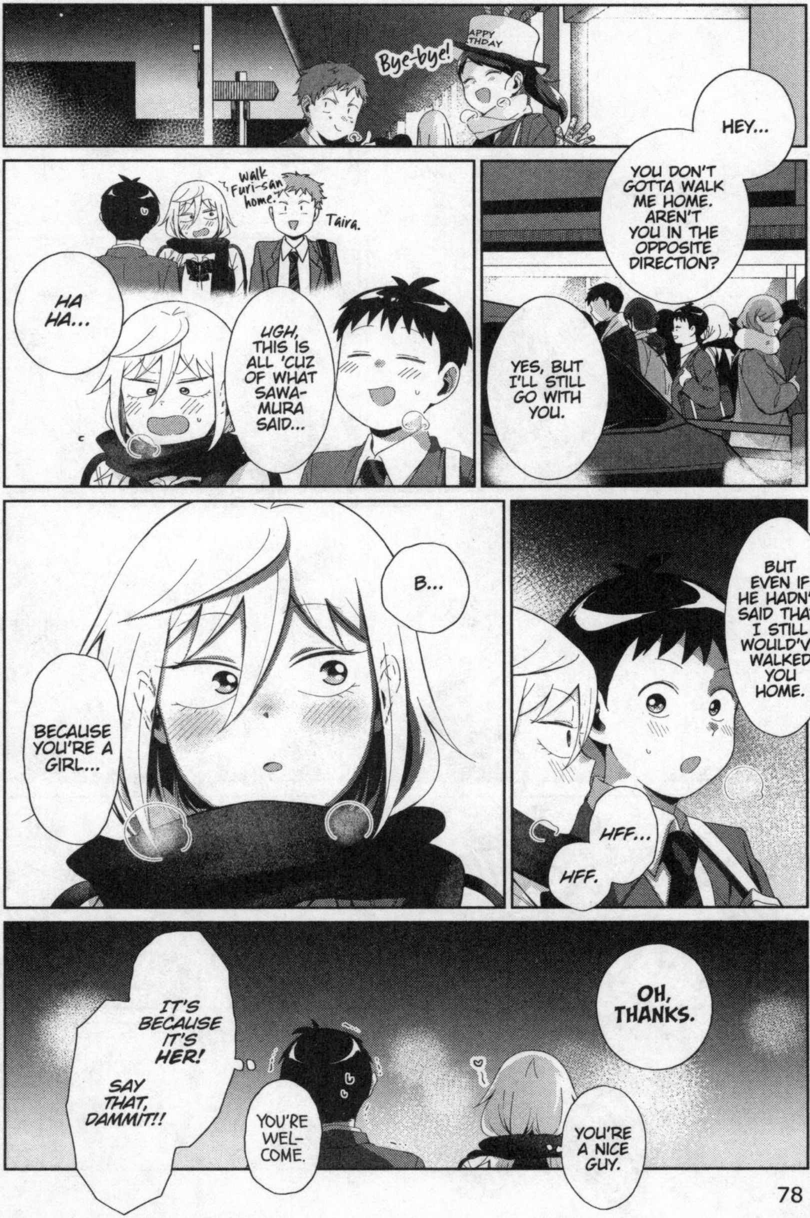
Bye-bye!
HEY...
YOU DON'T GOTTA WALK ME HOME. AREN'T YOU IN THE OPPOSITE DIRECTION?
YES, BUT I'LL STILL GO WITH YOU.
Walk Furi-san home.
Taira.
UGH, THIS IS ALL 'CUZ OF WHAT SAWAMURA SAID...
HA HA...
BUT EVEN IF HE HADN'T SAID THAT, I STILL WOULD'VE WALKED YOU HOME.
HFF...
HFF.
B...
BECAUSE YOU'RE A GIRL...
OH, THANKS.
YOU'RE A NICE GUY.
YOU'RE WEL-COME.
IT'S BECAUSE IT'S HER!
SAY THAT, DAMMIT!!

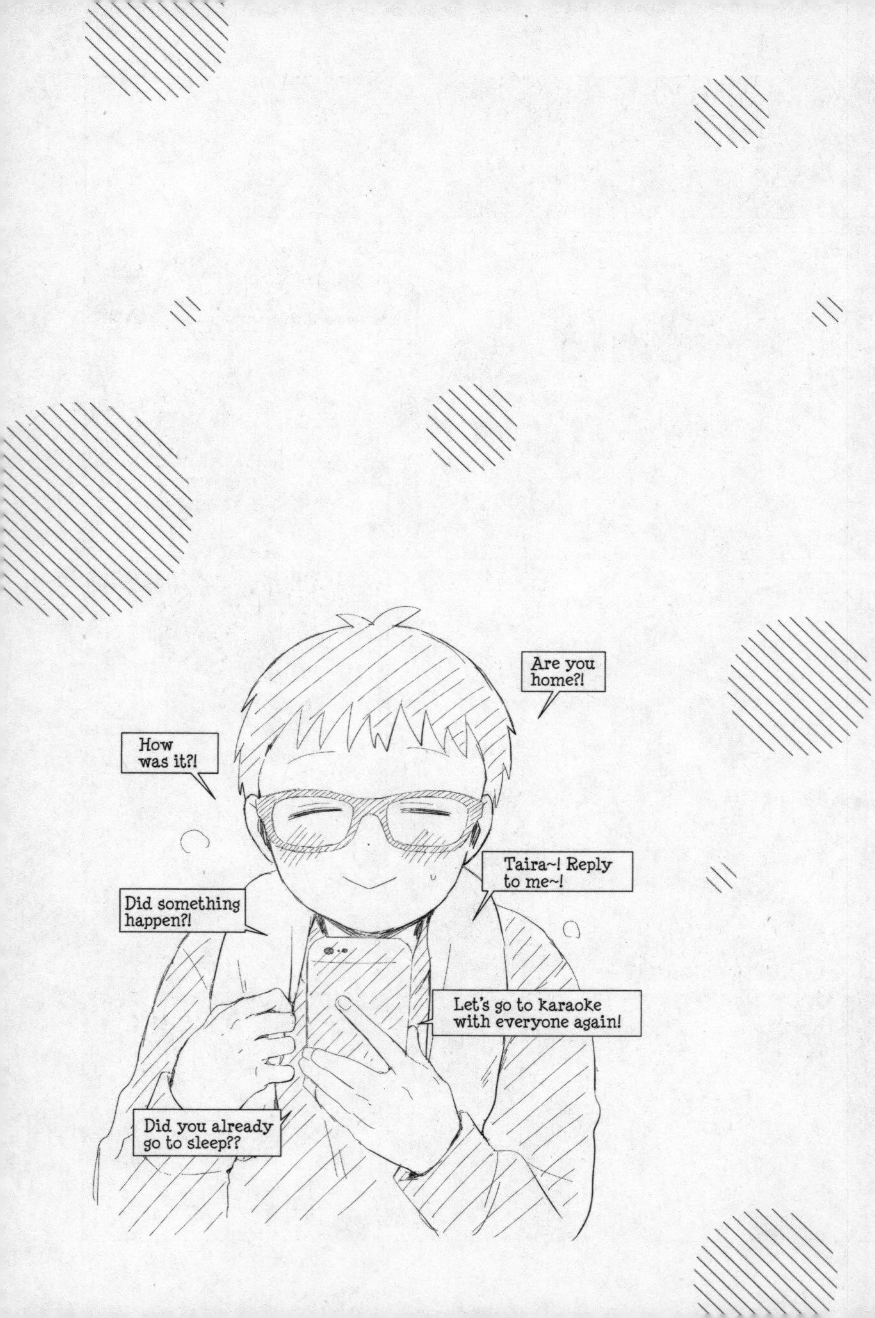
Are you home?!
How was it?!
Taira~! Reply to me~!
Did something happen?!
Let's go to karaoke with everyone again!
Did you already go to sleep??

Chapter 32

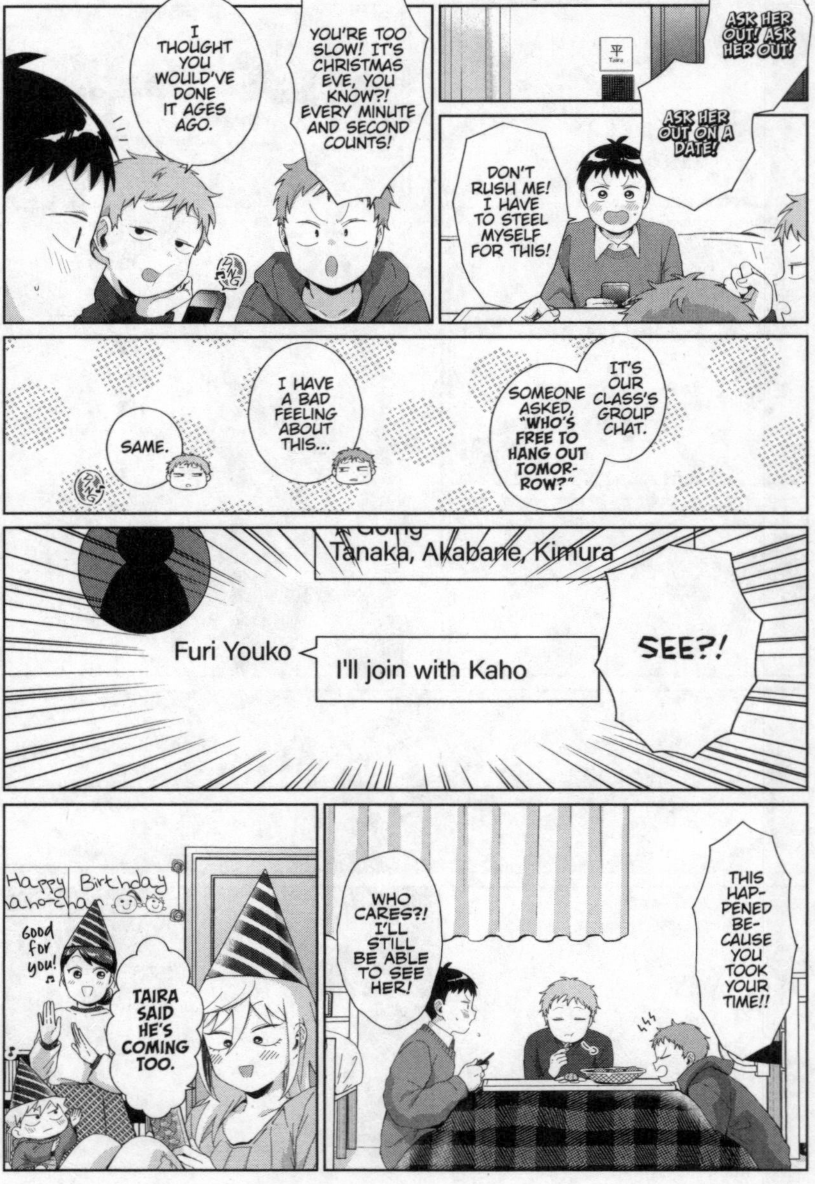

ASK HER OUT! ASK HER OUT!
ASK HER OUT ON A DATE!
DON'T RUSH ME! I HAVE TO STEEL MYSELF FOR THIS!
YOU'RE TOO SLOW! IT'S CHRISTMAS EVE, YOU KNOW?! EVERY MINUTE AND SECOND COUNTS!
I THOUGHT YOU WOULD'VE DONE IT AGES AGO.
ZING
IT'S OUR CLASS'S GROUP CHAT.
SOMEONE ASKED, "WHO'S FREE TO HANG OUT TOMOR-ROW?"
I HAVE A BAD FEELING ABOUT THIS...
SAME.
ZING
SEE?!
Tanaka, Akabane, Kimura
Furi Youko
I'll join with Kaho
THIS HAP-PENED BE-CAUSE YOU TOOK YOUR TIME!!
WHO CARES?! I'LL STILL BE ABLE TO SEE HER!
TAIRA SAID HE'S COMING TOO.
Good for you!
Happy Birthday

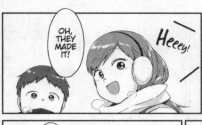

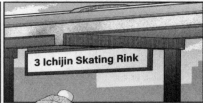

3 Ichijin Skating Rink
Heeey!
OH, THEY MADE IT!
WE'RE HERE~!
ARE WE LATE?!
NOPE, IT'S STILL FIVE MINUTES BEFORE THE MEETUP TIME.
EVERYONE'S HERE, RIGHT? WE'RE GETTING ON THE NEXT BUS!
Got it!
SHE'S CUTE TODAY, TOO...
M-MORNING, TAIRA.
Good morning.
...?
WHAT HAPPENED?

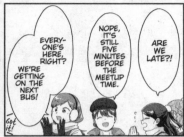

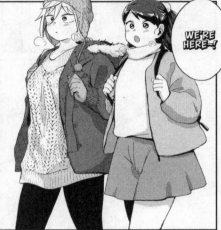

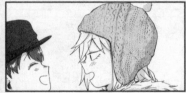

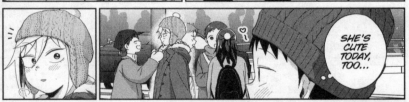

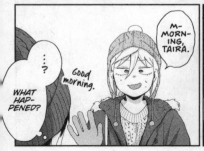

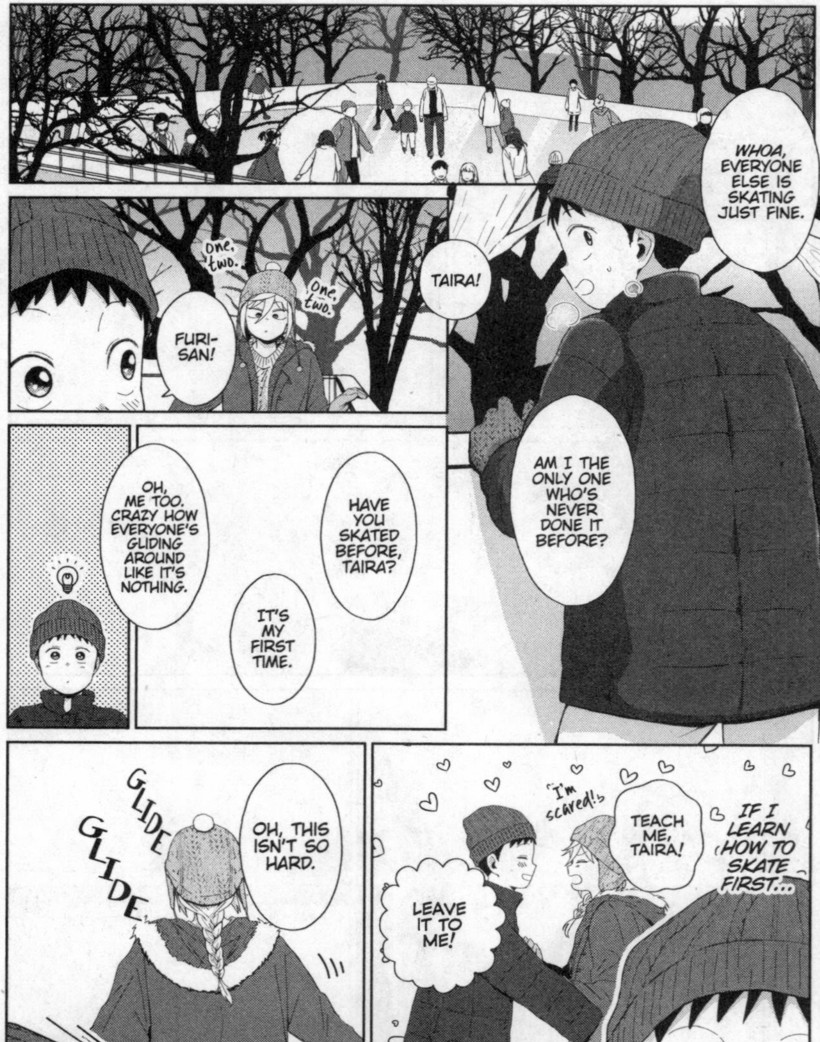
WHOA, EVERYONE ELSE IS SKATING JUST FINE.
TAIRA!
AM I THE ONLY ONE WHO'S NEVER DONE IT BEFORE?
One, two.
One, two.
FURI-SAN!
HAVE YOU SKATED BEFORE, TAIRA?
IT'S MY FIRST TIME.
OH, ME TOO. CRAZY HOW EVERYONE'S GLIDING AROUND LIKE IT'S NOTHING.
IF I LEARN HOW TO SKATE FIRST...
TEACH ME, TAIRA!
I'm scared!
LEAVE IT TO ME!
OH, THIS ISN'T SO HARD.
GLIDE
GLIDE
GLIDE

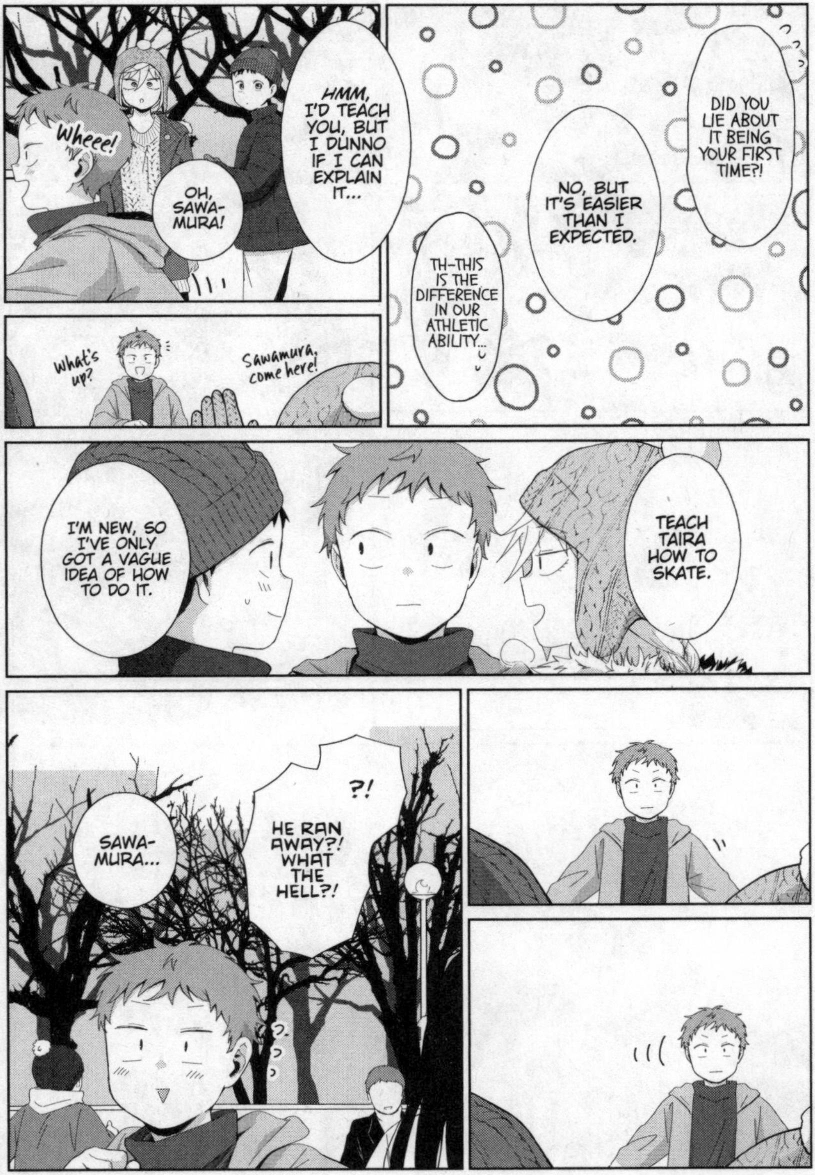
DID YOU LIE ABOUT IT BEING YOUR FIRST TIME?!
NO, BUT IT'S EASIER THAN I EXPECTED.
TH-THIS IS THE DIFFERENCE IN OUR ATHLETIC ABILITY...
HMM, I'D TEACH YOU, BUT I DUNNO IF I CAN EXPLAIN IT...
Wheee!
OH, SAWAMURA!
Sawamura, come here!
What's up?
TEACH TAIRA HOW TO SKATE.
I'M NEW, SO I'VE ONLY GOT A VAGUE IDEA OF HOW TO DO IT.
?!
HE RAN AWAY?! WHAT THE HELL?!
SAWAMURA...

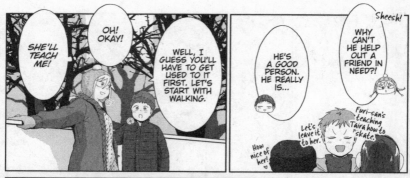

Sheesh!
WHY CAN'T HE HELP OUT A FRIEND IN NEED?!
HE'S A GOOD PERSON. HE REALLY IS...
Furi-san's teaching Taira how to skate.
Let's leave it to her.
How nice of her!
WELL, I GUESS YOU'LL HAVE TO GET USED TO IT FIRST. LET'S START WITH WALKING.
OH! OKAY!
SHE'LL TEACH ME!
POINT YOUR TOES OUT AND TAKE ONE STEP AT A TIME...
GO SLOWLY. DON'T FALL.
GOT IT!
I WANTED TO BE THE ONE TEACHING...
BUT THIS HAS ITS PERKS, TOO.
THIS REMINDS ME OF WHEN RYUU WAS LEARNING HOW TO WALK...
SHAKE
SHAKE
WOBBLE
WOBBLE

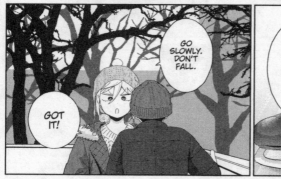

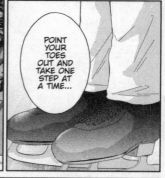

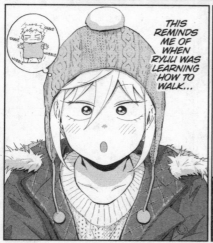

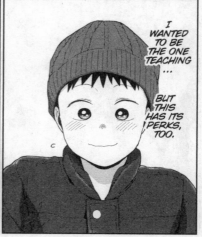

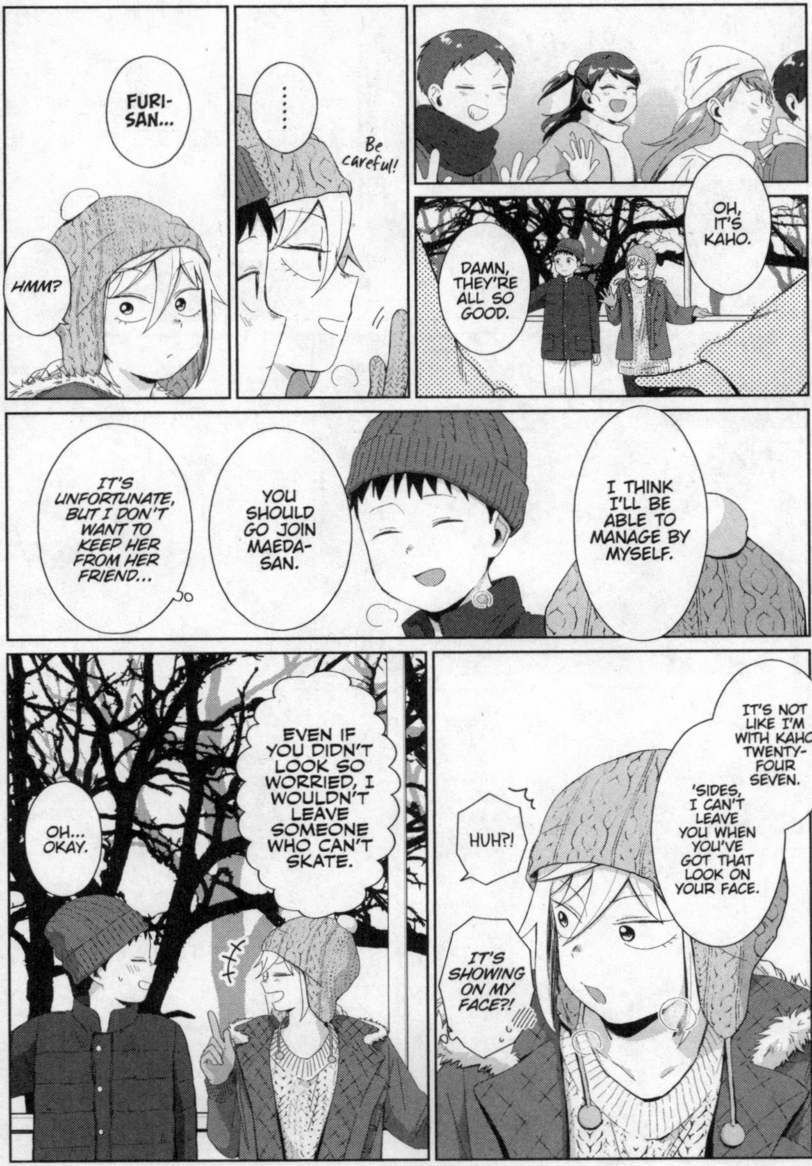
OH, IT'S KAHO.
DAMN, THEY'RE ALL SO GOOD.
......
Be careful!
FURI-SAN...
HMM?
I THINK I'LL BE ABLE TO MANAGE BY MYSELF.
YOU SHOULD GO JOIN MAEDA-SAN.
IT'S UNFORTUNATE, BUT I DON'T WANT TO KEEP HER FROM HER FRIEND...
IT'S NOT LIKE I'M WITH KAHO TWENTY-FOUR SEVEN.
'SIDES, I CAN'T LEAVE YOU WHEN YOU'VE GOT THAT LOOK ON YOUR FACE.
HUH?!
IT'S SHOWING ON MY FACE?!
EVEN IF YOU DIDN'T LOOK SO WORRIED, I WOULDN'T LEAVE SOMEONE WHO CAN'T SKATE.
OH... OKAY.

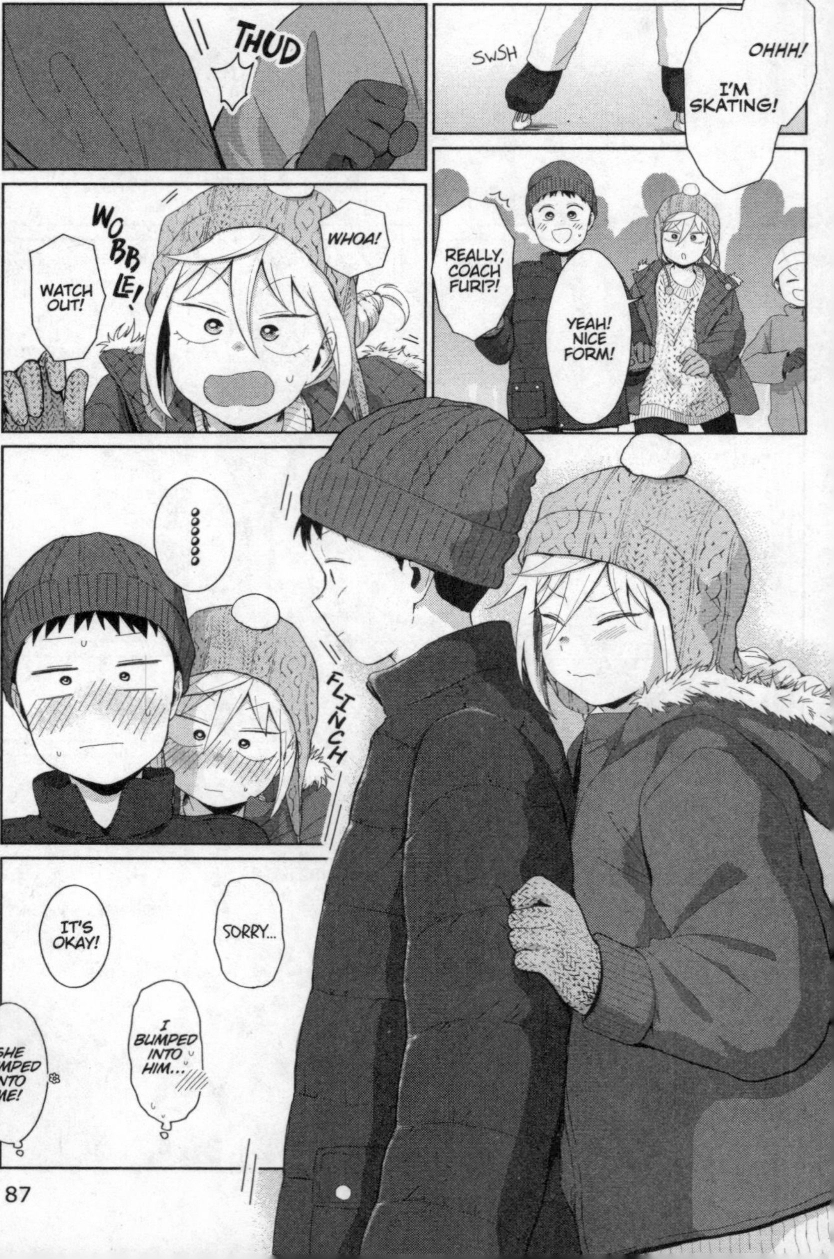

SWSH
OHHH! I'M SKATING!
THUD
REALLY, COACH FURI?!
YEAH! NICE FORM!
WHOA!
WOBBLE!
WATCH OUT!
FLINCH
......
SORRY...
IT'S OKAY!
I BUMPED INTO HIM...
SHE BUMPED INTO ME!

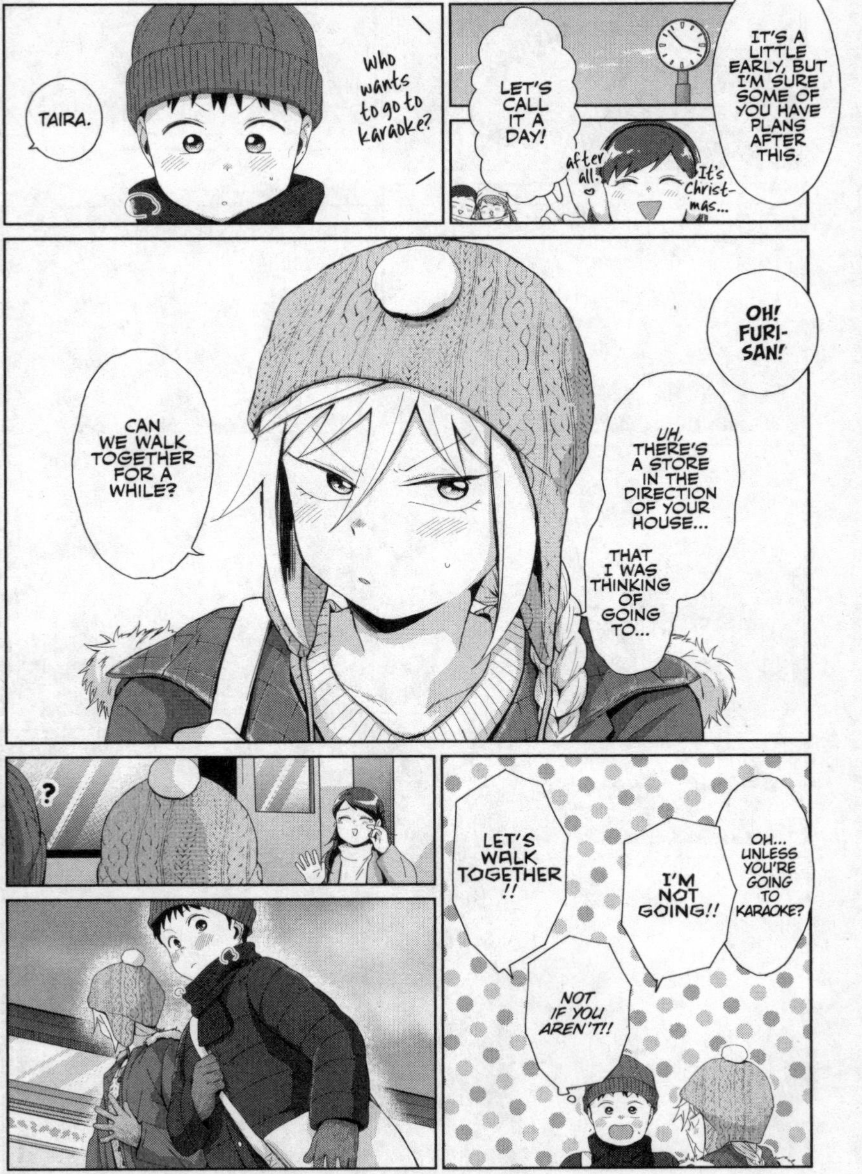
IT'S A LITTLE EARLY, BUT I'M SURE SOME OF YOU HAVE PLANS AFTER THIS.
It's Christmas...
after all.
LET'S CALL IT A DAY!
Who wants to go to karaoke?
TAIRA.
OH! FURI-SAN!
UH, THERE'S A STORE IN THE DIRECTION OF YOUR HOUSE...
THAT I WAS THINKING OF GOING TO...
CAN WE WALK TOGETHER FOR A WHILE?
OH... UNLESS YOU'RE GOING TO KARAOKE?
I'M NOT GOING!!
LET'S WALK TOGETHER!!
NOT IF YOU AREN'T!!
?

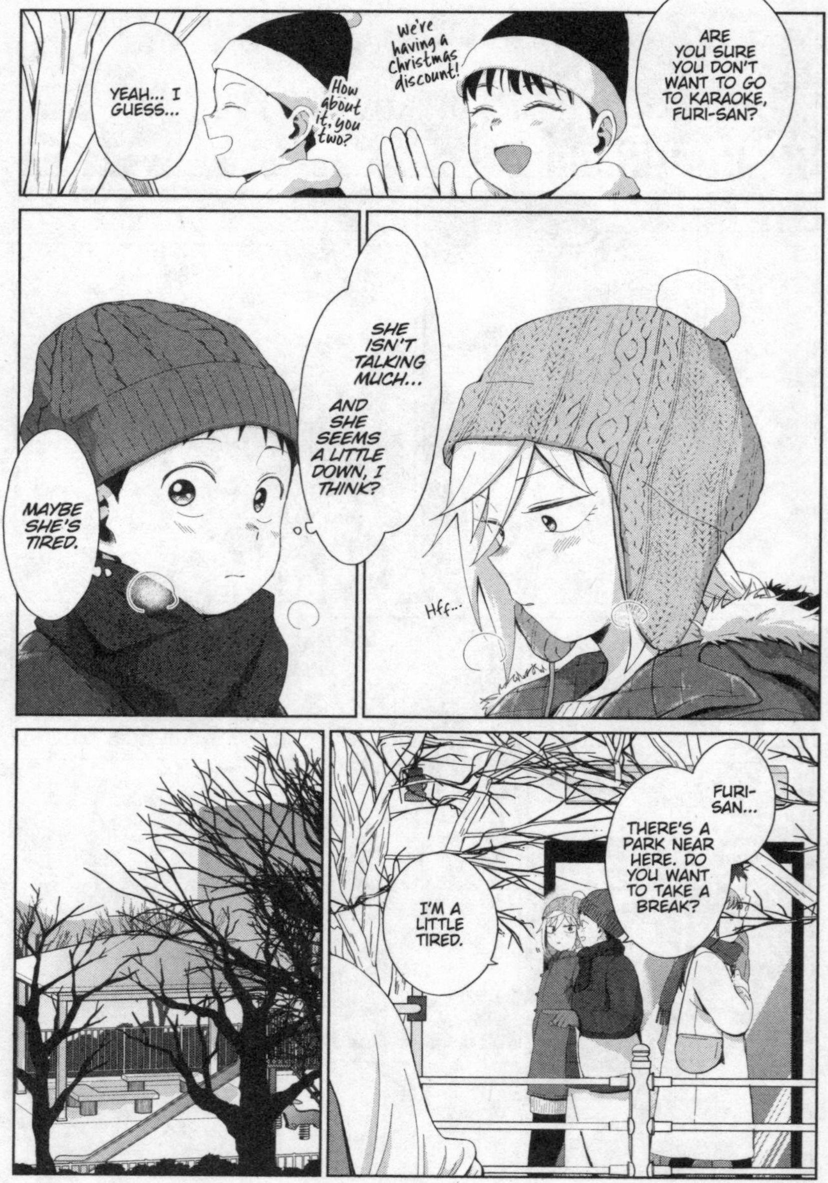
ARE YOU SURE YOU DON'T WANT TO GO TO KARAOKE, FURI-SAN?
We're having a Christmas discount!
How about it, you two?
YEAH... I GUESS...
Hff...
SHE ISN'T TALKING MUCH... AND SHE SEEMS A LITTLE DOWN, I THINK?
MAYBE SHE'S TIRED.
FURI-SAN... THERE'S A PARK NEAR HERE. DO YOU WANT TO TAKE A BREAK?
I'M A LITTLE TIRED.

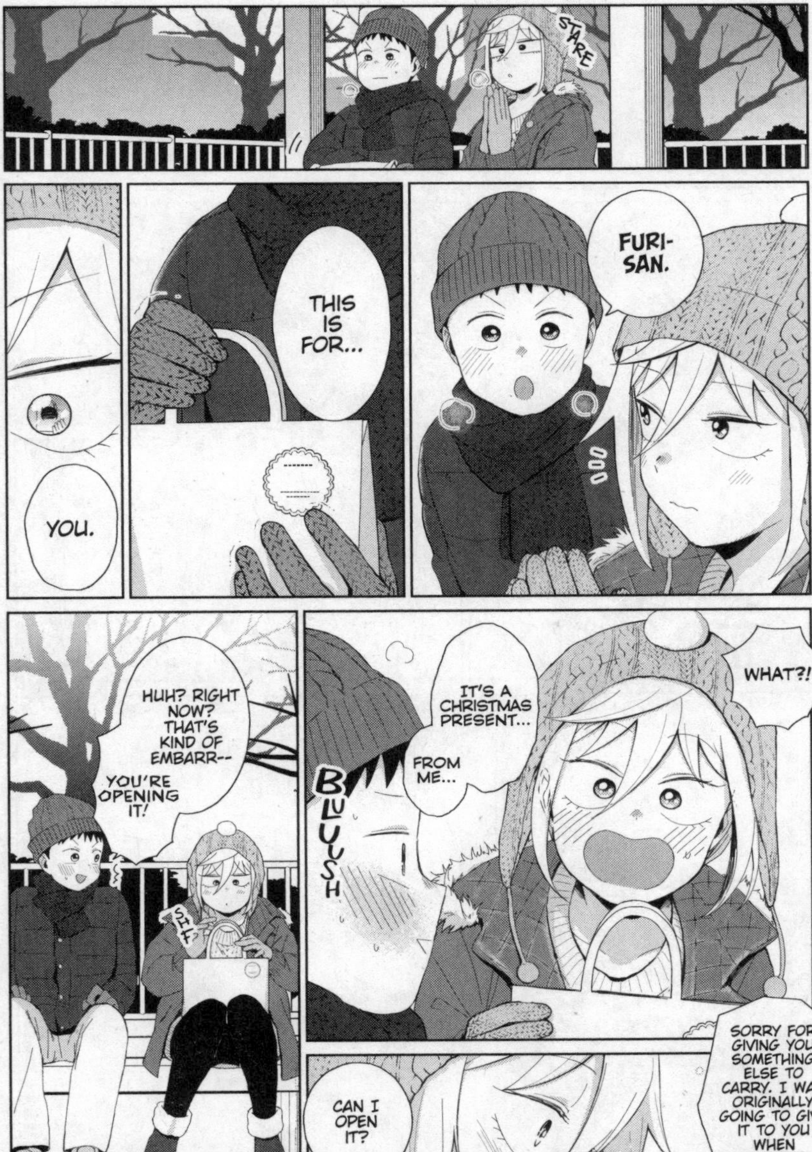
STARE
FURI-SAN.
THIS IS FOR...
YOU.
IT'S A CHRISTMAS PRESENT...
FROM ME...
BLUUSH
WHAT?!
SORRY FOR GIVING YOU SOMETHING ELSE TO CARRY. I WAS ORIGINALLY GOING TO GIVE IT TO YOU WHEN WE PARTED WAYS.
CAN I OPEN IT?
HUH? RIGHT NOW? THAT'S KIND OF EMBARR--
YOU'RE OPENING IT!
SHF

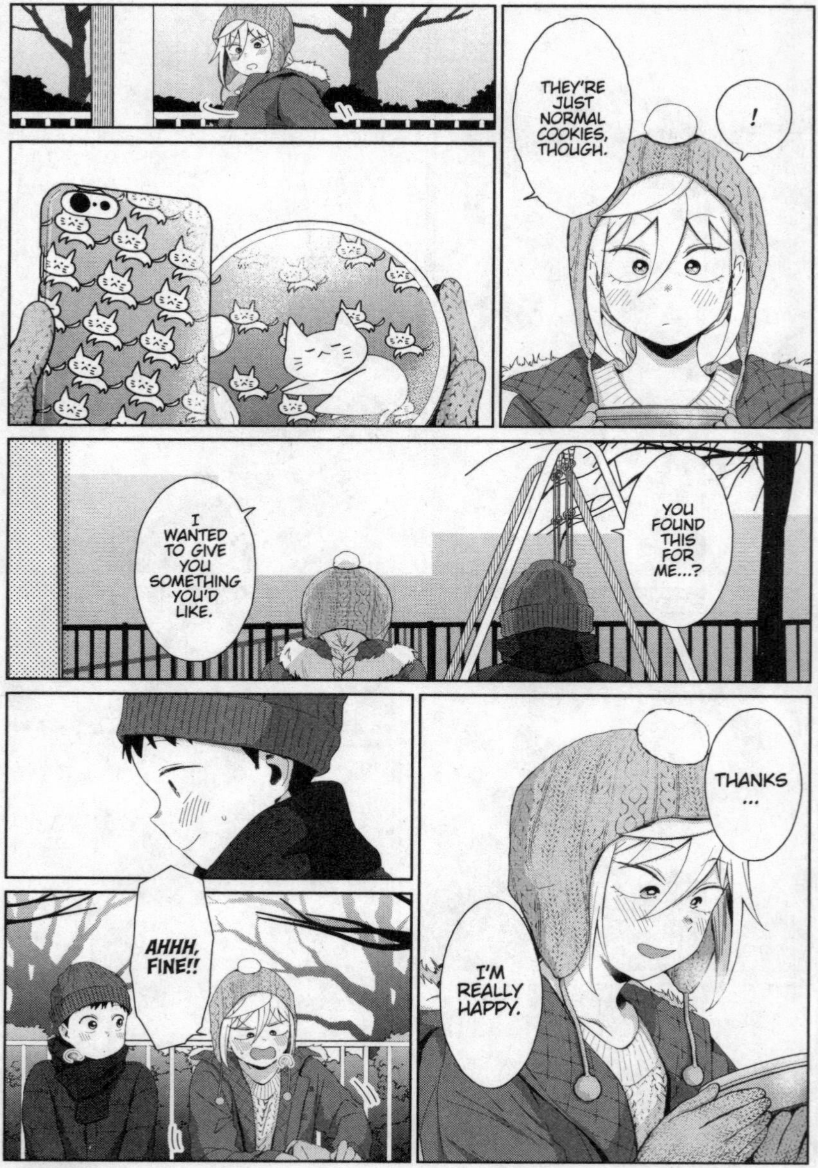
!
THEY'RE JUST NORMAL COOKIES, THOUGH.
YOU FOUND THIS FOR ME...?
I WANTED TO GIVE YOU SOMETHING YOU'D LIKE.
THANKS...
I'M REALLY HAPPY.
AHHH, FINE!!

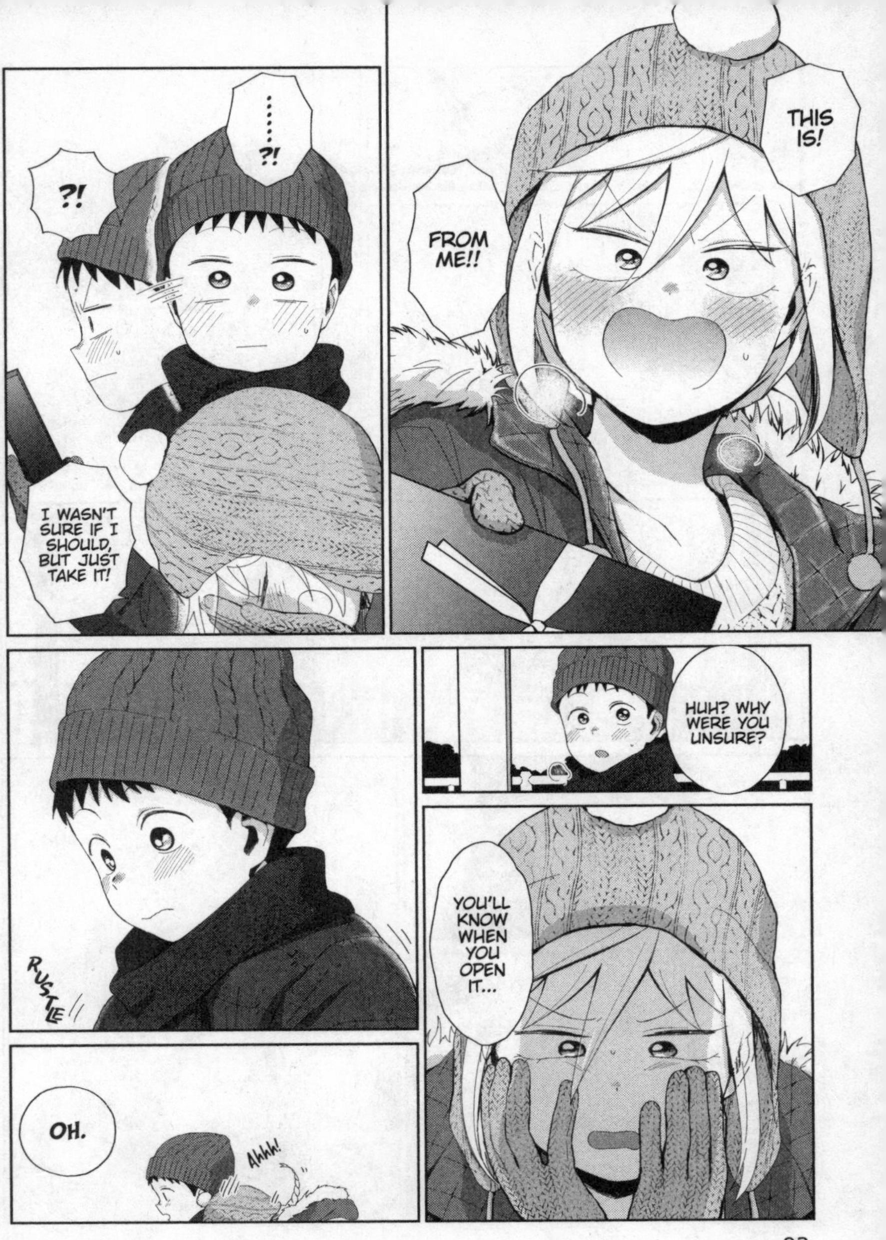
THIS IS!
FROM ME!!
......?!
?!
I WASN'T SURE IF I SHOULD, BUT JUST TAKE IT!
HUH? WHY WERE YOU UNSURE?
YOU'LL KNOW WHEN YOU OPEN IT...
RUSTLE
OH.
AHHH!

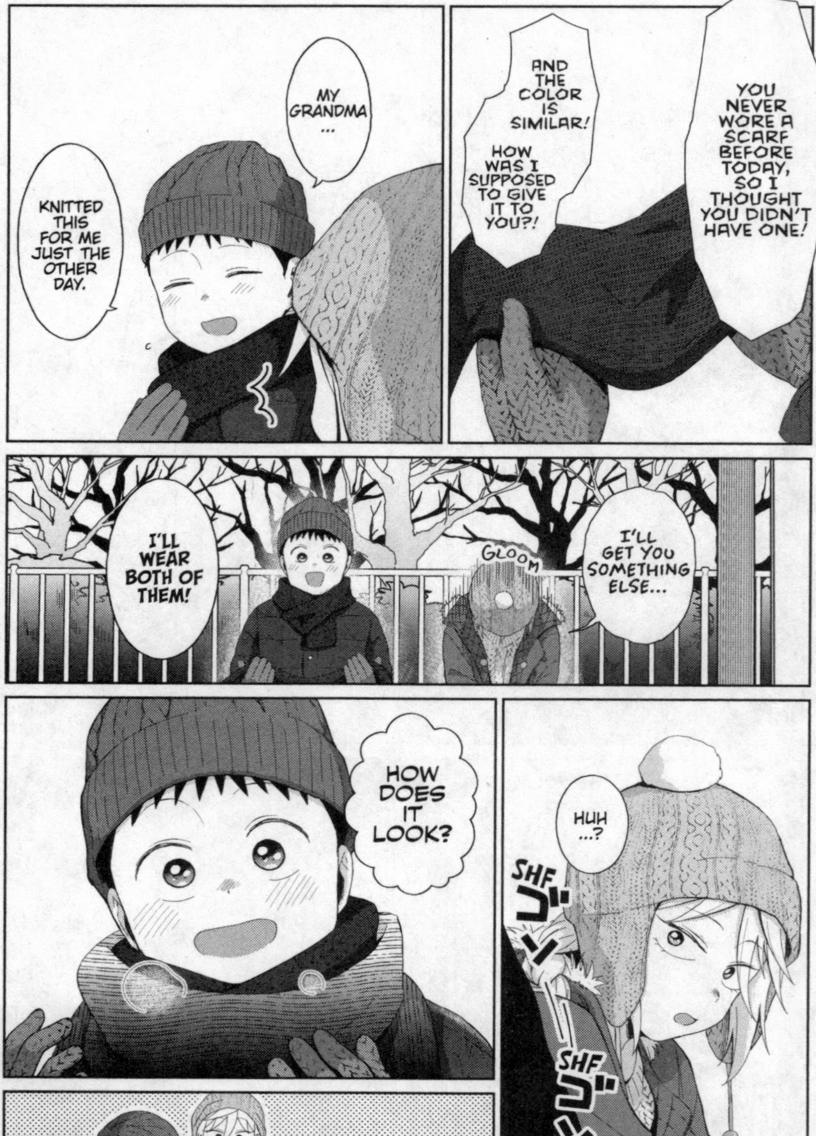

YOU NEVER WORE A SCARF BEFORE TODAY, SO I THOUGHT YOU DIDN'T HAVE ONE!
AND THE COLOR IS SIMILAR!
HOW WAS I SUPPOSED TO GIVE IT TO YOU?!
MY GRANDMA ...
KNITTED THIS FOR ME JUST THE OTHER DAY.
I'LL GET YOU SOMETHING ELSE...
GLOOM
I'LL WEAR BOTH OF THEM!
HUH ...?
SHF
SHF
HOW DOES IT LOOK?

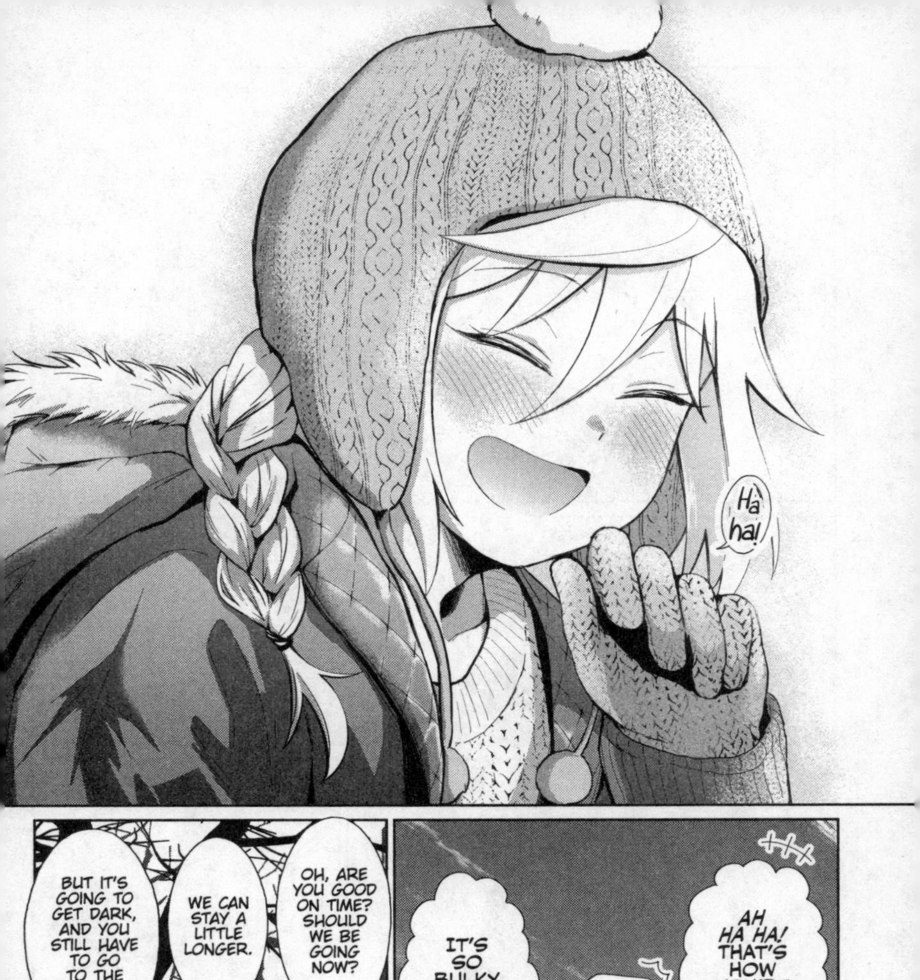
Ha ha!

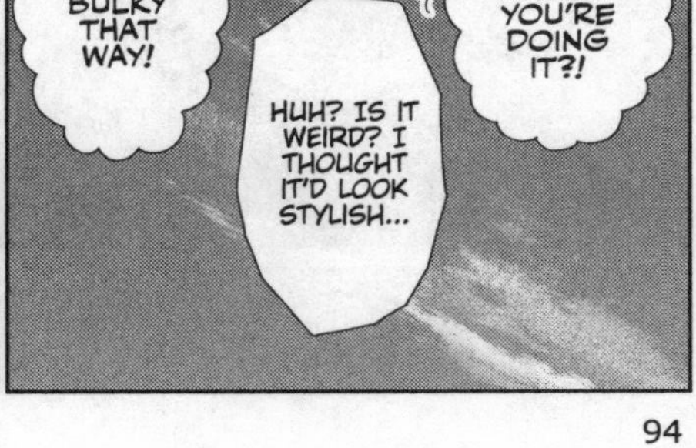
AH HA HA! THAT'S HOW YOU'RE DOING IT?!
IT'S SO BULKY THAT WAY!
HUH? IS IT WEIRD? I THOUGHT IT'D LOOK STYLISH...

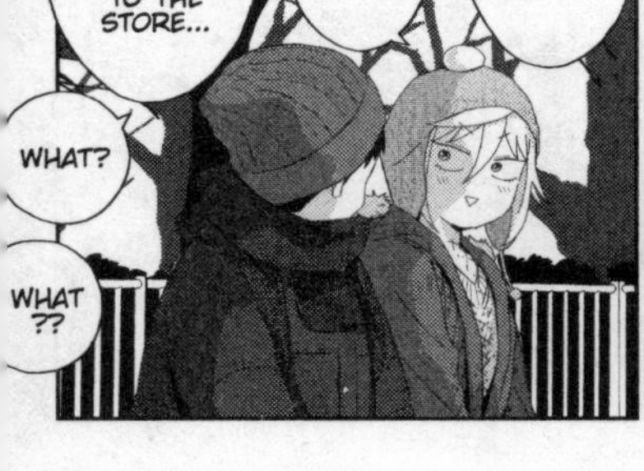
OH, ARE YOU GOOD ON TIME? SHOULD WE BE GOING NOW?
WE CAN STAY A LITTLE LONGER.
BUT IT'S GOING TO GET DARK, AND YOU STILL HAVE TO GO TO THE STORE...
WHAT?
WHAT??

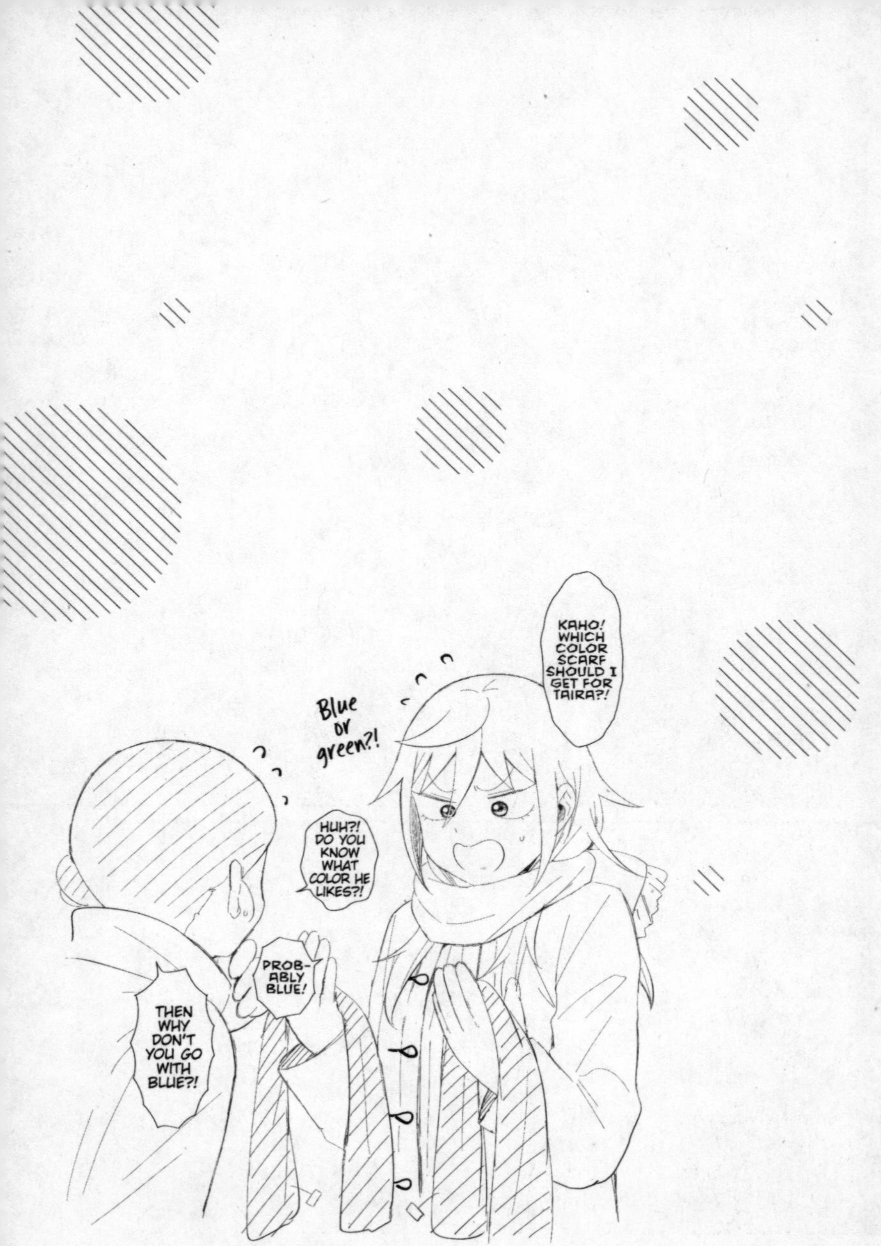
KAHO! WHICH COLOR SCARF SHOULD I GET FOR TAIRA?!
Blue or green?!
HUH?! DO YOU KNOW WHAT COLOR HE LIKES?!
PROB-ABLY BLUE!
THEN WHY DON'T YOU GO WITH BLUE?!

Chapter 33

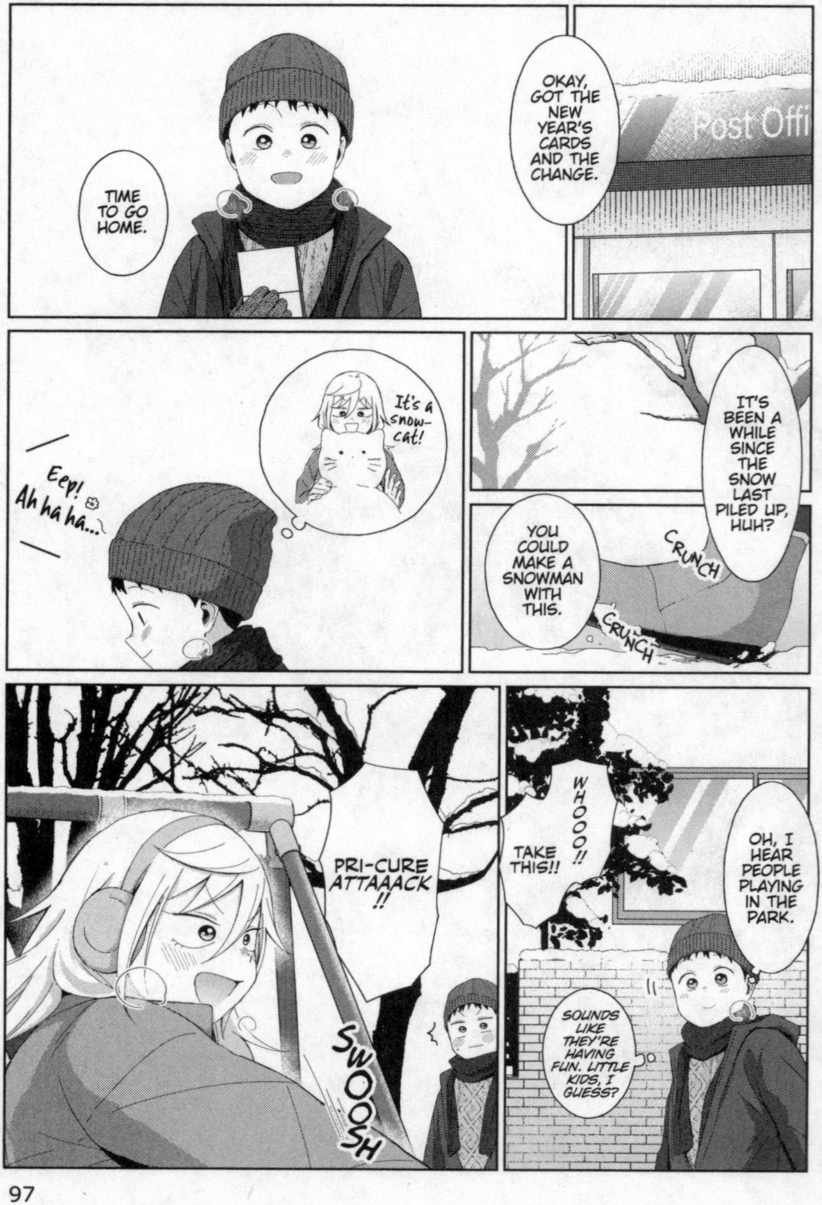

Post Offi
OKAY, GOT THE NEW YEAR'S CARDS AND THE CHANGE.
TIME TO GO HOME.
IT'S BEEN A WHILE SINCE THE SNOW LAST PILED UP, HUH?
CRUNCH
YOU COULD MAKE A SNOWMAN WITH THIS.
CRUNCH
It's a snow-cat!
Eep! Ah ha ha...
OH, I HEAR PEOPLE PLAYING IN THE PARK.
WHOOOO!!
TAKE THIS!!
SOUNDS LIKE THEY'RE HAVING FUN. LITTLE KIDS, I GUESS?
PRI-CURE ATTAAACK!!
SWOOSH

Chapter 33

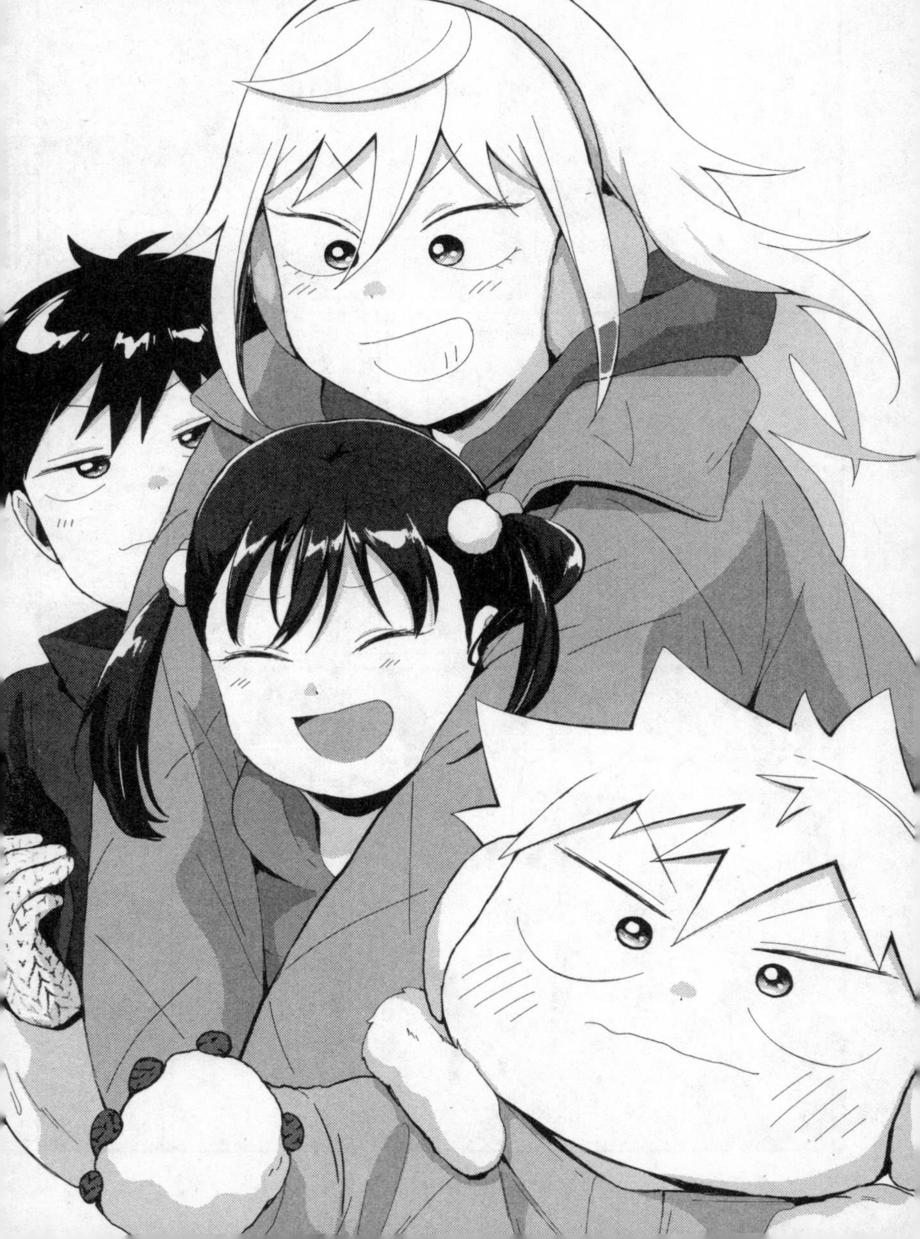

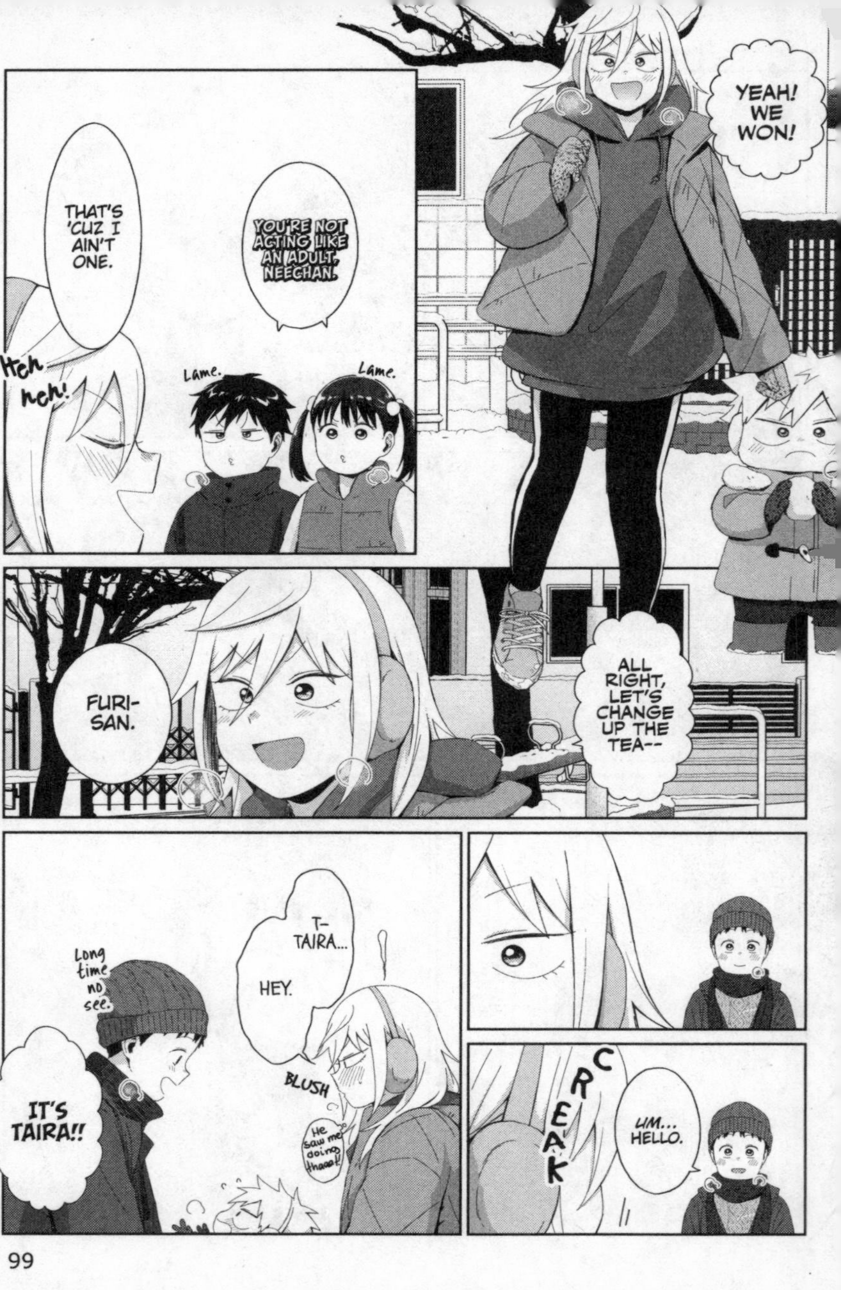
YEAH! WE WON!
YOU'RE NOT ACTING LIKE AN ADULT, NEECHAN.
THAT'S 'CUZ I AIN'T ONE.
Lame.
Lame.
Heh heh!
ALL RIGHT, LET'S CHANGE UP THE TEA--
FURI-SAN.
CREAK
UM... HELLO.
T-TAIRA...
HEY.
Long time no see.
BLUSH
He saw me doing thaaat!
IT'S TAIRA!!

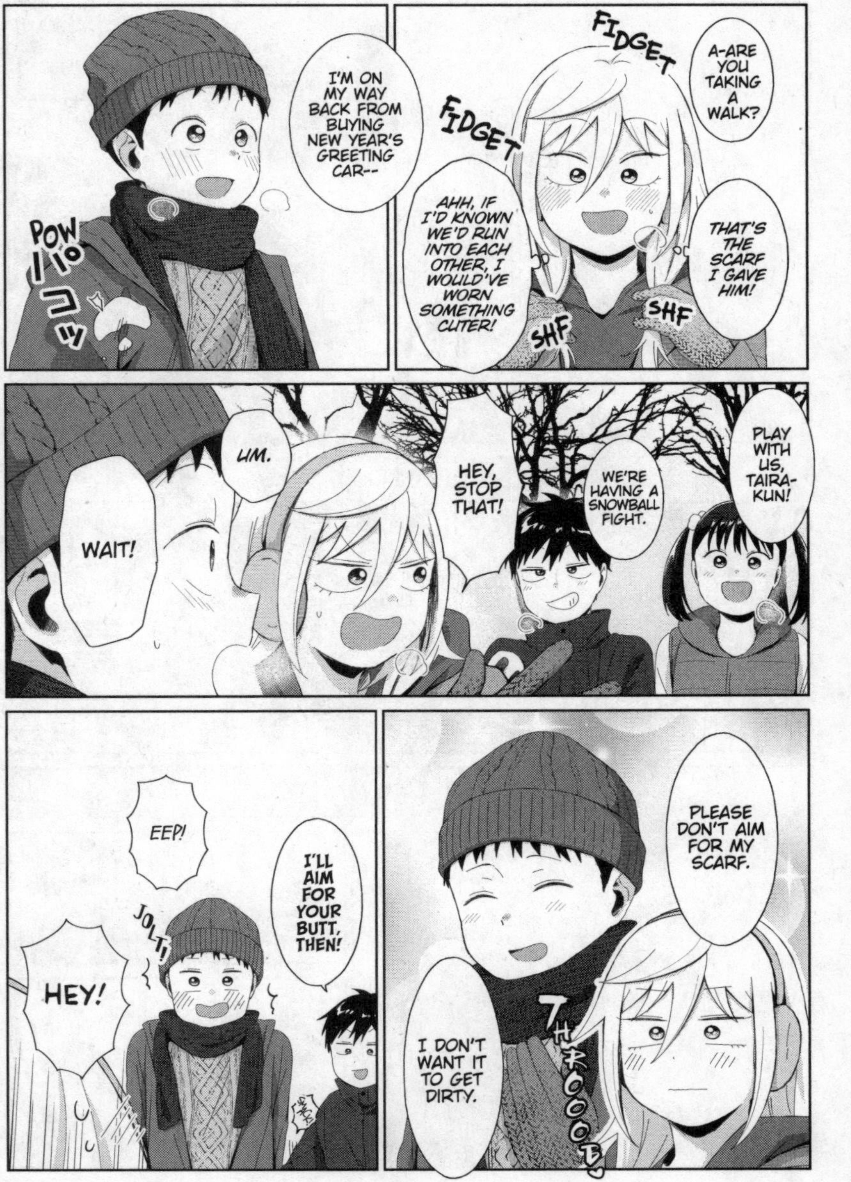
FIDGET
FIDGET
A-ARE YOU TAKING A WALK?
THAT'S THE SCARF I GAVE HIM!
AHH, IF I'D KNOWN WE'D RUN INTO EACH OTHER, I WOULD'VE WORN SOMETHING CUTER!
SHF
SHF
I'M ON MY WAY BACK FROM BUYING NEW YEAR'S GREETING CAR--
POW
PLAY WITH US, TAIRA-KUN!
WE'RE HAVING A SNOWBALL FIGHT.
HEY, STOP THAT!
UM.
WAIT!
PLEASE DON'T AIM FOR MY SCARF.
THROOOB
I DON'T WANT IT TO GET DIRTY.
I'LL AIM FOR YOUR BUTT, THEN!
EEP!
JOLT!
HEY!

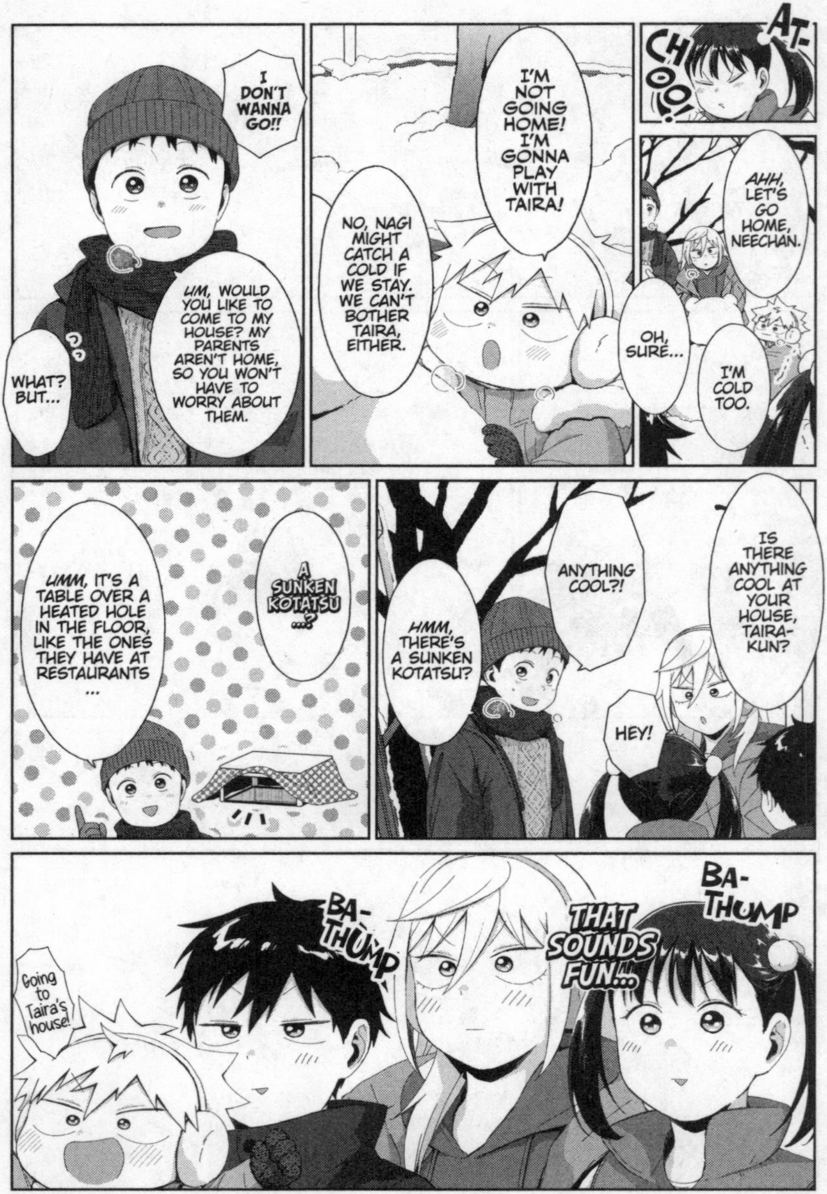
AT-CHOOO!!
AHH, LET'S GO HOME, NEECHAN.
OH, SURE...
I'M COLD TOO.
I'M NOT GOING HOME! I'M GONNA PLAY WITH TAIRA!
NO, NAGI MIGHT CATCH A COLD IF WE STAY. WE CAN'T BOTHER TAIRA, EITHER.
I DON'T WANNA GO!!
UM, WOULD YOU LIKE TO COME TO MY HOUSE? MY PARENTS AREN'T HOME, SO YOU WON'T HAVE TO WORRY ABOUT THEM.
WHAT? BUT...
IS THERE ANYTHING COOL AT YOUR HOUSE, TAIRA-KUN?
ANYTHING COOL?!
HEY!
HMM, THERE'S A SUNKEN KOTATSU?
A SUNKEN KOTATSU ...?
UMM, IT'S A TABLE OVER A HEATED HOLE IN THE FLOOR, LIKE THE ONES THEY HAVE AT RESTAURANTS ...
BA-THUMP
THAT SOUNDS FUN...
BA-THUMP
Going to Taira's house!

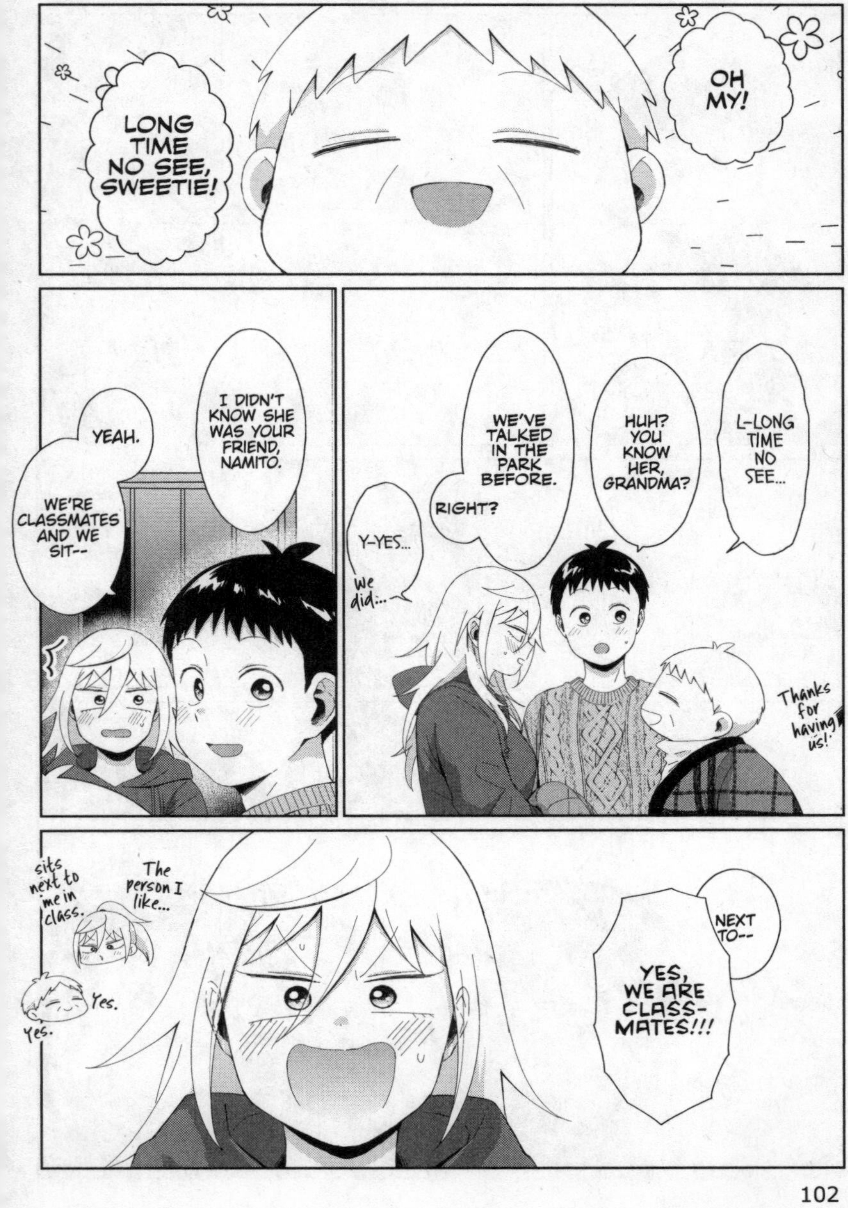
OH MY!
LONG TIME NO SEE, SWEETIE!
L-LONG TIME NO SEE...
Thanks for having us!
HUH? YOU KNOW HER, GRANDMA?
WE'VE TALKED IN THE PARK BEFORE.
RIGHT?
Y-YES...
we did...
I DIDN'T KNOW SHE WAS YOUR FRIEND, NAMITO.
YEAH.
WE'RE CLASSMATES AND WE SIT--
NEXT TO--
YES, WE ARE CLASS-MATES!!!
The person I like...
sits next to me in class.
Yes.
Yes.

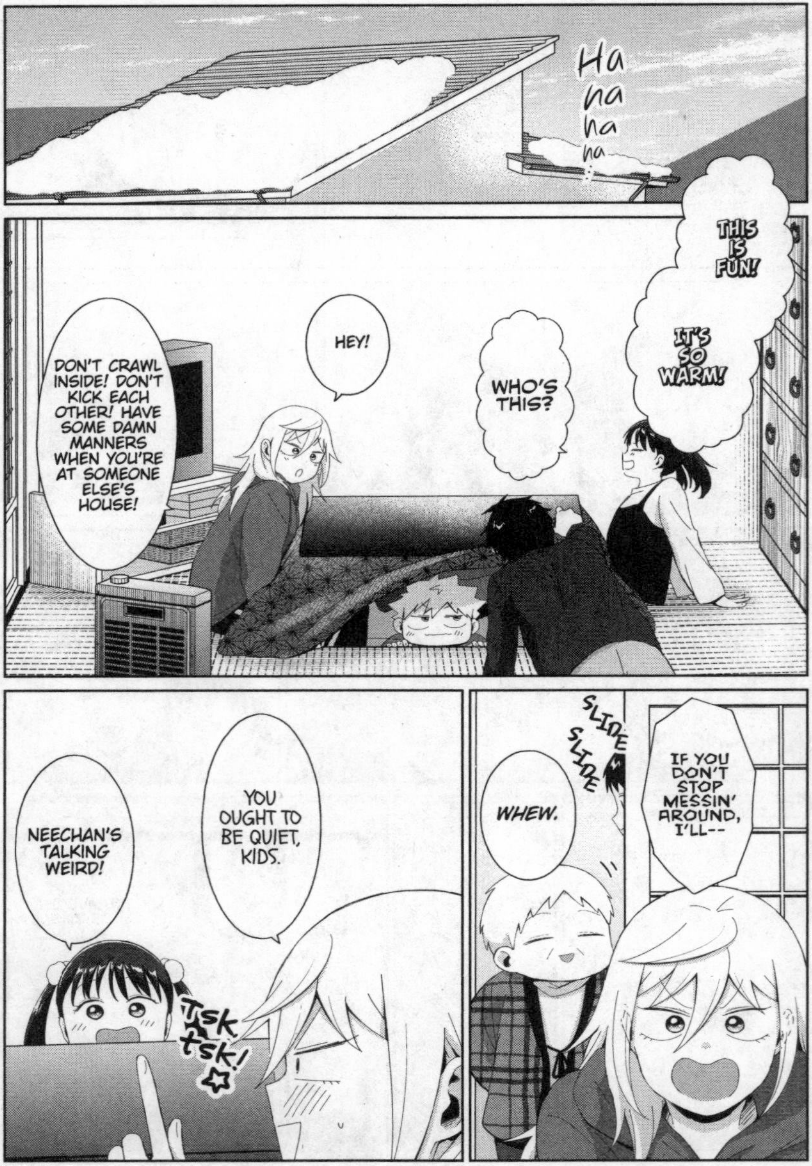
Ha na na na...
THIS IS FUN!
IT'S SO WARM!
WHO'S THIS?
HEY!
DON'T CRAWL INSIDE! DON'T KICK EACH OTHER! HAVE SOME DAMN MANNERS WHEN YOU'RE AT SOMEONE ELSE'S HOUSE!
IF YOU DON'T STOP MESSIN' AROUND, I'LL--
SLIDE SLIDE
WHEW.
YOU OUGHT TO BE QUIET, KIDS.
TSK TSK!
NEECHAN'S TALKING WEIRD!

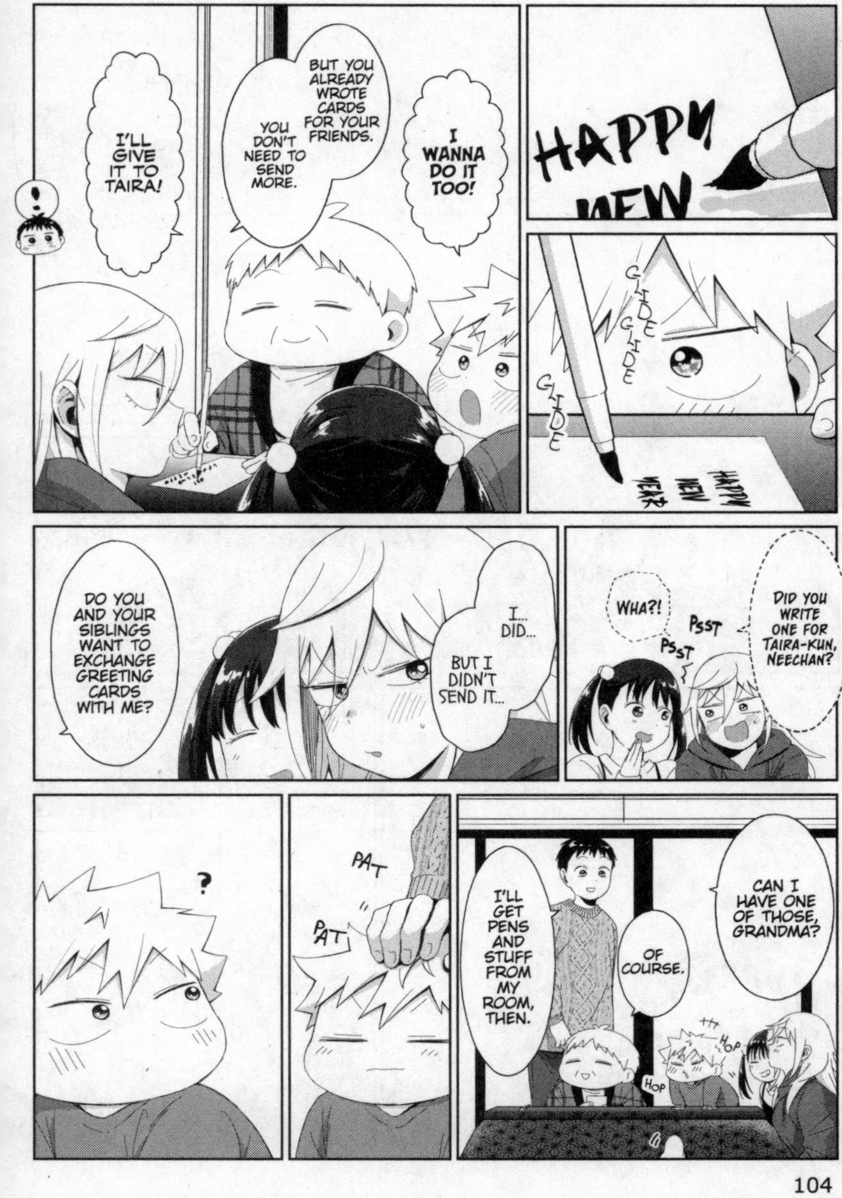
HAPPY NEW
GLIDE GLIDE GLIDE GLIDE
HAPPY NEW YEAR
I WANNA DO IT TOO!
BUT YOU ALREADY WROTE CARDS FOR YOUR FRIENDS.
YOU DON'T NEED TO SEND MORE.
I'LL GIVE IT TO TAIRA!
!
DID YOU WRITE ONE FOR TAIRA-KUN, NEECHAN?
WHA?!
PSST PSST
I... DID...
BUT I DIDN'T SEND IT...
DO YOU AND YOUR SIBLINGS WANT TO EXCHANGE GREETING CARDS WITH ME?
CAN I HAVE ONE OF THOSE, GRANDMA?
OF COURSE.
I'LL GET PENS AND STUFF FROM MY ROOM, THEN.
HOP HOP
PAT PAT
?

Chiyo
Namito-sama
Furi Youko
Minato
Nagisa
Ryuuji
ROCK, PAPER...
SCISSORS!!
RYUU USED SCISSORS!! WHO TAUGHT HIM HOW TO DO THAT?!
WE ONLY GET ONE CARD BETWEEN THE FOUR OF US, ALL RIGHT?! DON'T DRAW ANYTHING BIG!
I'M SORRY THEY'RE SO NOISY...
SCRITCH
SCRITCH
SCRATCH
I SAID DON'T!!
YOU'RE NOT ALLOWED TO DRAW ANYMORE, RYUU!!
Gyah! Gyah!
BOW
I'M SO SORRY! I'M SO SORRY!
BOW
IT'S NICE AND LIVELY.

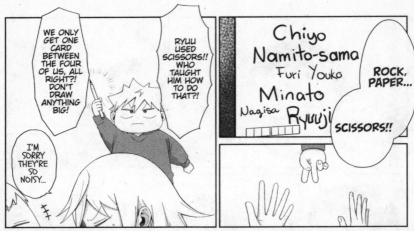

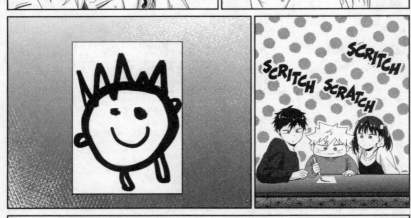

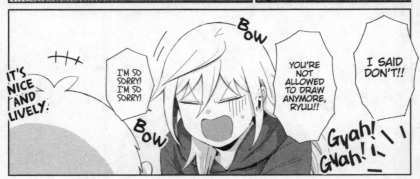

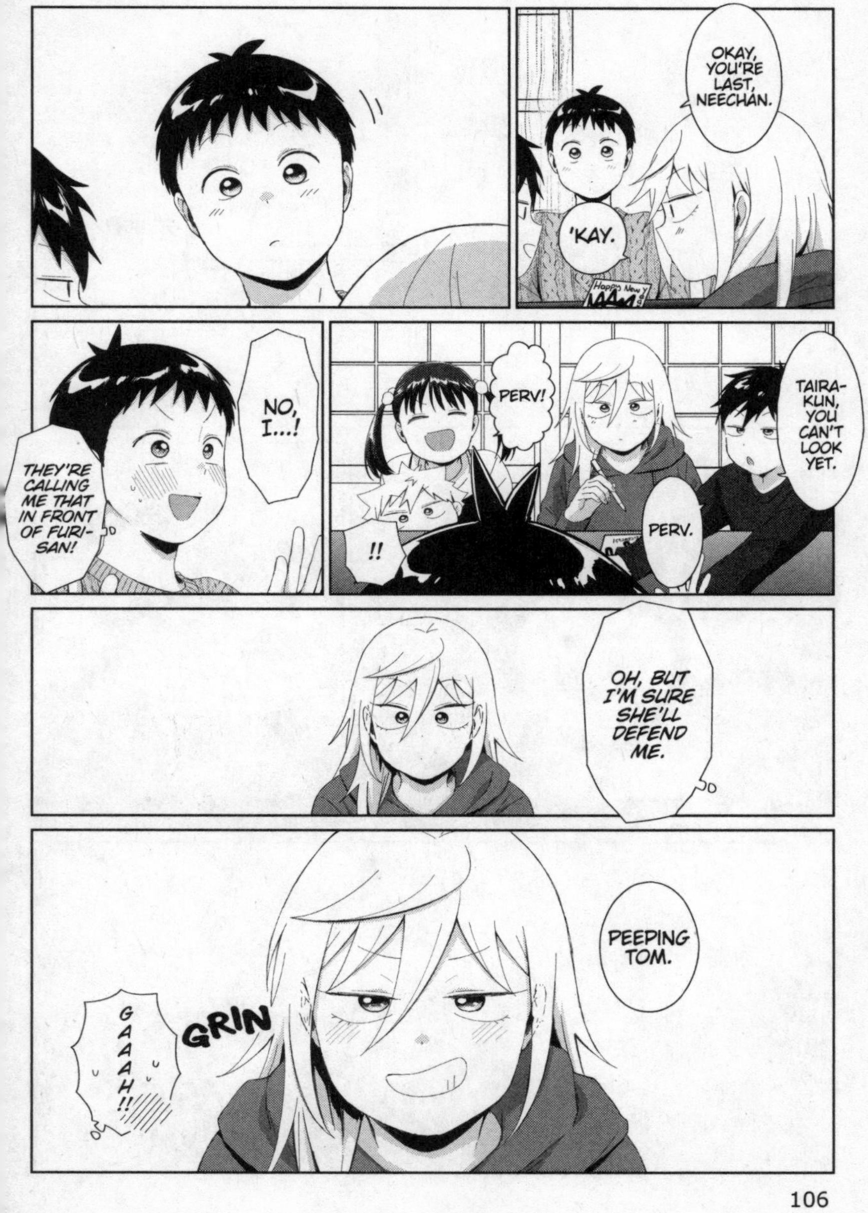
OKAY, YOU'RE LAST, NEECHAN.
'KAY.
TAIRA-KUN, YOU CAN'T LOOK YET.
PERV!
PERV.
!!
NO, I...!
THEY'RE CALLING ME THAT IN FRONT OF FURI-SAN!
OH, BUT I'M SURE SHE'LL DEFEND ME.
PEEPING TOM.
GRIN
GAAAAH!!

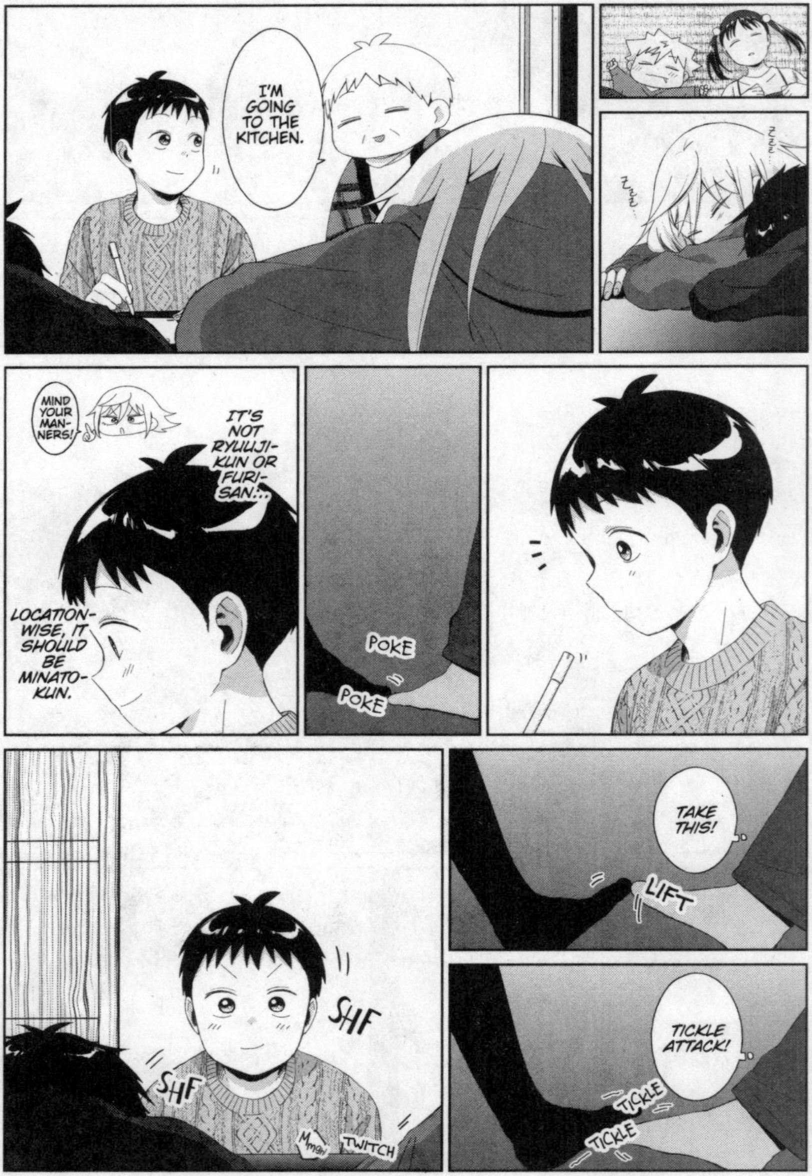
Zzz...
Zzz...
I'M GOING TO THE KITCHEN.
POKE
POKE
IT'S NOT RYUUJI-KUN OR FURI-SAN...
MIND YOUR MANNERS!
LOCATION-WISE, IT SHOULD BE MINATO-KUN.
TAKE THIS!
LIFT
TICKLE ATTACK!
TICKLE
TICKLE
SHF
SHF
MMGH
TWITCH

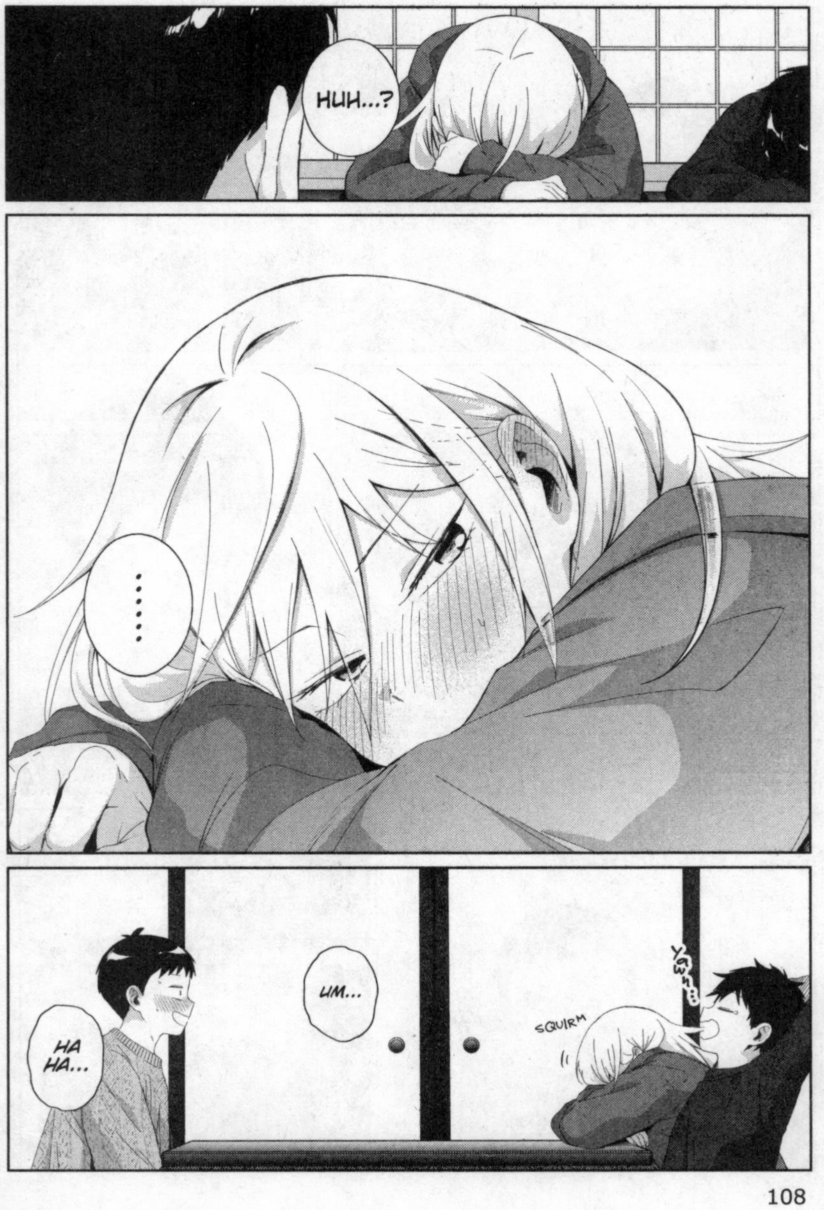
HUH...?
......
Yawn...
SQUIRM
UM...
HA HA...

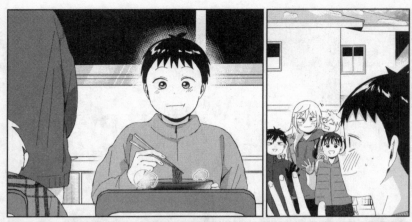

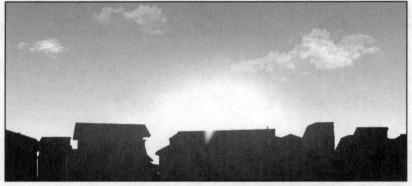

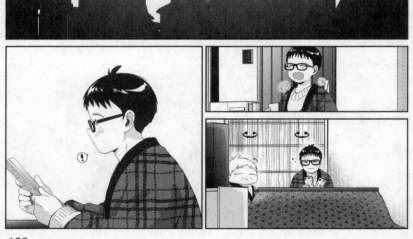

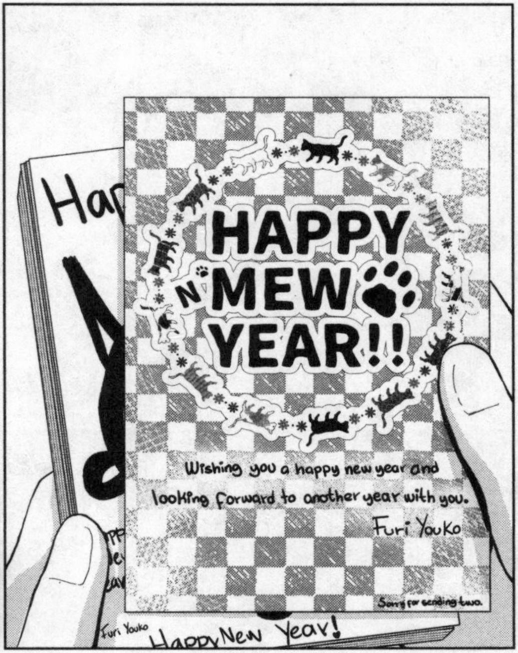
HAPPY MEW YEAR!!
N'
Wishing you a happy new year and looking forward to another year with you.
Furi Youko
Sorry for sending two.
Furi Youko
Happy New Year!
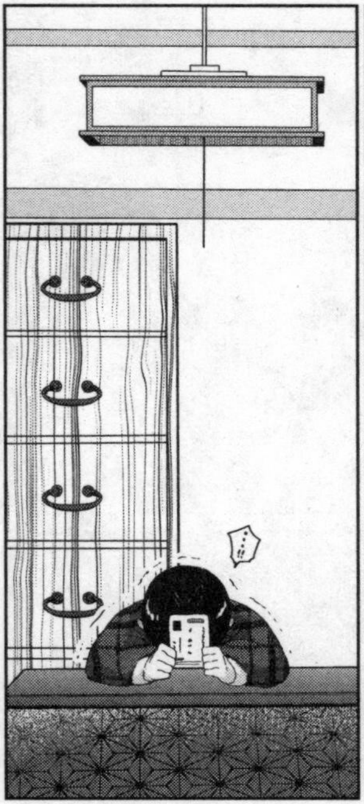
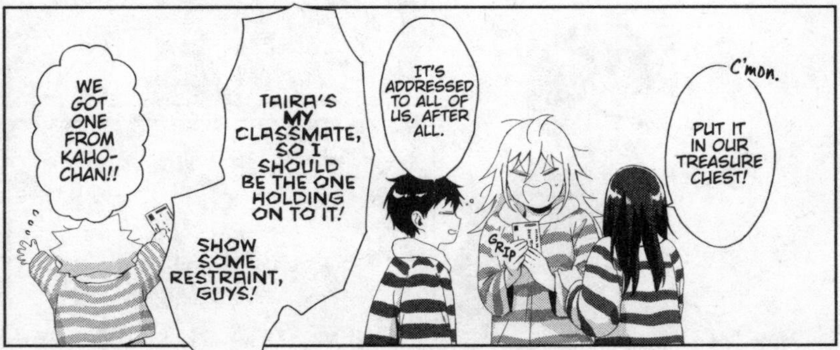
C'mon.
PUT IT IN OUR TREASURE CHEST!
IT'S ADDRESSED TO ALL OF US, AFTER ALL.
GRIP
TAIRA'S **MY** CLASSMATE, SO I SHOULD BE THE ONE HOLDING ON TO IT!
SHOW SOME RESTRAINT, GUYS!
WE GOT ONE FROM KAHO-CHAN!!

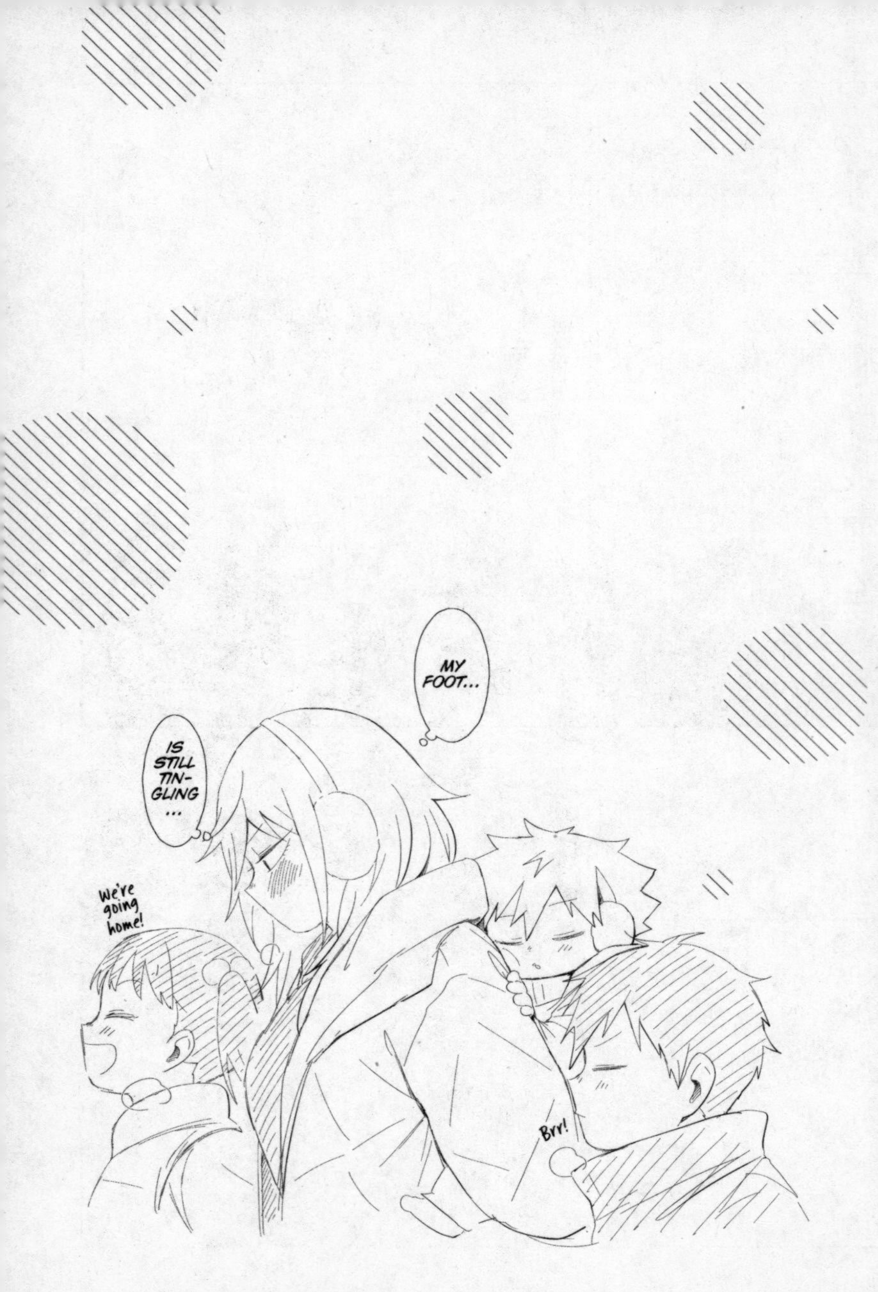
MY FOOT...
IS STILL TIN-GLING...
We're going home!
Brr!

Chapter 34

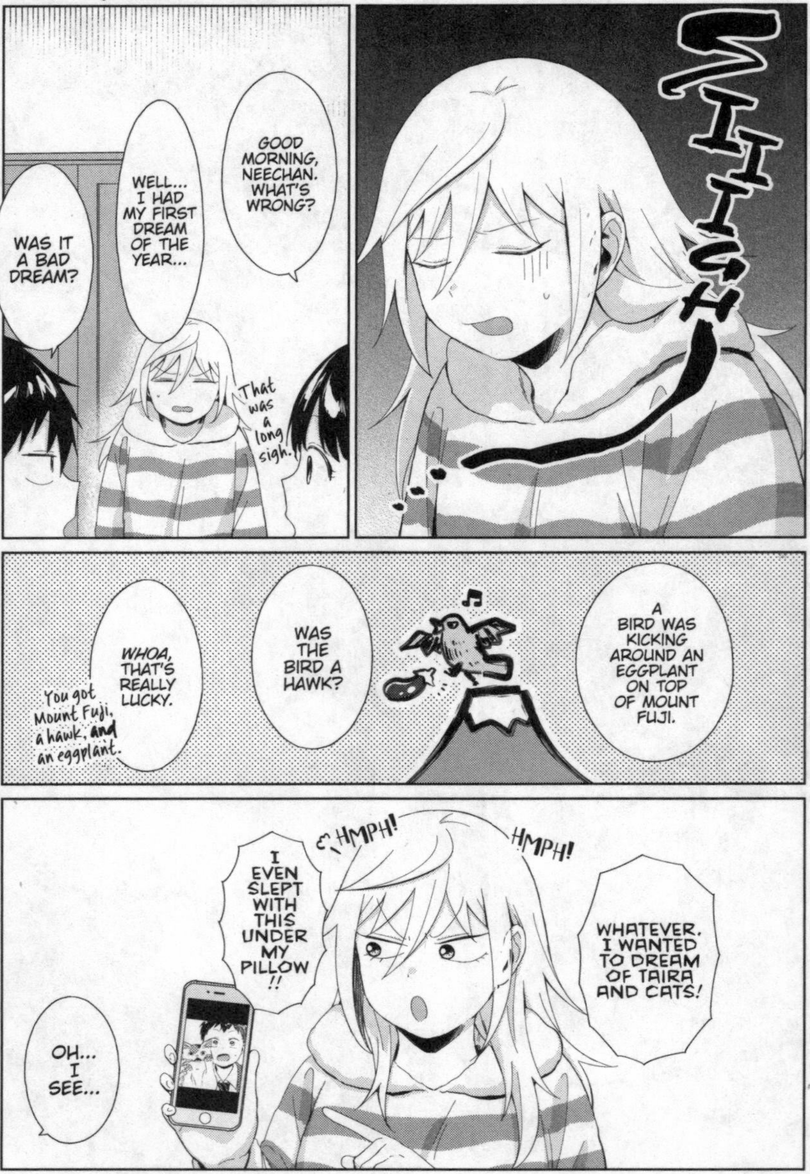
SIIIGH
GOOD MORNING, NEECHAN. WHAT'S WRONG?
WELL... I HAD MY FIRST DREAM OF THE YEAR...
WAS IT A BAD DREAM?
That was a long sigh.
A BIRD WAS KICKING AROUND AN EGGPLANT ON TOP OF MOUNT FUJI.
WAS THE BIRD A HAWK?
WHOA, THAT'S REALLY LUCKY.
You got Mount Fuji, a hawk, and an eggplant.
HMPH!
HMPH!
WHATEVER. I WANTED TO DREAM OF TAIRA AND CATS!
I EVEN SLEPT WITH THIS UNDER MY PILLOW!!
OH... I SEE...

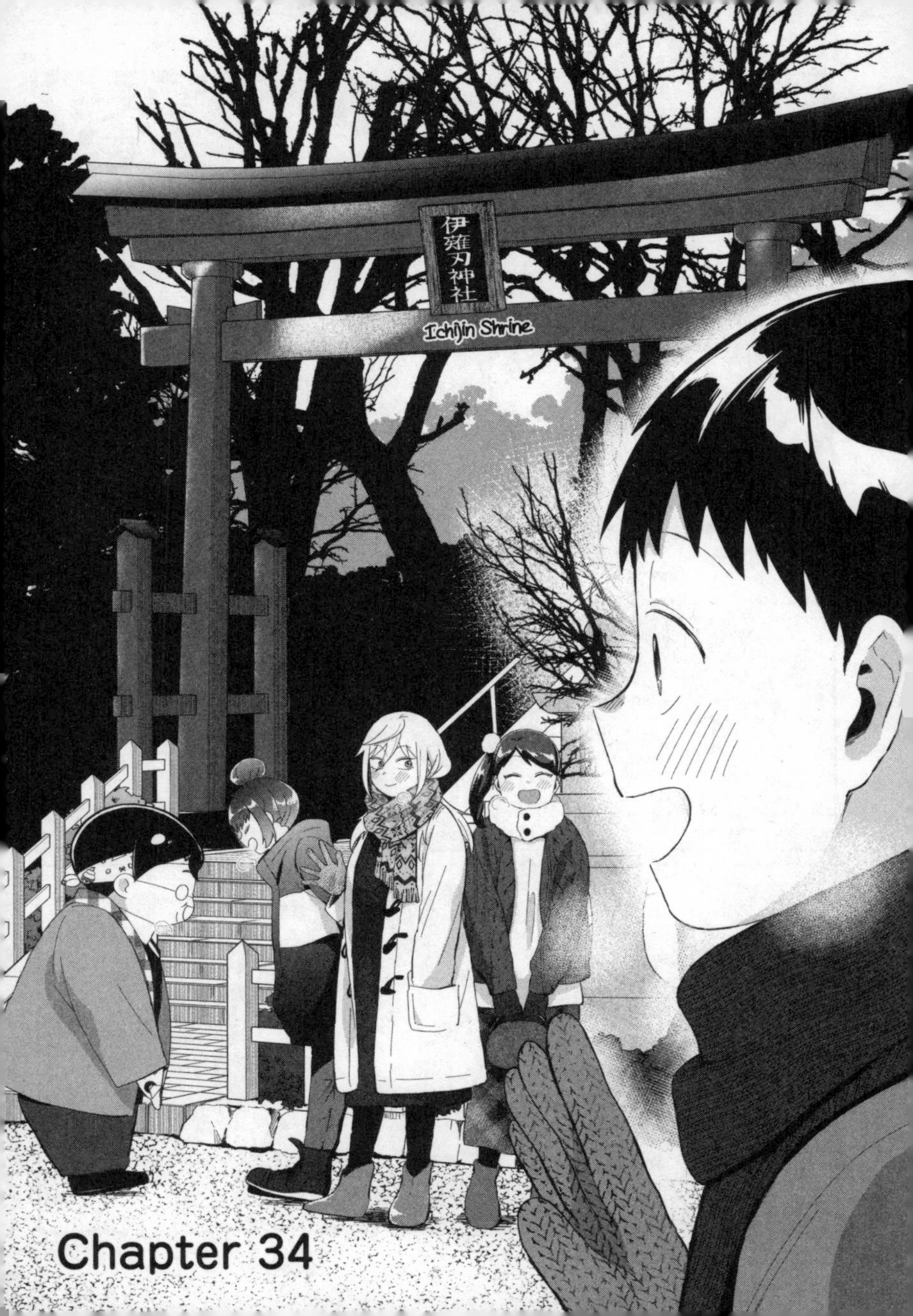
伊薙刃神社
Ichijin Shrine

Chapter 34

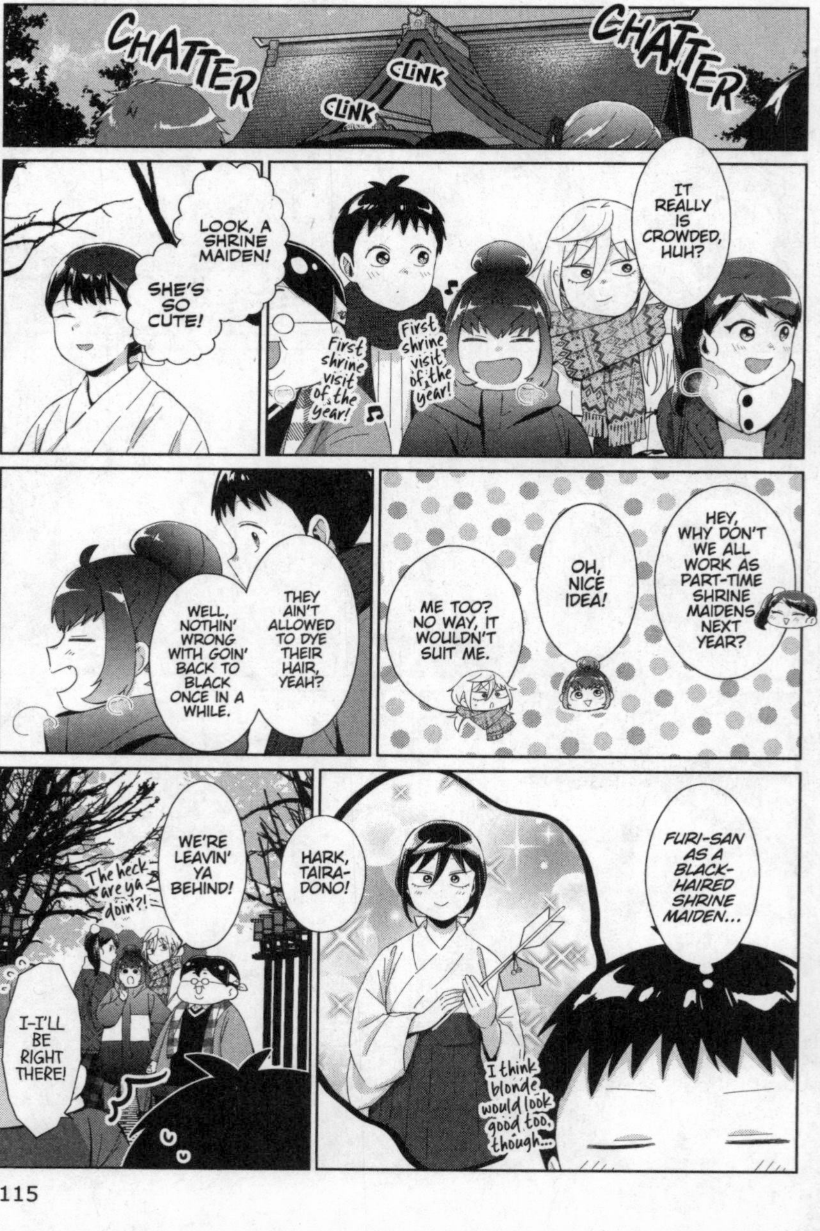
CHATTER
CLINK
CLINK
CHATTER
IT REALLY IS CROWDED, HUH?
First shrine visit of the year!
First shrine visit of the year!
LOOK, A SHRINE MAIDEN!
SHE'S SO CUTE!
HEY, WHY DON'T WE ALL WORK AS PART-TIME SHRINE MAIDENS NEXT YEAR?
OH, NICE IDEA!
ME TOO? NO WAY, IT WOULDN'T SUIT ME.
THEY AIN'T ALLOWED TO DYE THEIR HAIR, YEAH?
WELL, NOTHIN' WRONG WITH GOIN' BACK TO BLACK ONCE IN A WHILE.
FURI-SAN AS A BLACK-HAIRED SHRINE MAIDEN...
I think blonde would look good too, though...
HARK, TAIRA-DONO!
WE'RE LEAVIN' YA BEHIND!
The heck are ya doin'?!
I-I'LL BE RIGHT THERE!

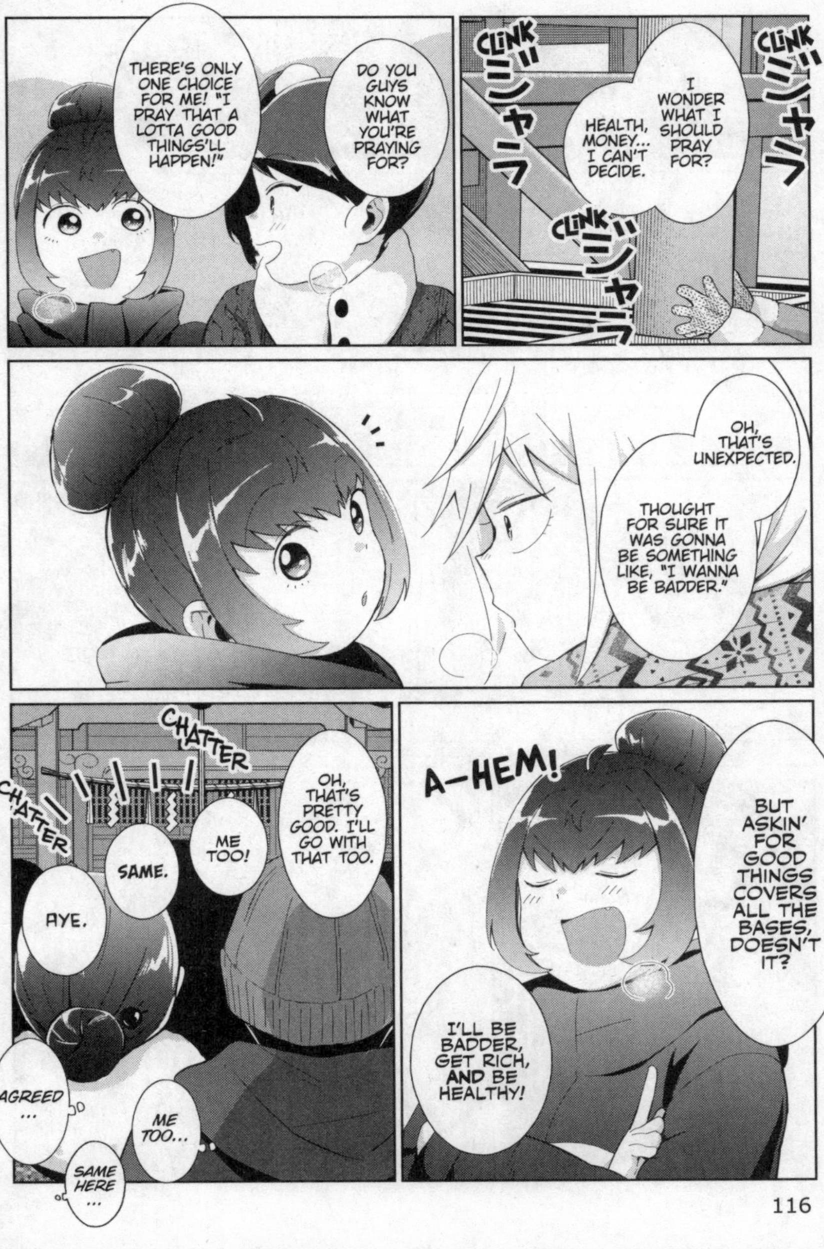

CLINK ジャラ
I WONDER WHAT I SHOULD PRAY FOR?
HEALTH, MONEY... I CAN'T DECIDE.
CLINK ジャラ
CLINK ジャラ
DO YOU GUYS KNOW WHAT YOU'RE PRAYING FOR?
THERE'S ONLY ONE CHOICE FOR ME! "I PRAY THAT A LOTTA GOOD THINGS'LL HAPPEN!"
OH, THAT'S UNEXPECTED.
THOUGHT FOR SURE IT WAS GONNA BE SOMETHING LIKE, "I WANNA BE BADDER."
A-HEM!
BUT ASKIN' FOR GOOD THINGS COVERS ALL THE BASES, DOESN'T IT?
I'LL BE BADDER, GET RICH, AND BE HEALTHY!
CHATTER
CHATTER
OH, THAT'S PRETTY GOOD. I'LL GO WITH THAT TOO.
ME TOO!
SAME.
AYE.
AGREED...
ME TOO...
SAME HERE...

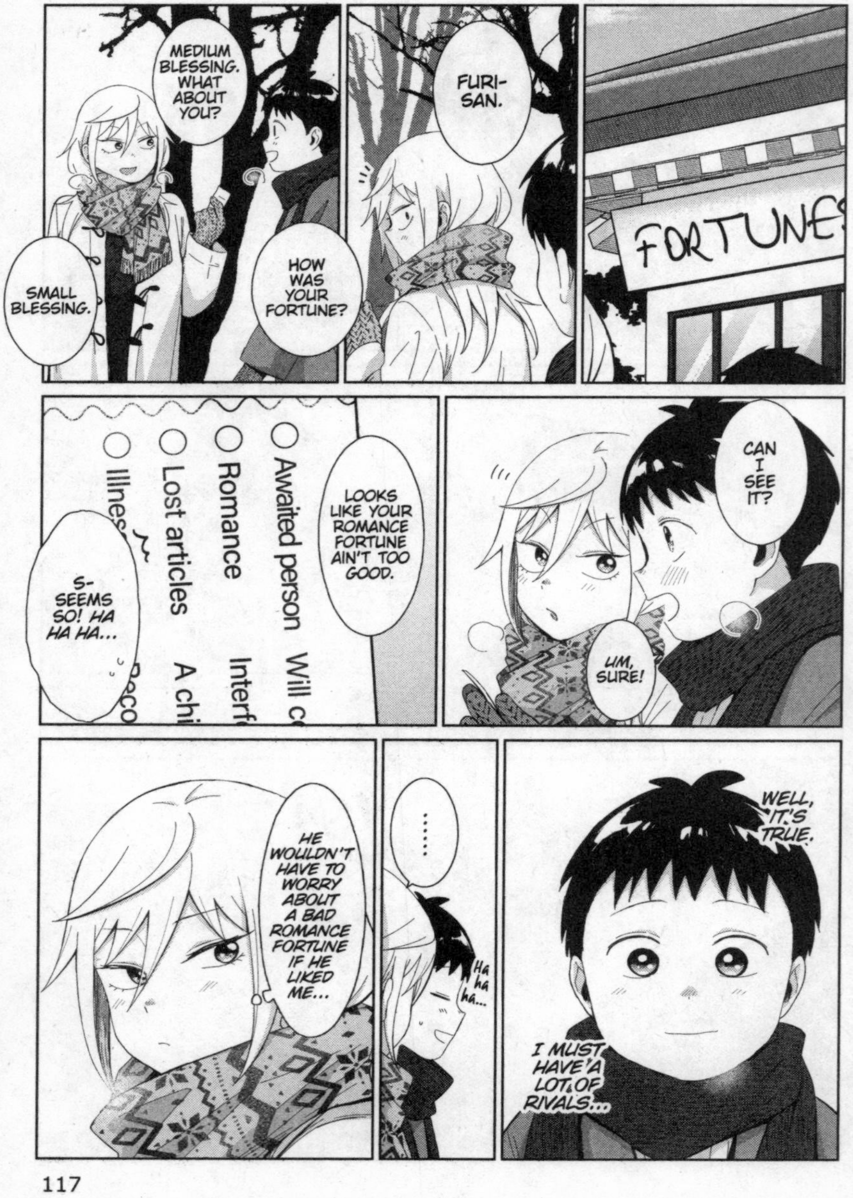
FORTUNES
FURI-SAN.
HOW WAS YOUR FORTUNE?
MEDIUM BLESSING. WHAT ABOUT YOU?
SMALL BLESSING.
CAN I SEE IT?
UM, SURE!
LOOKS LIKE YOUR ROMANCE FORTUNE AIN'T TOO GOOD.
Awaited person
Romance
Lost articles
S-SEEMS SO! HA HA HA...
WELL, IT'S TRUE.
I MUST HAVE A LOT OF RIVALS...
......
Ha ha ha...
HE WOULDN'T HAVE TO WORRY ABOUT A BAD ROMANCE FORTUNE IF HE LIKED ME...

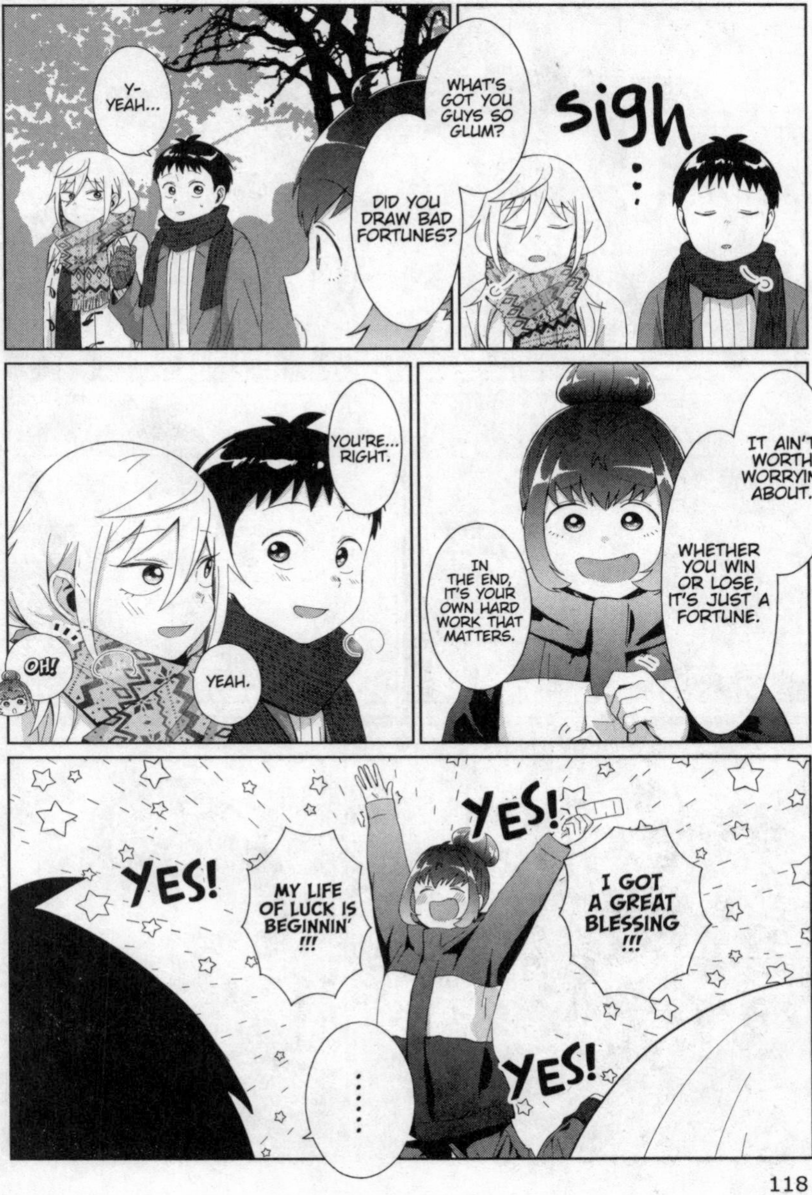

sigh
...
WHAT'S GOT YOU GUYS SO GLUM?
DID YOU DRAW BAD FORTUNES?
Y-YEAH...
IT AIN'T WORTH WORRYIN' ABOUT.
WHETHER YOU WIN OR LOSE, IT'S JUST A FORTUNE.
IN THE END, IT'S YOUR OWN HARD WORK THAT MATTERS.
YOU'RE... RIGHT.
YEAH.
OH!
YES!
I GOT A GREAT BLESSING !!!
MY LIFE OF LUCK IS BEGINNIN' !!!
YES!
YES!
......

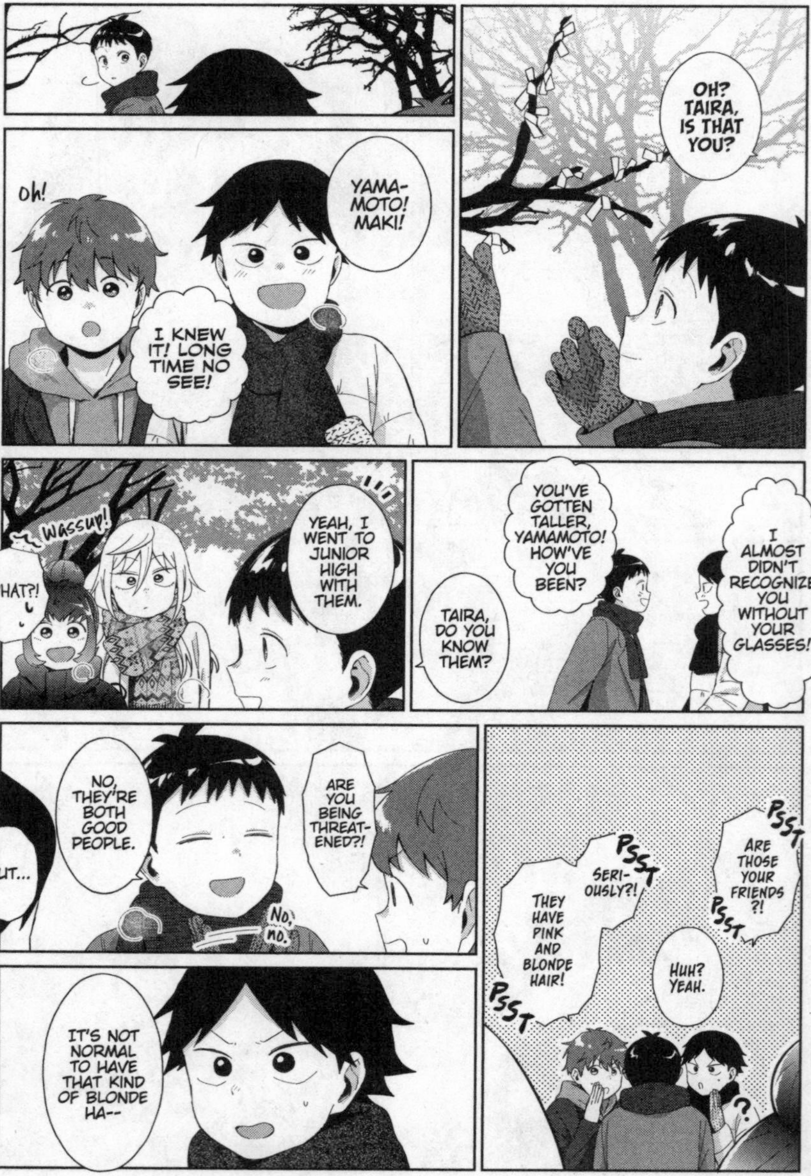
OH? TAIRA, IS THAT YOU?
YAMA-MOTO! MAKI!
Oh!
I KNEW IT! LONG TIME NO SEE!
I ALMOST DIDN'T RECOGNIZE YOU WITHOUT YOUR GLASSES!
YOU'VE GOTTEN TALLER, YAMAMOTO! HOW'VE YOU BEEN?
TAIRA, DO YOU KNOW THEM?
YEAH, I WENT TO JUNIOR HIGH WITH THEM.
Wassup!
WHAT?!
PSST
ARE THOSE YOUR FRIENDS?!
PSST
PSST
SERI-OUSLY?!
THEY HAVE PINK AND BLONDE HAIR!
HUH? YEAH.
PSST
ARE YOU BEING THREAT-ENED?!
NO, THEY'RE BOTH GOOD PEOPLE.
No, no.
BUT...
IT'S NOT NORMAL TO HAVE THAT KIND OF BLONDE HA--

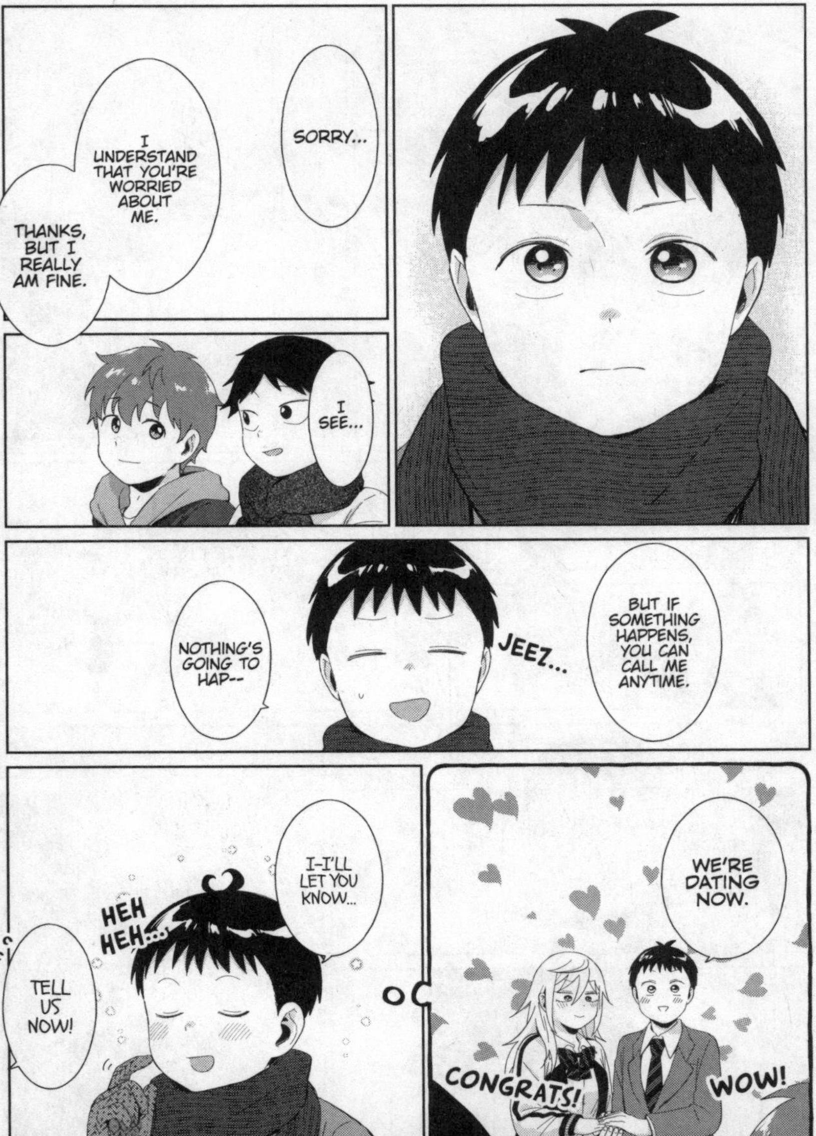
SORRY...
I UNDERSTAND THAT YOU'RE WORRIED ABOUT ME.
THANKS, BUT I REALLY AM FINE.
I SEE...
BUT IF SOMETHING HAPPENS, YOU CAN CALL ME ANYTIME.
JEEZ...
NOTHING'S GOING TO HAP--
WE'RE DATING NOW.
WOW!
CONGRATS!
I-I'LL LET YOU KNOW...
HEH HEH...
TELL US NOW!

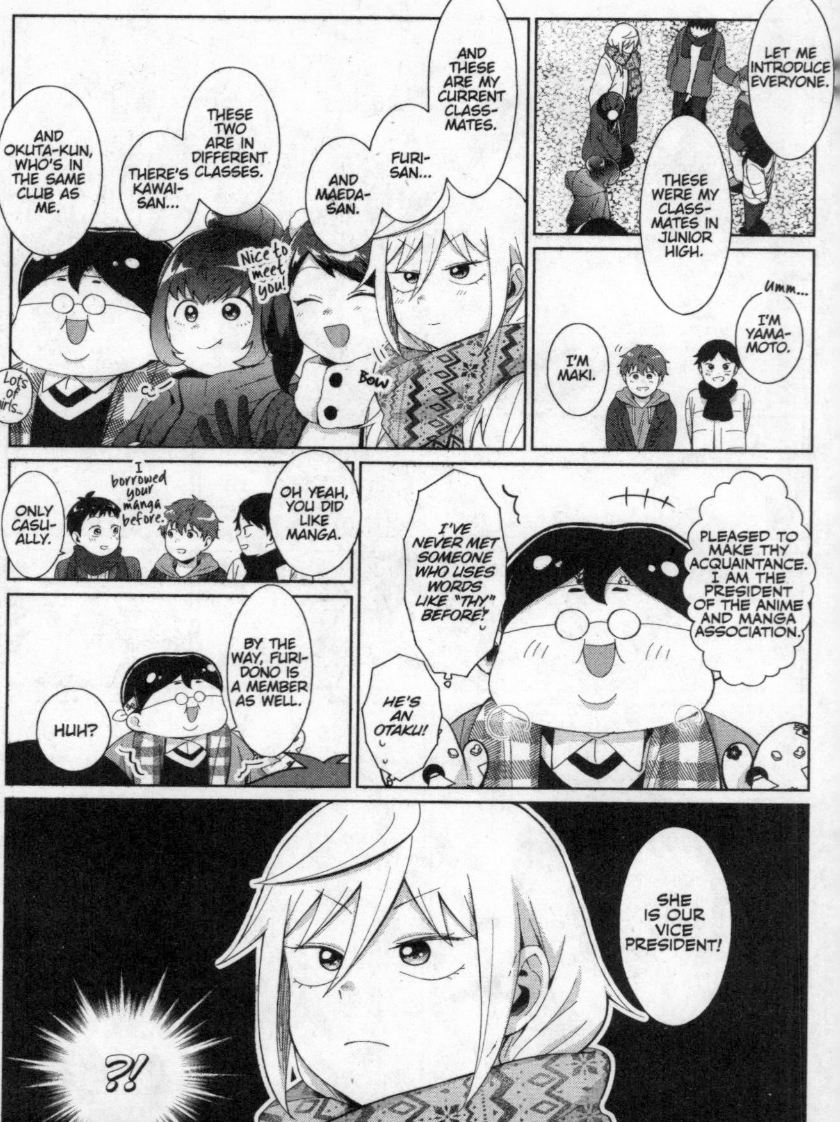
LET ME INTRODUCE EVERYONE.
THESE WERE MY CLASSMATES IN JUNIOR HIGH.
Umm...
I'M YAMAMOTO.
I'M MAKI.
AND THESE ARE MY CURRENT CLASSMATES.
FURI-SAN...
AND MAEDA-SAN.
Nice to meet you!
BOW
THESE TWO ARE IN DIFFERENT CLASSES.
THERE'S KAWAI-SAN...
AND OKUTA-KUN, WHO'S IN THE SAME CLUB AS ME.
Lots of girls...
PLEASED TO MAKE THY ACQUAINTANCE. I AM THE PRESIDENT OF THE ANIME AND MANGA ASSOCIATION.
I'VE NEVER MET SOMEONE WHO USES WORDS LIKE "THY" BEFORE!
HE'S AN OTAKU!
OH YEAH, YOU DID LIKE MANGA.
I borrowed your manga before.
ONLY CASUALLY.
BY THE WAY, FURI-DONO IS A MEMBER AS WELL.
HUH?
SHE IS OUR VICE PRESIDENT!
?!

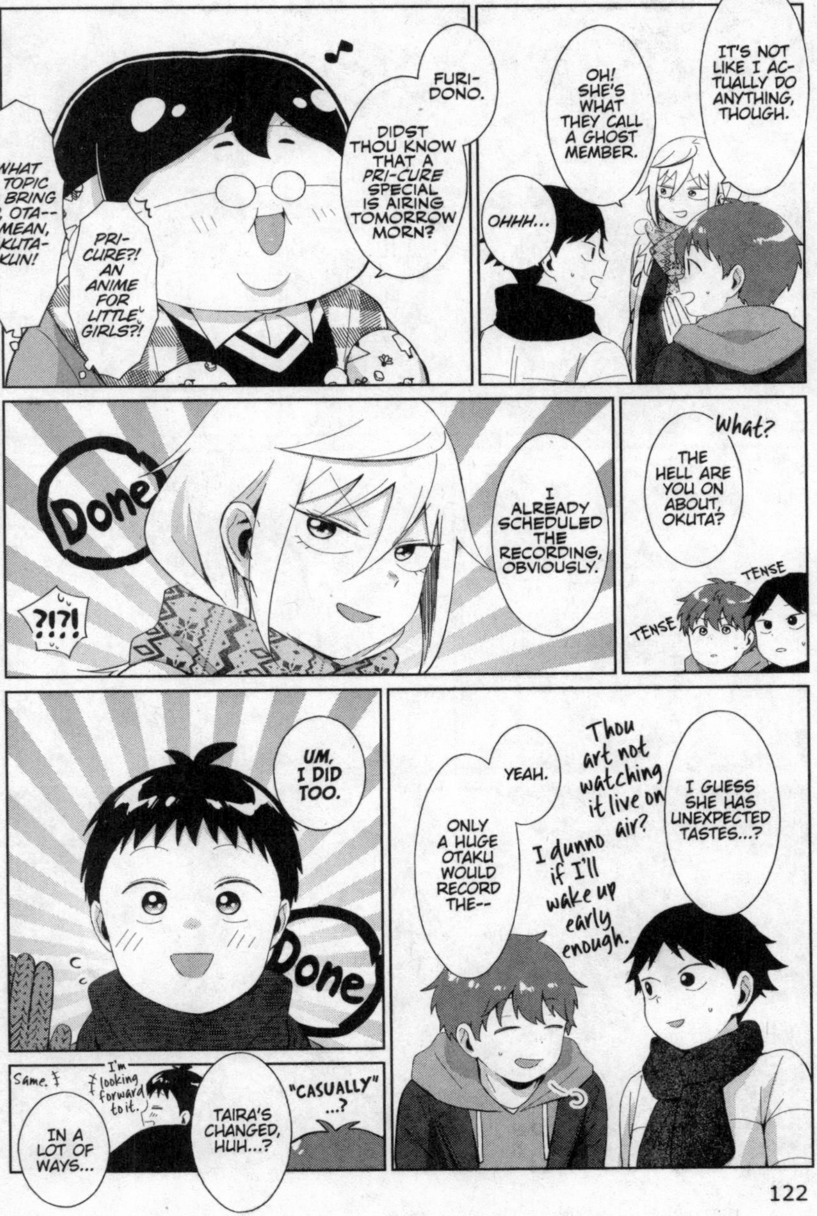
IT'S NOT LIKE I ACTUALLY DO ANYTHING, THOUGH.
OH! SHE'S WHAT THEY CALL A GHOST MEMBER.
OHHH...
FURI-DONO.
DIDST THOU KNOW THAT A PRI-CURE SPECIAL IS AIRING TOMORROW MORN?
PRI-CURE?! AN ANIME FOR LITTLE GIRLS?!
WHAT A TOPIC TO BRING UP, OTA-- I MEAN, OKUTA-KUN!
What?
THE HELL ARE YOU ON ABOUT, OKUTA?
TENSE
TENSE
I ALREADY SCHEDULED THE RECORDING, OBVIOUSLY.
Done
?!?!
I GUESS SHE HAS UNEXPECTED TASTES...?
Thou art not watching it live on air?
YEAH.
ONLY A HUGE OTAKU WOULD RECORD THE--
I dunno if I'll wake up early enough.
UM, I DID TOO.
Done
"CASUALLY" ...?
TAIRA'S CHANGED, HUH...?
I'm looking forward to it.
Same.
IN A LOT OF WAYS...

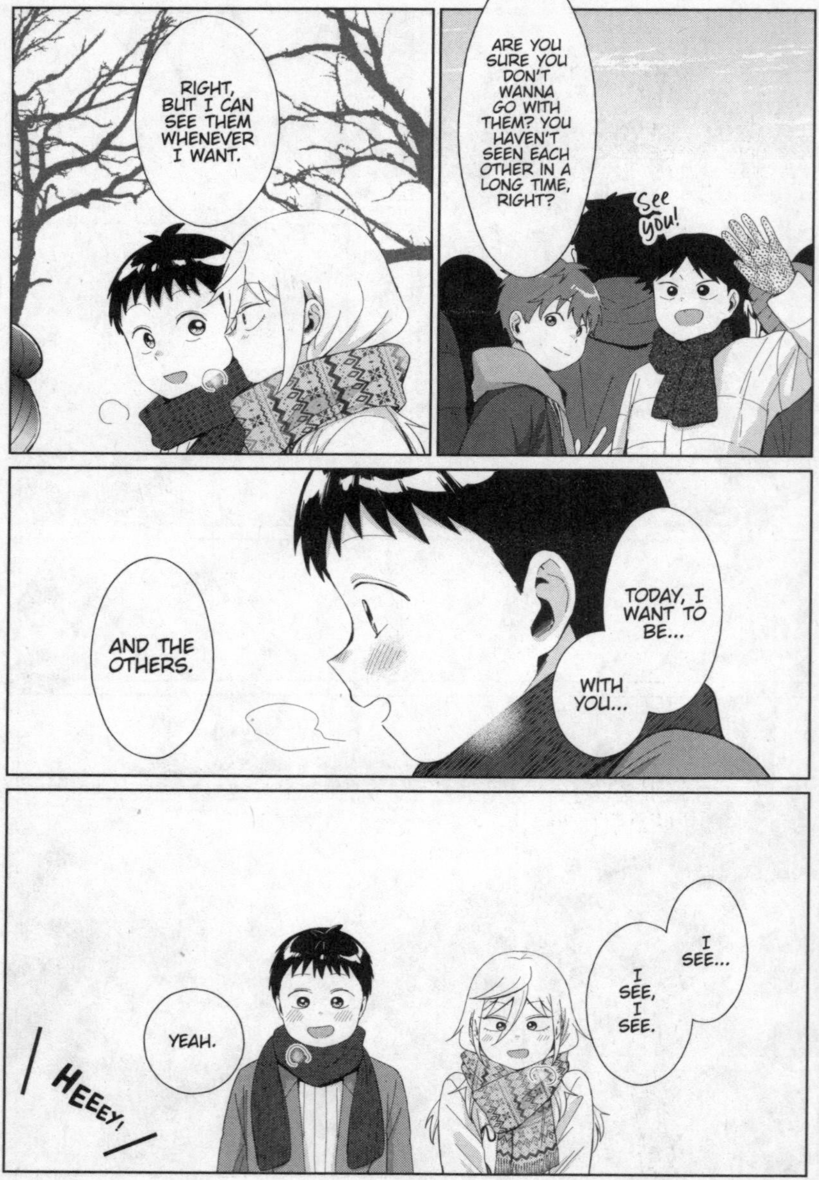
ARE YOU SURE YOU DON'T WANNA GO WITH THEM? YOU HAVEN'T SEEN EACH OTHER IN A LONG TIME, RIGHT?
See you!
RIGHT, BUT I CAN SEE THEM WHENEVER I WANT.
TODAY, I WANT TO BE...
WITH YOU...
AND THE OTHERS.
I SEE...
I SEE, I SEE.
YEAH.
HEEEY!

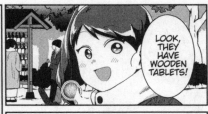

LOOK, THEY HAVE WOODEN TABLETS!
I WAS LAZY WITH THE PRAYER ...
Oh!
BUT I'M GOING TO WRITE MY NUMBER ONE WISH ON THIS!
LET'S KEEP OUR WISHES A SECRET, THEN. THAT WAY, WE CAN TAKE IT MORE SERIOUSLY.
Agreed!

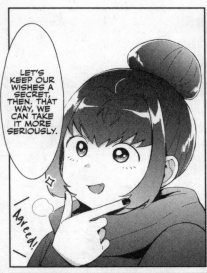

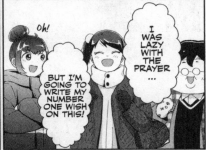

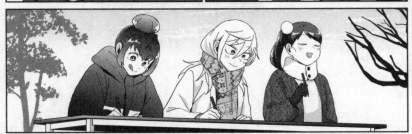

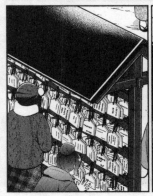

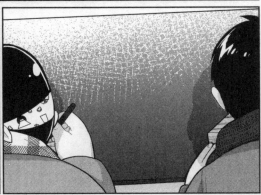

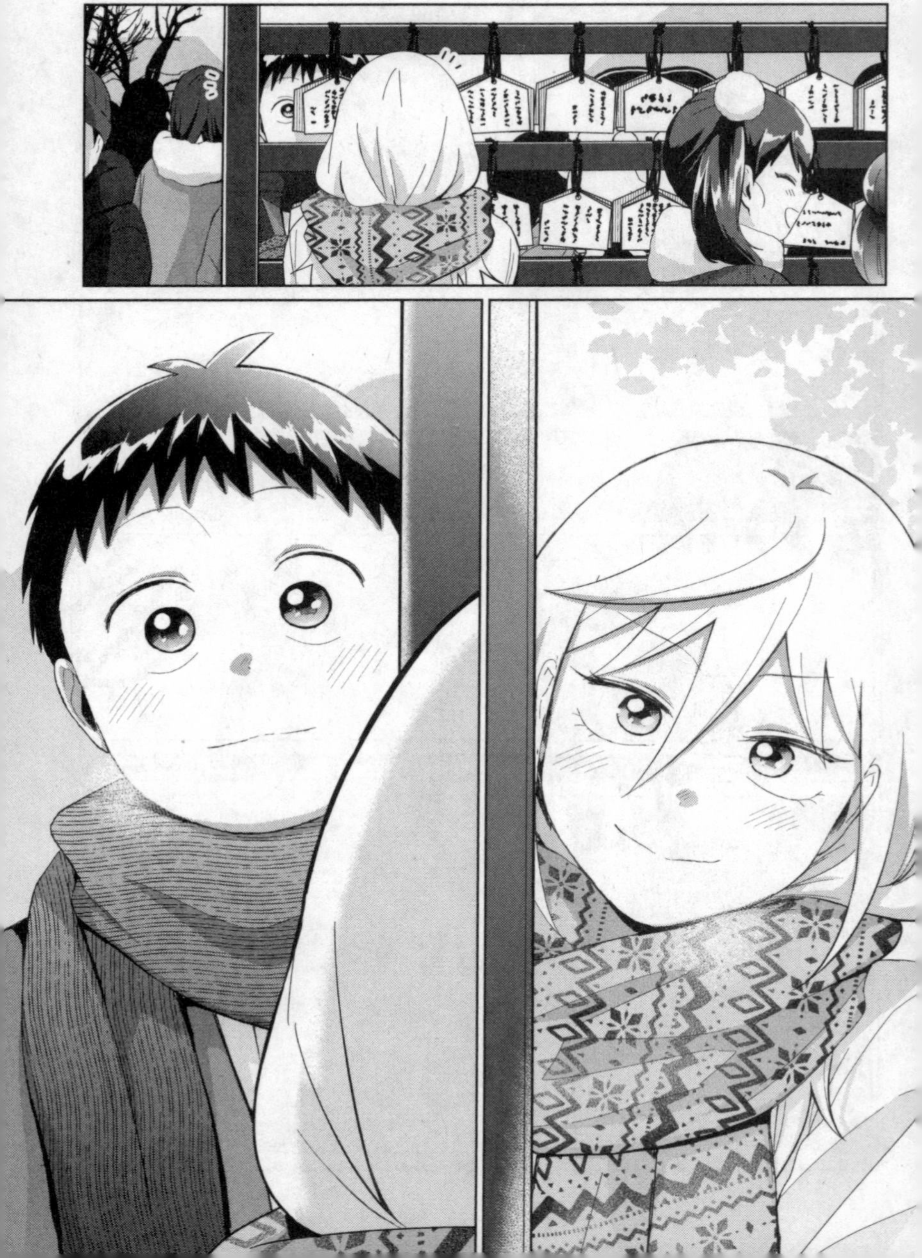

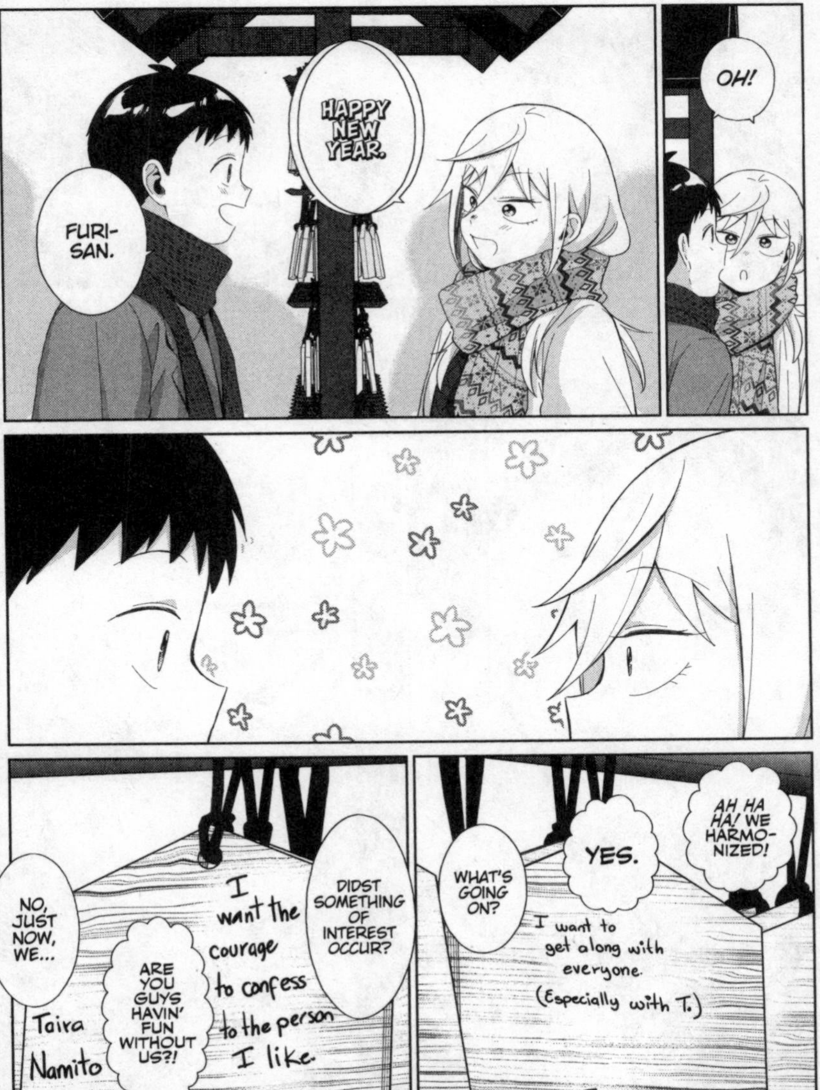
OH!
HAPPY NEW YEAR.
FURI-SAN.
AH HA HA! WE HARMONIZED!
YES.
WHAT'S GOING ON?
I want to get along with everyone. (Especially with T.)
Furi Youko
DIDST SOMETHING OF INTEREST OCCUR?
I want the courage to confess to the person I like.
NO, JUST NOW, WE...
ARE YOU GUYS HAVIN' FUN WITHOUT US?!
Taira Namito

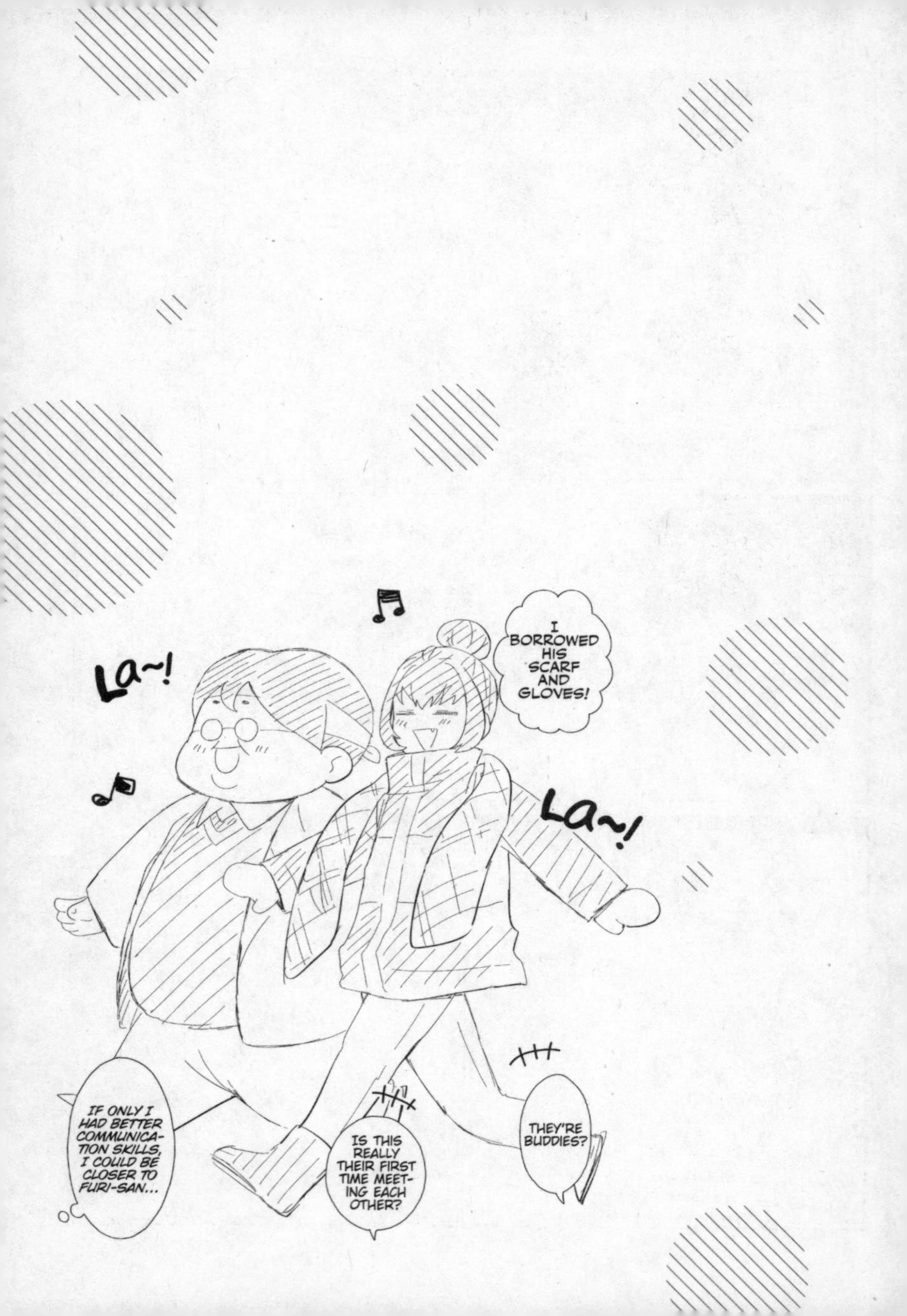
I BORROWED HIS SCARF AND GLOVES!
La~!
La~!
THEY'RE BUDDIES?
IS THIS REALLY THEIR FIRST TIME MEETING EACH OTHER?
IF ONLY I HAD BETTER COMMUNICATION SKILLS, I COULD BE CLOSER TO FURI-SAN...

Bonus Chapter (31.5)

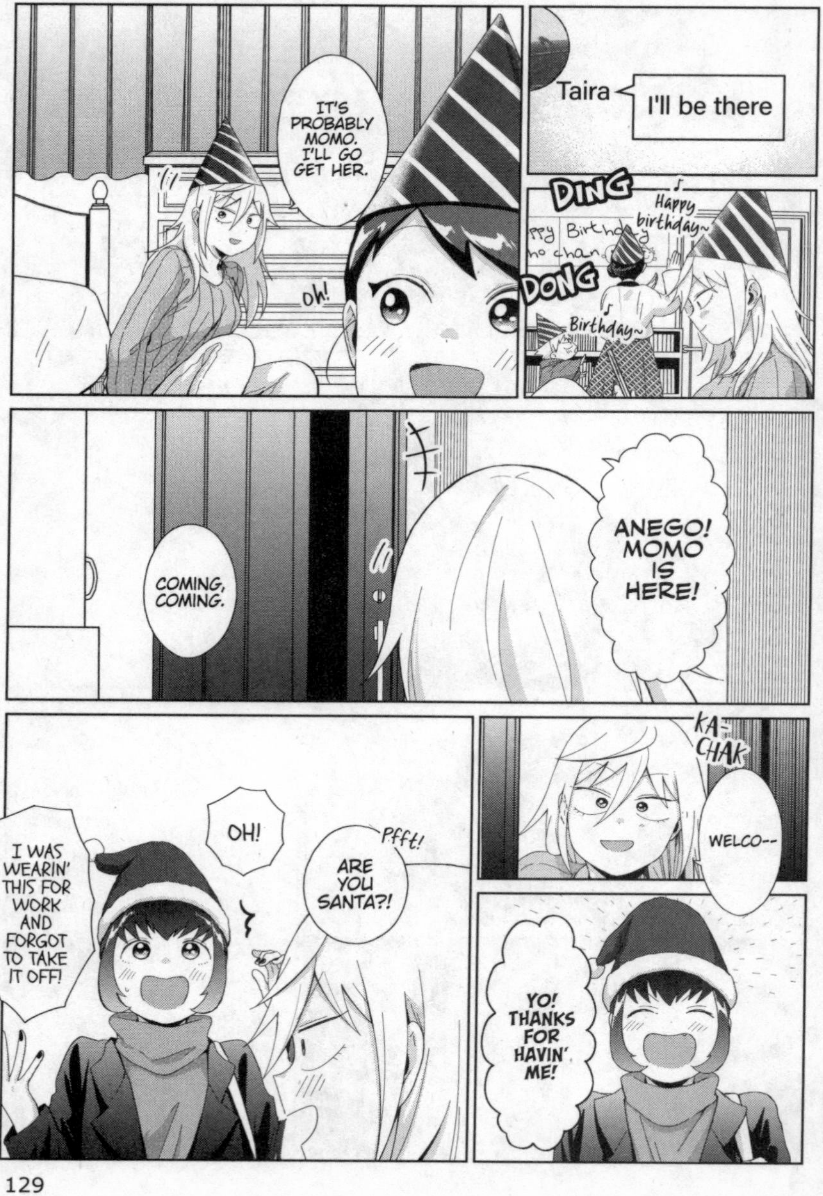
Taira
I'll be there
DING
Happy birthday~
ppy Birthday
no chan
DONG
Birthday~
IT'S PROBABLY MOMO. I'LL GO GET HER.
OH!
ANEGO! MOMO IS HERE!
COMING, COMING.
KA-CHAK
WELCO--
YO! THANKS FOR HAVIN' ME!
Pfft!
ARE YOU SANTA?!
OH!
I WAS WEARIN' THIS FOR WORK AND FORGOT TO TAKE IT OFF!

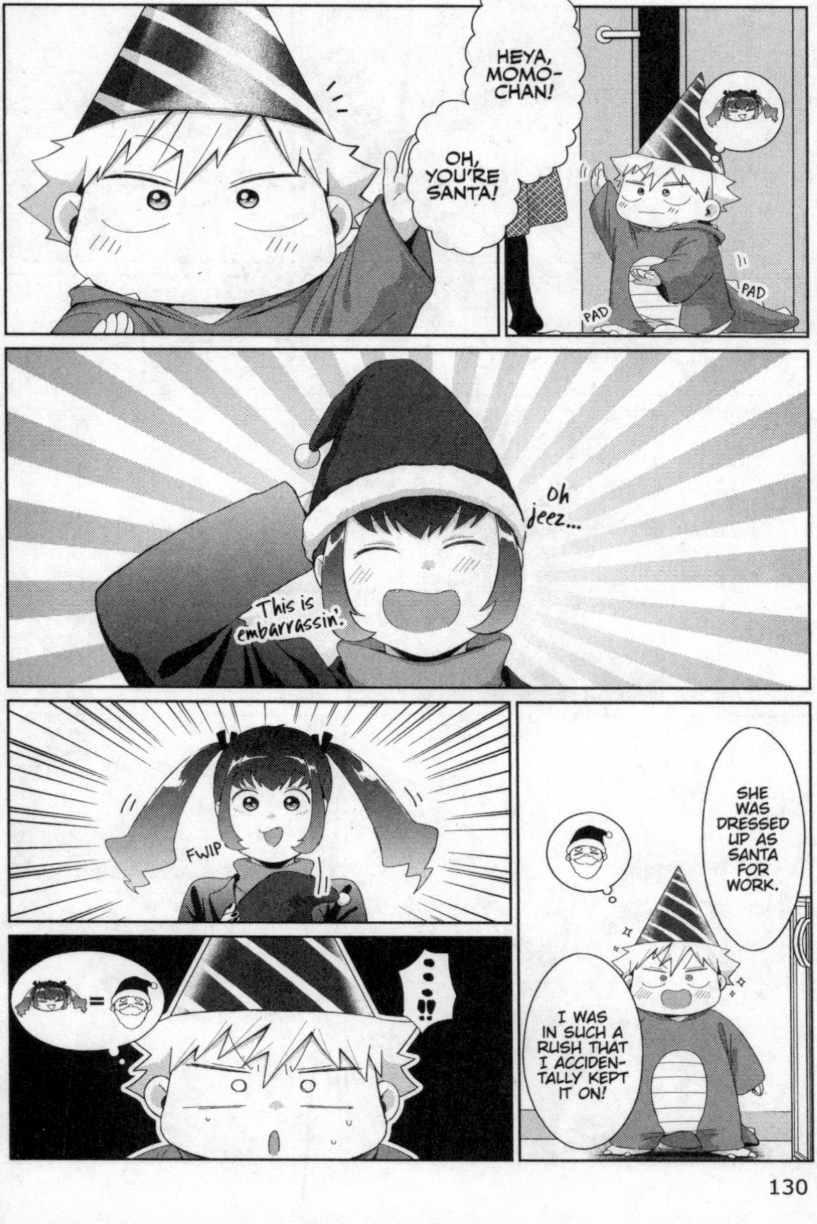
PAD
PAD
HEYA, MOMO-CHAN!
OH, YOU'RE SANTA!
Oh jeez...
This is embarrassin'.
SHE WAS DRESSED UP AS SANTA FOR WORK.
I WAS IN SUCH A RUSH THAT I ACCIDENTALLY KEPT IT ON!
FWIP
....!!

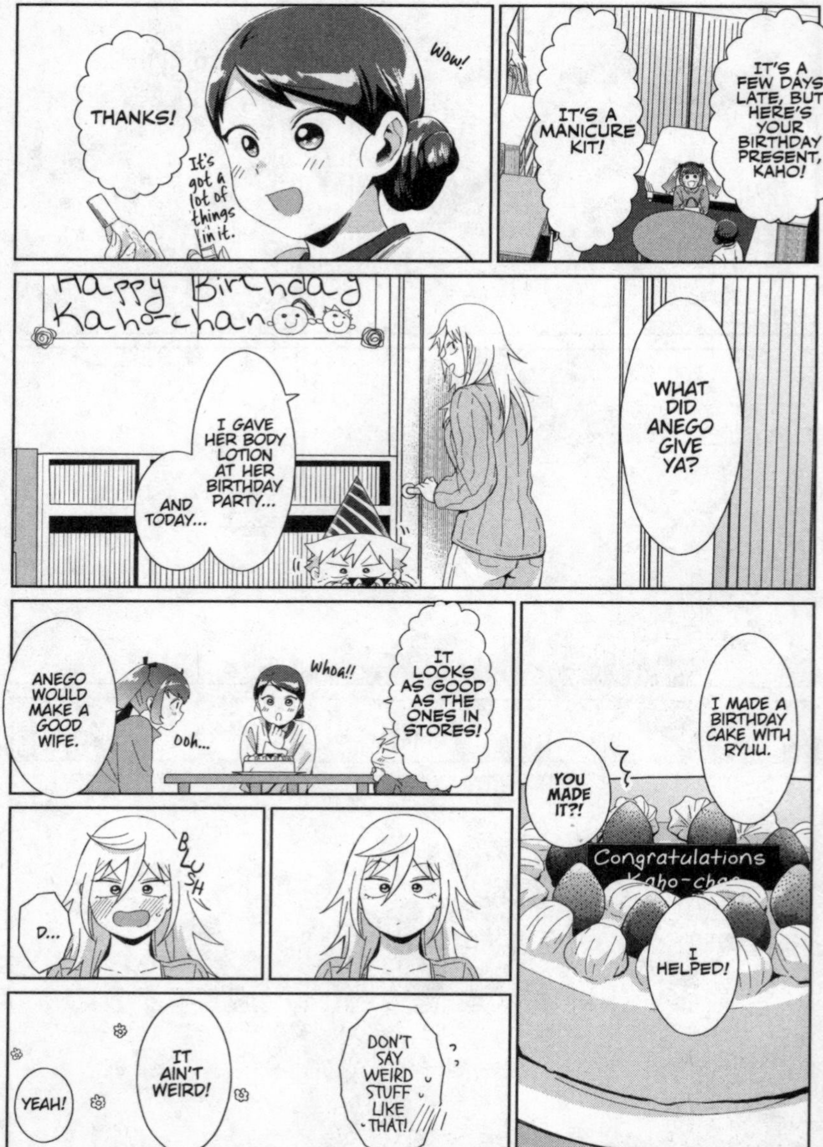
IT'S A FEW DAYS LATE, BUT HERE'S YOUR BIRTHDAY PRESENT, KAHO!
IT'S A MANICURE KIT!
WOW!
THANKS!
It's got a lot of things in it.
Happy Birthday Kaho-chan
WHAT DID ANEGO GIVE YA?
I GAVE HER BODY LOTION AT HER BIRTHDAY PARTY... AND TODAY...
I MADE A BIRTHDAY CAKE WITH RYUU.
YOU MADE IT?!
Congratulations
I HELPED!
IT LOOKS AS GOOD AS THE ONES IN STORES!
Whoa!!
Ooh...
ANEGO WOULD MAKE A GOOD WIFE.
BLUSH
D...
DON'T SAY WEIRD STUFF LIKE THAT!
IT AIN'T WEIRD!
YEAH!

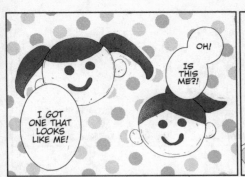

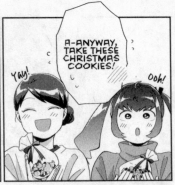

A-ANYWAY, TAKE THESE CHRISTMAS COOKIES!
Ooh!
Yay!
OH! IS THIS ME?!
I GOT ONE THAT LOOKS LIKE ME!
RYUU MADE THOSE.
RIGHT?
NOD
I LIKE YOU BOTH...
SO I TRIED MY BEST.
C-CAN I HAVE HIM AS A LITTLE BRO...?
My heart!
NO! I'M TAKING HIM BACK TO THE MAEDA FAMILY!
THROOOB
NEITHER OF YOU CAN HAVE HIM!

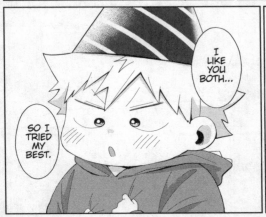

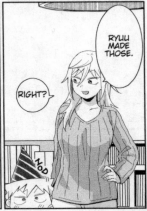

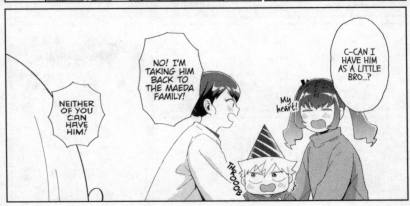

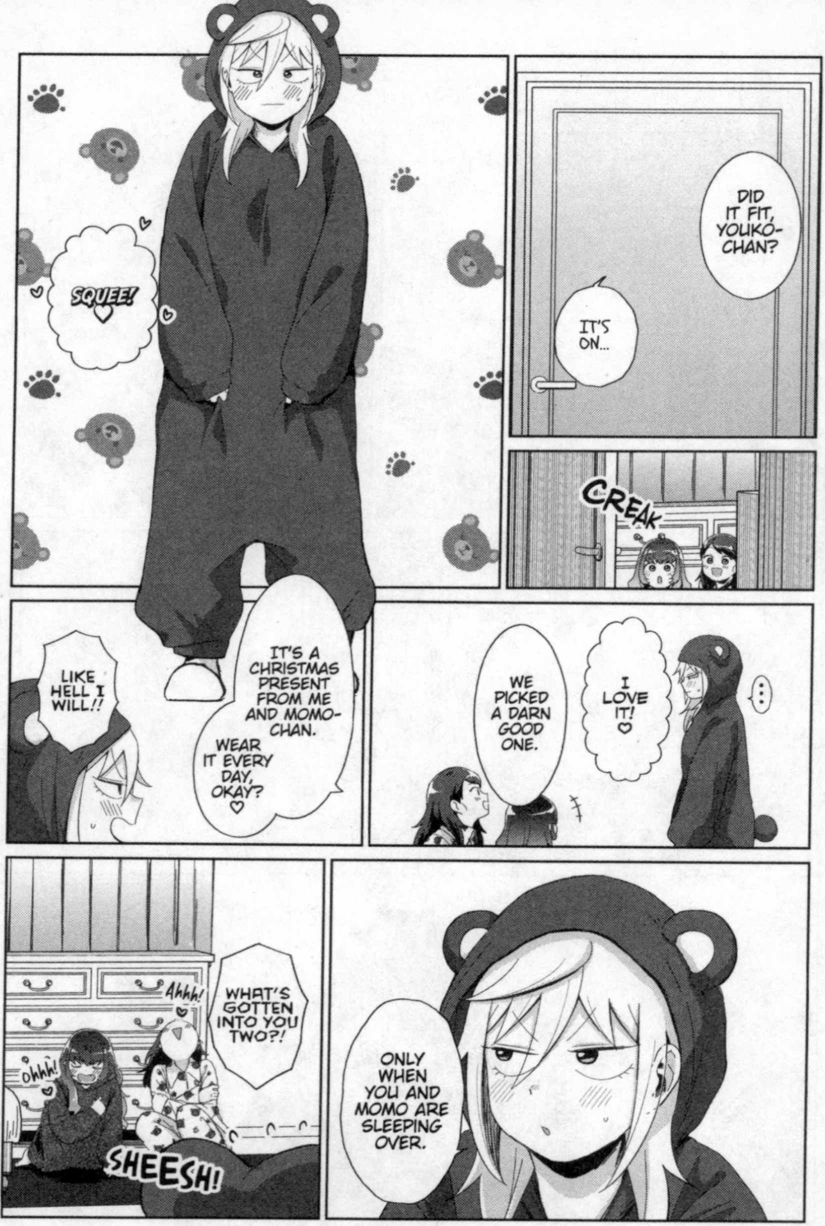
DID IT FIT, YOUKO-CHAN?
IT'S ON...
CREAK
SQUEE! ♡
...
I LOVE IT! ♡
WE PICKED A DARN GOOD ONE.
IT'S A CHRISTMAS PRESENT FROM ME AND MOMO-CHAN.
WEAR IT EVERY DAY, OKAY? ♡
LIKE HELL I WILL!!
ONLY WHEN YOU AND MOMO ARE SLEEPING OVER.
WHAT'S GOTTEN INTO YOU TWO?!
Ahhh! ♡
ohhh! ♡
SHEESH!

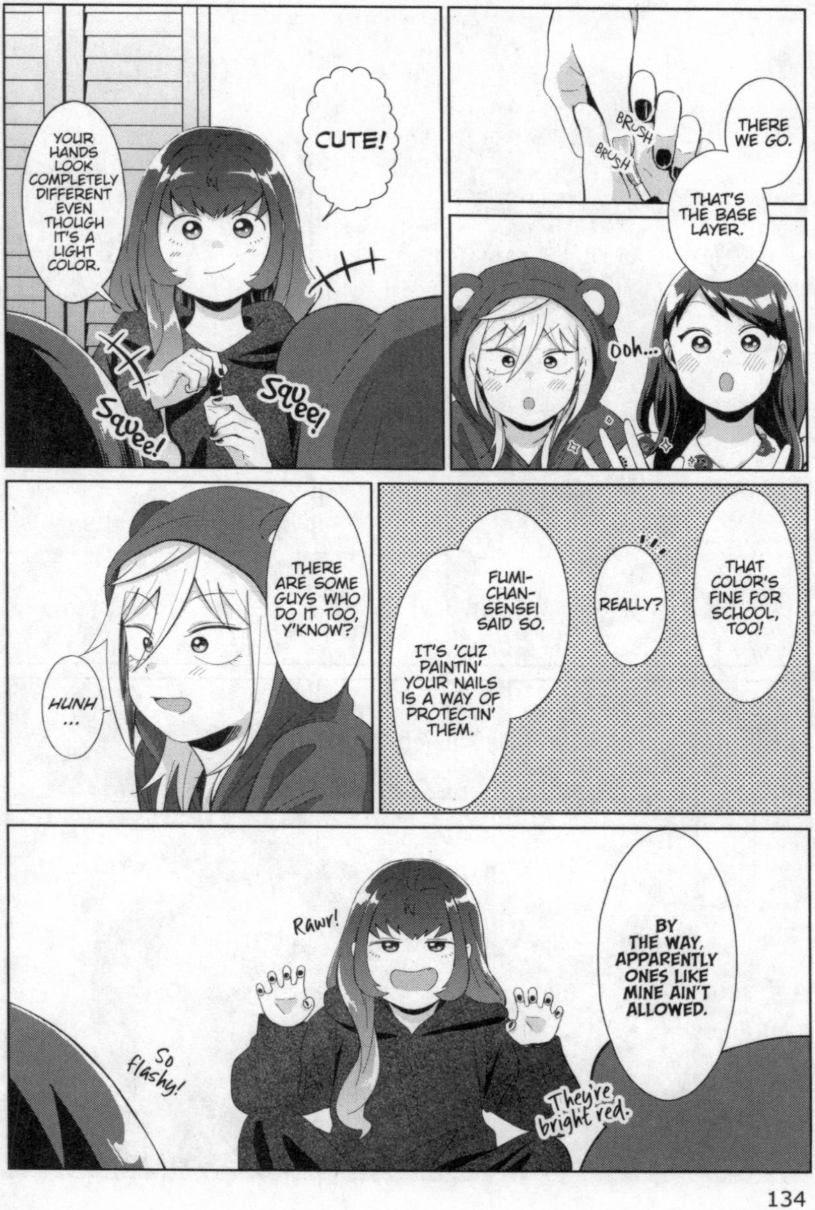

THERE WE GO.
THAT'S THE BASE LAYER.
BRUSH
BRUSH
Ooh...
CUTE!
YOUR HANDS LOOK COMPLETELY DIFFERENT EVEN THOUGH IT'S A LIGHT COLOR.
Squee!
Squee!
THAT COLOR'S FINE FOR SCHOOL, TOO!
REALLY?
FUMI-CHAN-SENSEI SAID SO.
IT'S 'CUZ PAINTIN' YOUR NAILS IS A WAY OF PROTECTIN' THEM.
THERE ARE SOME GUYS WHO DO IT TOO, Y'KNOW?
HUNH ...
BY THE WAY, APPARENTLY ONES LIKE MINE AIN'T ALLOWED.
Rawr!
They're bright red.
So flashy!

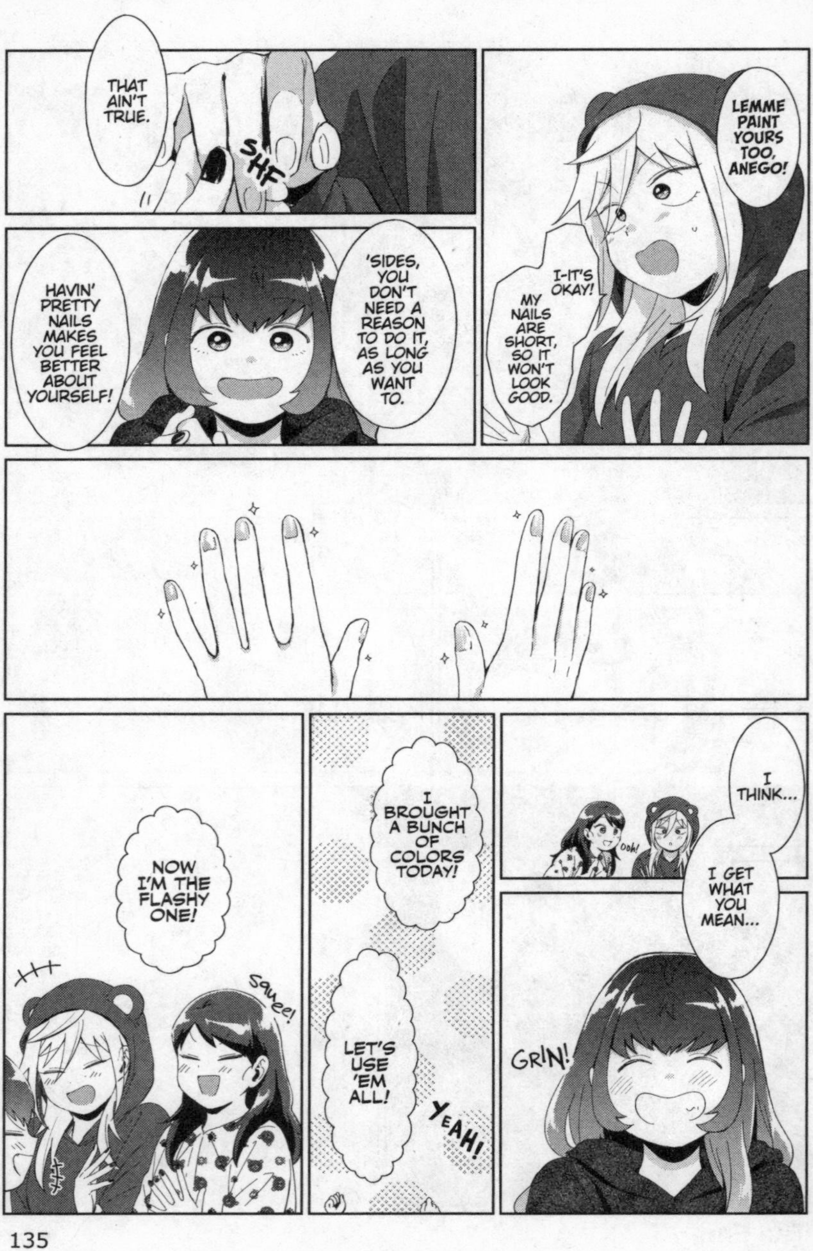
LEMME PAINT YOURS TOO, ANEGO!
I-IT'S OKAY!
MY NAILS ARE SHORT, SO IT WON'T LOOK GOOD.
THAT AIN'T TRUE.
SHF
'SIDES, YOU DON'T NEED A REASON TO DO IT, AS LONG AS YOU WANT TO.
HAVIN' PRETTY NAILS MAKES YOU FEEL BETTER ABOUT YOURSELF!
I THINK...
Ooh!
I GET WHAT YOU MEAN...
GRIN!
I BROUGHT A BUNCH OF COLORS TODAY!
LET'S USE 'EM ALL!
YEAH!
NOW I'M THE FLASHY ONE!
Squee!

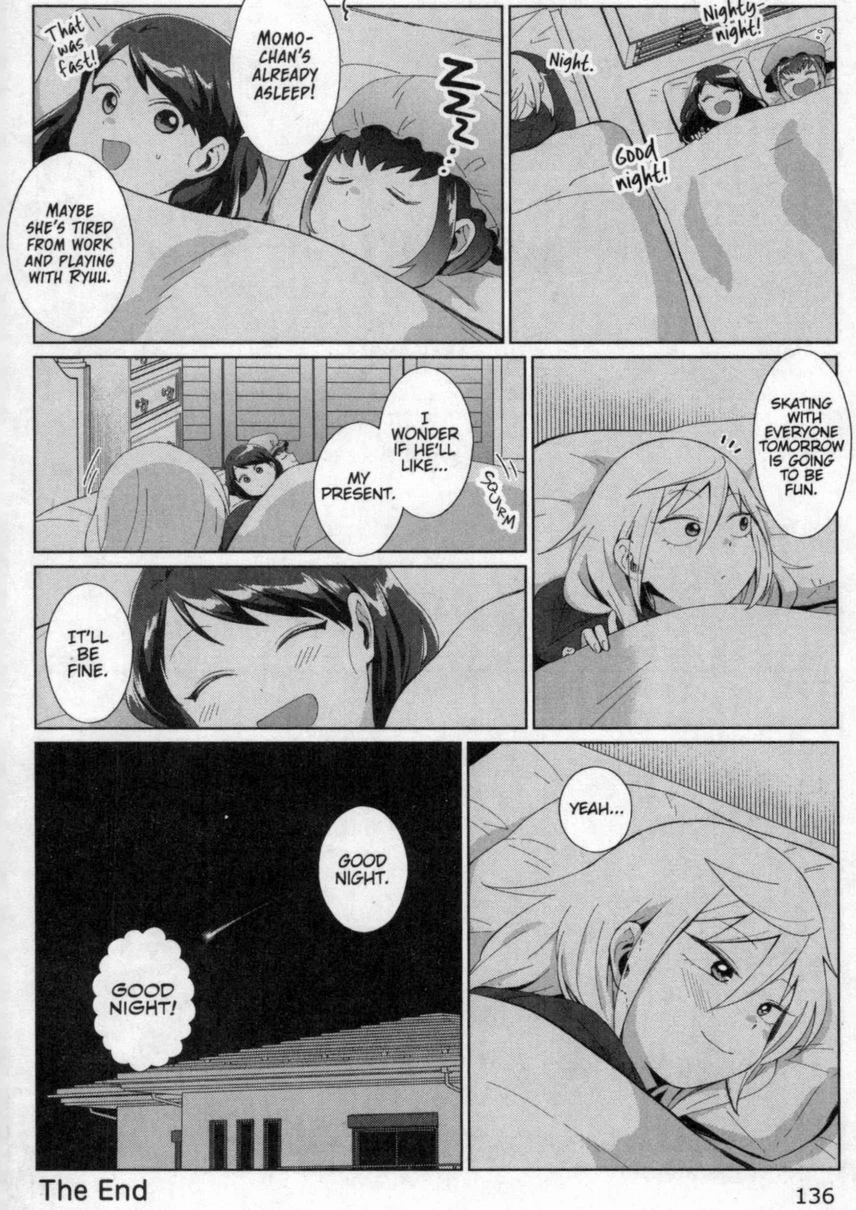
Nighty-night!
Night.
Good night!
Momo-chan's already asleep!
ZZZ...
That was fast!
Maybe she's tired from work and playing with Ryuu.
Skating with everyone tomorrow is going to be fun.
SQUIRM
I wonder if he'll like...
my present.
It'll be fine.
Yeah...
Good night.
Good night!

The End

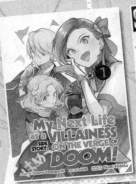
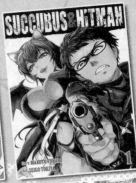
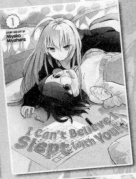
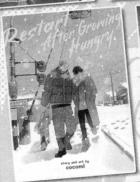
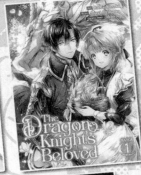
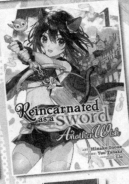
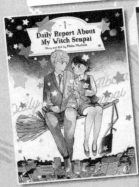
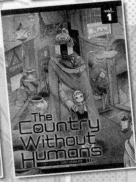
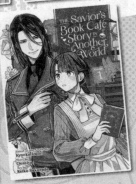

SEVEN SEAS ENTERTAINMENT PRESENTS

NO MATTER WHAT YOU SAY, FURi-SAN is SCARY!

Vol. 4

story and art by SEIICHI KINOUE

TRANSLATION
Minna Lin

LETTERING
Carolina Hernández Mendoza

COVER AND LOGO DESIGN
H. Qi

PROOFREADER
Kurestin Armada

SENIOR COPY EDITOR
Dawn Davis

EDITOR
K. McDonald

PRODUCTION DESIGNER
Christinaa McKenzie

PRODUCTION MANAGER
Lissa Pattillo

PREPRESS TECHNICIAN
Jules Valera

PRINT MANAGER
Rhiannon Rasmussen-Silverstein

EDITOR-IN-CHIEF
Julie Davis

ASSOCIATE PUBLISHER
Adam Arnold

PUBLISHER
Jason DeAngelis

Seven Seas press and purchase enquiries can be sent to Marketing Manager Lianne Sentar at press@gomanga.com. Information regarding the distribution and purchase of digital editions is available from Digital Manager CK Russell at digital@gomanga.com.

ISBN: 978-1-63858-641-8
Printed in Canada
First Printing: August 2022
10 9 8 7 6 5 4 3 2 1

READING DIRECTIONS

This book reads from ***right to left***, Japanese style. If this is your first time reading manga, you start reading from the top right panel on each page and take it from there. If you get lost, just follow the numbered diagram here. It may seem backwards at first, but you'll get the hang of it! Have fun!!

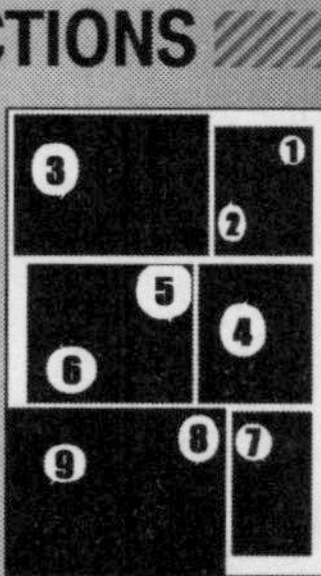
1
2
3
4
5
6
7
8
9

Follow us online: www.SevenSeasEntertainment.com